SWANTON
IN AUSTRALIA

SWANTON
IN AUSTRALIA

with MCC 1946 - 1975

E.W. SWANTON

WITH FOREWORD BY
Sir Robert Menzies

AND INTRODUCTION BY
Sir Donald Bradman

COLLINS
St. James's Place, London
1975

William Collins Sons & Co Ltd
London · Glasgow · Sydney · Auckland
Toronto · Johannesburg

First published 1975
© E.W. Swanton

ISBN 0 00 216236 9

Set in Linotype Imprint
Made and Printed in Great Britain by
William Collins Sons & Co Ltd Glasgow

I have deprived myself of the joint dedication I would otherwise have made to Sir Robert Menzies and Sir Donald Bradman, who have kindly contributed the Foreword and Introduction. For this I am deeply grateful. However, it does give me the chance to dedicate this book to all my Australian friends, past and present, who have made my eight MCC tours in their country so happy and rewarding.

Contents

Acknowledgements

The chief source of this book has been my writings in the *Daily Telegraph*, and I am grateful for permission to quote therefrom. Thus I have filled in the detail and confirmed general impressions.

detect, perhaps, any change in my writing style!

Wisden as ever has been a constant source of reference, as has *Test Cricket – England v. Australia* by Ralph Barker and Irving Rosenwater. I have refreshed my memory by re-reading several tour books, notably those by Jack Fingleton, Ian Peebles and Alan Ross. I am indebted to my secretary, Miss Wendy Wimbush, for much labour on the book, and especially for compiling the full and detailed Appendix. My thanks, too, to Jim Coldham, who meticulously prepared the Index. The scores of the forty-two Test Matches played by England in Australia between 1946 and 1975 will be found in the Appendix, and a book-marker is provided for easier reference as between the text and the scores.

Illustration Credits

Foreword

BY SIR ROBERT MENZIES

Of the making of cricket books there is apparently no end. But this is to be understood, because at their best books about cricket have a literary quality which makes them stand out from books about other sports.

Cricket is a reflective game, a game which above all things lends itself to writing in the lovely flexible English which we have inherited from our ancestors. Some cricket books are good, some are bad, and some are indifferent. Some are written by the people whose names appear on them, others by 'ghosts'.

A few years back I added to my cricket library a book by a celebrated English cricketer. Later I added to the same library a book about another celebrated cricketer who was a contemporary and colleague of the first player, and I was horrified to find each book contained very damaging and critical remarks about the other man. I spoke to an eminent cricket writer of my acquaintance and said 'You know, I was nauseated by this – to have these men, each of whom had added so magnificently to the history of English cricket, snarling at each other.' He smiled and said: 'Well, yes, but I happen to know the chap who wrote both books!'

I can now smell a 'ghost' as clearly as the eye of a medieval witch could have seen him. But I do not mind. Each person has his own job in life, and if somebody writes a book for a great cricketer, well, that is all right so long as the financial arrangements are adequate. But to an old cricket lover like myself there is no smell so obvious as the smell of a 'ghost'.

Against that kind of writing are three cricket writers who command my instant attention and, indeed, my affection.

One of them is no longer writing, and that is the late Neville Cardus. Neville was a remarkable writer about cricket because he was a remarkable writer about music. He was a music critic and a cricket critic, and he introduced the one into the other elegantly. All the great passages in his cricket books were in some way derived from music and the melodies of music. He had the great advantage of having been trained on the old *Manchester Guardian* under C. P. Scott, who was, in terms of literary expression, a perfectionist. He trained quite a few wonderful writers of English, and Neville, of course, was one of them.

But there was also C. E. Montague, and Howard Spring, and that great clutch of writers who learned their trade on the *Manchester Guardian*. These were wonderful days in the history of journalism.

Of the other two cricket writers I have in mind one is an Australian – Jack Fingleton. It is true that he writes for a newspaper in London and represents them not only on cricket but on political affairs. It is also happily true that he appears in the press in Australia during the current series of Test Matches. But whatever he does he writes with unique knowledge of the 'man in the middle'. Fingleton was an opening batsman for Australia of great note and he knows all about body-line bowling and things of that kind – these odd excrescences on modern cricket. In other words, he is an expert witness. He writes from first-hand knowledge. Very few people can do this, and when he writes he does so in what I call a fine 'muscular' English – he speaks his mind. I have a great respect for Fingleton as a commentator on the cricket of today.

So far I have written of Neville Cardus, a great music critic turned cricket writer, and about Jack Fingleton who, of all the people who have played in Test Matches of a hard-fought kind, is the one who speaks so clearly and so well. Among Englishmen E. W. Swanton stands supreme. Jim Swanton, of course, has written a great deal about cricket and has, indeed, played cricket himself extremely well. He is not one of your keyhole reporters who serve to destroy cricket, but one of those men of intellect and wisdom who dignify cricket when they write about it. He lives in Sandwich, one of my Cinque Ports, of which I am the Lord Warden, and I have many times been to his house – very much a reflection of the man. To reach the front door you step over a little moat and in the back garden there are fruit trees. You feel isolated from the world – out of the noise into the silence. He has entertained me there many times – he and his wife, Ann, who is a fine artist and whose portrait of Frank Woolley I once bought in Sandwich and presented to the Melbourne Cricket Club, in whose library it now hangs.

He is familiar with and has written in a most illuminating way about the history of cricket, and understands the game from the grass roots up. He seems never to arrive at a conclusion in a hurry, but when he has arrived at it he states it quietly, with emphasis, with dignity and with judgement. Nobody now writing in English could possibly have brought me the same joy as his writings, either in the *Cricketer* or in his books.

The great element about Jim Swanton is that he is not only a man of intelligence but also of maturity. He does not fall for the latest stunt in cricket writing or in cricket, or in anything else. The people who fall for stunts, who are accustomed or willing to use the jargon of the moment, have always left me cold. But Jim is one of those rare people in sporting writing, a man of intelligence and education. Always a man of good temper, never one to give way to the latest cry, he is a man whose maturity will be of value to those who read about cricket in a hundred years' time. It is for these reasons that I have agreed that I would write, to a book of his, probably my last Foreword.

Melbourne,   ROBERT MENZIES
20th January 1975

Introduction

BY SIR DONALD BRADMAN

It is an honour that I should have been asked to write the Introduction to Jim Swanton's book, *Swanton in Australia*. Nevertheless, I accepted the charge with reluctance, first because I questioned my ability to do justice to the foremost cricket writer extant, and, second, because I dislike encouraging a valedictory effort which I suspect is the case now that E.W.S. has retired from daily journalism. But I suppose writers must lay aside their pens albeit at a more mature age than cricketers lay down their bats; and no doubt E.W.S. feels he has had a good innings.

Today, as he looks at his somewhat corpulent figure in a mirror, E.W.S. must reflect that during his traumatic days in a Japanese prison camp in the 1940s he had never dreamt that his future as a cricket writer would extend to 1975. But faith has always been one of his characteristics, and in those desperate days he never gave up hope. The miracle to him is that the Japanese did not take his 'well-thumbed' *Wisden* from him, thinking it must surely be a code book – for at best a *Wisden* must be double-Dutch to a Japanese.

Swanton is obviously making an attempt in his book to give a picture of the 'earthy' Australian and in that context, not inappropriately, starts off by quoting comments from a taxi driver. The Australian variety is not a bad source from which to glean the views of the rank and file.

Swanton then goes on to give a penetrating analysis of many great cricket personalities. Some of them have passed to the great beyond, others are at an age when criticism no longer causes them to bristle, and I can tell E.W.S. has freed himself from some of the restrictions which surround contemporaneous comment. Indeed the same would be valid, even as applied to current players.

Throughout his writing career Jim Swanton has tended to be a diplomatic critic. Not weak, I hasten to add, but his writings have seldom carried the barbed, abrasive comment which is the style of so many 'sensational' writers. For instance, E.W.S. once described Trevor Bailey's batting as 'lacking in aggressive intent', when of course he really meant 'not playing a bloody stroke all day.'

In this style of writing has lain much of his value. His views are carefully weighed before being delicately phrased, and he has made it his business to be as well-informed as possible, particularly when dealing with events involving relations between countries and with matters of administrative significance. In such contexts I value his considered opinions on some of the more controversial matters which have plagued cricket during his era.

His condemnation of suspect bowling actions, for instance, leaves nobody in doubt where he stands. Here it is not a question of who sinned and who didn't, but rather the agreement on the vital principles that there is no place in cricket for throwers, irrespective of their country of origin.

Personally I particularly welcome his forthright attack on Bodyline, which he brands as a shameful episode in which Australia was the aggrieved party. This ought to be now accepted by all Englishmen, but regrettably one still occasionally finds instances where the old charge of 'squealing' is revived.

Very early on the book touches a nostalgic note, for it gives an absorbing picture of Arthur Mailey, that whimsical and lovable character, with whom I had a long and rewarding association. Someone dubbed him the man who bowled like a millionaire, and how true it was! Arthur's objective was to take wickets, and the spending of runs in the process bothered him little. For a relatively small man Arthur had abnormally large hands, soft as silk to the touch, and he once told me that he didn't know what it was to have tired or sore fingers. Which was quite remarkable, for I doubt if any man in history spun the ball more, or achieved greater deception with his 'wrong-un'. Men of his calibre adorn cricket beyond measure.

From that absorbing commencement Swanton goes on to trace most of the great matches and events up to the present day. As a participant in so many happenings and an observer of most others I read the accounts with perhaps more than normal interest and relish.

From an Australian point of view I don't think it unfair to say our people usually felt that Swanton tended to be less critical (certainly in the heat of battle) of his countrymen than ours. Whether that stricture was justified or not, I feel sure it cannot be levelled at the contents of this book, wherein all and sundry are taken to task when the need arises. For instance, there is his treatment of Hammond's moody captaincy in 1946/7, his trenchant disapproval of Hutton and Washbrook's dismal 237 in a full day's batting against South Australia in 1946, and the even more dismal total of 161 for 4 wickets, which was all Australia could show for a full day's batting at Adelaide in January 1955.

However, he puts his finger right on the sore spot when he says that slow scoring rates are not always the fault of the batsmen, and he unreservedly condemns the period when England deliberately reduced the rate of bowling so that only 54 overs were delivered in a full day's play. Tactics such as these are responsible for administrative retaliation. Indeed, many of the laws of cricket stem from abuses of a freedom, not the least the LBW law, which was not wanted until 'Ring was shabby enough' to use his pads for defence of his stumps, not protection of his person from injury (as was the purpose of their invention).

On the bright side we find references to some marvellous performances which conjure up visions such as Tyson's 6 for 16 one morning before lunch, Iverson's 6 for 27 off 19.4 overs, some ecstatic writing on Godfrey Evans's hey-day and a generous tribute to Colin Cowdrey's career. Swanton was always a great supporter of Cowdrey and Jim must have had misgivings on MCC's last tour watching Colin manfully struggling with a task which should in all fairness have been allotted to a younger and more active player.

Descriptions of many wonderful performances bring back memories. Humour abounds, mostly subtle but delightful, such as his references to Dexter being left out because his critics said 'he has too much to learn about slow bowling.' As Dexter was a batsman, not a slow bowler, they obviously meant 'he has a lot to learn about *batting against* slow bowling.'

But the humour came in the telling comment that Harry Vardon had much to learn about putting to the end of his life. He nevertheless won six open championships. That buoyed me up somewhat, because putting has always been my weakness at golf. I shall go forward with renewed hope, Vardon's name on my lips.

Great humour too *in re* J.J. Warr's taking 1 wicket for 281 runs in the 1950/51 tests, and his subsequent reference to appropriate words of a hymn. But J.J. was rewarded – he is now Australia's distinguished representative at International Cricket Conferences.

Even journalists get their mention, notably on the hilarious occasion when that wonderful batsman Sid Barnes, later to achieve some notoriety through the raw comments in his column 'Like It or Lump It,' asked Neville Cardus to put in an extra carbon copy because, as Sid put it, 'our styles are much the same.'

I notice that Swanton gives me the 'credit', if such be the right word, for the historic decision to pick Benaud as Australian captain in preference to Neil Harvey. Certainly I was a party to the decision, but with respect, I prefer all selection decisions to be given joint acclaim or condemnation. It is seldom fair or accurate for one person to be singled out. I say that advisedly, because in a very long career as selector and administrator I have been outvoted far more often than anyone would reasonably contemplate. This is not to criticize or blame my contemporaries, who had their full measure of success, but I want to make it clear I was never associated with sycophants.

One matter which surprised me was Jim Swanton's suggestion that on the famous occasion of the so-called 'sweated' pitch in Melbourne the Australian Board of Control (now the Australian Cricket Board) was considering offering to play the match again if Australia had won. I was a member of the Board at the time and can recall no such idea being canvassed. If someone did think of it then I hope the idea of such a precedent has long since been forgotten. Memories are fresh of three misadventures affecting pitches in the 1974/5 tour, of the recent disaster at Lord's which so upset the Pakistanis, and many other happenings going back in my knowledge to the leaking pipe at Lord's in 1926. No doubt many others occurred even before that. It will be a sad day if ever legislators try to alter a result brought about by chance.

Certain aspects of the laws still cause discussion and widely differing views exist. They embrace the LBW law, on-side limitation, control of short-pitched deliveries, time-wasting, gamesmanship, and a need which is, I think, universally acknowledged, that it would be to the advantage of cricket if leg spin bowling could be restored to its former eminence.

Strangely enough one of the great problems of the latter is that modern watering systems are providing us with better grassed outfields – and often more grassy pitches. These things, which are extraordinarily difficult for the administrator to control, are meat and drink to the medium pace seamer (especially in England). It is a trend which is not in the best interests of cricket. The problem is how to cope with it.

The synthetic limited-over matches compound the difficulty, because any match where victory may be achieved by denying runs to your opponent without having to dismiss him is made to order for the negative captain. Here is a most fruitful field for study; the problem is urgent but the answer obscure.

Swanton has an understandable swipe at what is termed 'chequebook' journalism. It is a knotty problem. He means, I presume, the person who sells his fame as a cricketer for the lucrative peddling of sensationalism at the risk of damaging human relationships.

The professional journalist whose writing is out of the top drawer may well buck at what a wholly incompetent writer may be paid merely to be ghosted. By its very nature sport lends itself to such treatment. But here we enter a field of great complexity affecting human rights and privileges. Moreover, the cricketer of today may be the journalist of tomorrow, given the opportunity. Australia's foremost cricket writer at present (or at worst second best) is an ex-Australian XI batsman, and even though I am aware that there are very mixed feelings about current players writing for the press some of the most reasoned, sensible, best informed and best expressed comments in 1974/5 came from a current player.

But I am in danger of writing a book, not an introduction and must not succumb to this temptation. My prime task is to commend *Swanton in Australia*. It covers a long period in cricket history, an era of change probably without precedent, and indeed covers momentous issues still with us. Jim Swanton's writings do much to mould public opinion, and readers should be grateful for a faithful and illuminating description, from the ringside, of these fascinating years in cricket history.

I

Sentimental Journey

This last MCC tour of Australia was for me a tour with a difference, for it was my eighth and final visit as a cricket writer, and as such something of a sentimental journey. One was about to revisit remembered places, to relive on the spot many of the old battles, to encounter old friends probably for the last time: at any rate for the last time in Australia as a 'working journalist', as our kind is sometimes strangely described. (Has anyone, by the way, met a non-working journalist?)

What ground these all-but-thirty years had covered from Hammond's men in 46/7 to Denness's in 74/5, with those of Brown, Hutton, May, Dexter, Smith and Illingworth intervening! Each tour had been so different even if the chief places and the general itinerary had been broadly similar: the course of each was conditioned, naturally, by the strength or otherwise of Australian cricket at the moment: the spirit and 'flavour' of each reflected its particular leadership, both in captaincy and management.

My strongest feeling as I prepared for this final journey was thankfulness for being still in harness and so able to make it. Of the fourteen cricket writers who set out from Southampton with MCC on the *Stirling Castle* on 31 August 1946 no one else was fulfilling the job that he was doing then. Most had retired, three were dead. The only other member of the 1946 MCC party due to take part in 1974/5 was Alec Bedser, then England's bowling hope, now the manager.

Not the least of the contrasts between 1946 and 1974 was the greater sophistication of the foremost cricketers of today. True, Michael Denness would be new to Australia, but ten of his side had been before, while all the rest bar one had been with him on one or other of the two tours immediately preceding in India, Pakistan and the West Indies, if not on both. The solitary exception was David Lloyd, the Lancashire captain, at 27 one of the youngest spirits.

Wally Hammond, by contrast, in 1946 took only three who had seen Australia before, Bill Voce, Joe Hardstaff, and Laurie Fishlock.

Most of the remainder of his team must have qualified for the tour which would have sailed from home in 1940: notably, of course, the bright young things of the thirties, Hutton, Compton, Edrich, and Wright.

If the MCC cricketers of 1974 were a more knowing lot than their predecessors (I did not say better players) what about the country they were going to? Needless to say, the face of Australia had changed vastly. One wondered afresh each time at the physical expansion, of Perth especially but of all the capital cities, as population increased. There was a growing sophistication, too, in the art of living, quickened by the immigrant strains from Europe. Sadly, also, if inevitably, there was no disguising that Commonwealth bonds had weakened somewhat, as Australia looked across the Pacific to America. There had been a change in the relationship certainly, but surely old associations must be preserved – and one of the most ancient of these was cricket.

Plum Warner's favourite saying, that cricket cements the bond of Empire – for which read Commonwealth – is an old cliché, but it is only half-true. If a Test series well fought and conducted brings countries closer the converse is undeniable. There is a constant ebb and flow in the relationship between England and Australia. The story of these ups and downs, in so far as cricket has affected them, is the theme – and, I hope, will be considered the justification – for this book. My aims are to bring Australia and Australians just a little closer to English readers, and to give those in Australia a version of MCC tours there from an English point of view. Hence this opening chapter which deals only incidentally with cricket.

My eighth tour would, of course, proceed in the tempo of the seventies, jetting here, jetting there, in and out of motels with their fridges and telly and all mod. cons. wherein no doubt players can spend quietly such brief and valuable hours of relaxation as the programme allows. No such lovely, leisurely, luxurious start as the old sea voyages through the Med and Suez and with the stretching of sea-legs in the one-day game at Colombo: no dusty train-journeys (except one special air-conditioned one for me), no putting-up at faded old country hotels, seemingly not redecorated since the gold rush where the welcome was uniformly warm even if the plumbing and ablutionary arrangements were sometimes rudimentary.

I recall a communal wash-room, I think at Kalgoorlie, which had several hand-basins but a single mirror so that only one of us could shave at a time. The Australian patrons, unaccustomed to such intimate proximity to an Earl-Marshal and premier duke, let alone in pyjamas and before breakfast, made polite noises.

'After you, your Grace.'

'Not at all, it's your turn.'

(Author thinks: ' "Grace"? they didn't say that, they said "Grice." Yes, but if I write that won't they write me off on page 3 as just another toffee-nosed Pom? Maybe, I don't know. Anyway, let's ease them in gently to the possibility that *some* Australians, like some English, aren't too particular about some of the vowel sounds.')

The ice was soon broken around the MCC manager, as it always was on this, the tour of 1962/3, one of the happiest of the eight.

A thought, by the way, about the sea voyages: among other beneficial things they enabled our MCC cricketers to meet and become acquainted with a variety of Australians returning home, generally as a family after a summer in Great Britain and Europe. Friendships developed which were renewed in homes right around the coast as we progressed from Perth to Adelaide, to Melbourne, to Sydney, and finally up to Brisbane. If they were countrymen, visits to properties were proposed, and sometimes there was time for these to be accepted when we came within travelling range. Not many friendships are forged on airplanes or in motels. Indeed the tourist to Australia nowadays is largely insulated from social contact. The loss is his.

However, it is no good repining. The P & O no longer run a regular passenger service between England and Australia, and if they did the fares as well as the time involved would make a return to the old way of travel prohibitive. And at least the world's great airways have inherited the tradition of service and care for the passenger which were always the pride of the shipping companies. Such were my thoughts, as, settling into my seat on QF2 at London Airport at 18.00 hours on Thursday, 21 November 1974, I was promptly offered the choice of pineapple juice, champagne or beer. Travelling Qantas this time I had stepped out of Heathrow straight, as it were, into Australian territory: of which that cold antipodean beer was the first intimation. It eases the steward's depressing if necessary drill with the life-jackets, and the information as to the use of whistles and red lights if by chance we should find ourselves in the water. A firm injunction that international regulations forbid us to smoke in the 'toilets', and we are away: to Amsterdam, Bahrein, and my first destination, Singapore. The dawn comes up over the Persian Gulf, and a little later one hears sleepily the captain's voice saying over the intercom that we are approaching the Gulf of Oman and on our right is the oil-port of Dubai. I dimly recall our refuelling there a couple of years before, flying home from India.

At Singapore Airport I am met by Cecil Cooke, who as chairman of the Singapore Cricket Association keeps the flag flying there among that prosperous multi-national community. 'We're so relieved to see you,' he says. 'We weren't sure which flight you were on, and there's been a hi-jacking at Dubai.' It was a VC10 destined for Singapore which had set off from London an hour or two ahead of us. If Thomas Cook had not booked me Qantas I should certainly have been on the hi-jacked flight.

I imagine that Singapore beckons all travellers to the Far East who, like me, were caught up in the defence of Malaya and finally, on 15 February 1942, became prisoners of the Japs as a result of the biggest British capitulation in history. The prospect of a brief return had for me a certain macabre fascination, though in reality one is at once absorbed by the modern development of Singapore, its evident thriving well-being. There was a reception for me at the Singapore Cricket Club, that prosperous social-cum-sporting institution marvellously situated within a stone's throw of the Anglican Cathedral and the Supreme Court. (They got their priorities right, those nineteenth-century empire-builders.) And I lunched at the Island Golf Club with my friend Dr Ong Swee Law, president of the Malaysian Cricket Association when my Commonwealth team toured there in 1964, now 'as evidence of his versatility' chairman of the Singapore Zoo. It amused me to be entertained in that red-roofed club-house on which I had rained so many 25-pounder shells (with what effect I never knew) thirty-odd years before. I tried hard but in vain to find a crossroads below the Chinese cemetery in the Adam-road area which has often been in my thoughts since for a strictly personal reason.

Towards the end of the battle I was picked up, after having been wounded, by an improvised ambulance, which lumbered off, ostensibly to a dressing-station. Suddenly to my horror I saw that the driver was within a few yards of a crossroads proceeding smartly towards the enemy, 180° in the wrong direction. The Japs had knocked out several of our vehicles at this precise spot, having, we thought, a gun on fixed lines trained for this purpose. A yell to the driver

4

caused him to use the crossroads to turn the ambulance round. To me those seconds while he did so were an eternity: however, not a shot came our way. Presumably the Jap gunners were having a tea (or mishi-mishi) break. What luck!

Talking of guns on fixed lines (that is to say permanently set on a particular target) there is a story of a well-known Army and Oxford cricketer of other days, Colonel A. C. Wilkinson, who, by the way, to give his presence in this chapter rather more relevance, is half-Australian, half-English. Alex was a soldier reputedly without fear, and has two D.S.O.s and M.C. and George Medal to testify thereto. At a quiet time on the Italian front in the last war his early evening habit was to collect some reluctant bridge-playing fellow-officer from his mess to make a four with two friends of his quartered on the other side of the adjacent river. The snag was that crossing the river-bridge invariably attracted fire from a lone German machine-gun. A Cranleighan friend of mine, named Peter Black, was duly selected one evening and made his nervous way at his commanding officer's side. When they reached the bridge, sure enough the gun started up, whereupon the colonel raised his walking-stick above his head. A bullet promptly took a couple of inches off the end of it.

'There you are,' said Alex, 'I knew it – perfectly safe! It's on fixed lines.'

How many times young Black revoked that evening is not recorded. He could at least thank his stars he would be making the homeward journey in the dark.

I started my last book with a number of personal 'ifs' to illustrate the part that luck plays in all our lives and fortunes, and you will note that a couple of quite serious personal 'ifs' have already found their way into this opening chapter. If the Jap gunners had been on the job at the crossroads this book would no more have been written than if the fellow shooting from a tree had despatched instead of winging me just previously. Talking, incidentally, of Japs up trees Fred Titmus, who lost all four small toes of one foot in a boating accident in Barbados some years ago, may be interested to know that their staple footwear in the jungle was a rubber-boot so cloven that the big toe has a compartment to itself. So Nippon was ahead of him in discovering that it is the big toe that does all the work, whether bowling or climbing trees.

Again, what if I had taken the VC10 flight to Singapore? At one point in the negotiations the hi-jackers took a prosperous-looking

German travelling first-class and shot him. There but for the grace of God . . .

But it is time we were heading again for Australia, and making via Darwin the night hop to Brisbane. Only its dim outlines were to be seen as we flew out of Australia's most northerly outpost – the city that was to be so tragically devastated by Cyclone Tracy a bare month later – but soon at 30,000 feet we were flying into a golden dawn – the most humbling and wonderful sight – and soon again were being served barramundi for breakfast. Barramundi is a superb fish caught in the waters of the Northern Territory, and is something between a turbot and a mackerel. Not many breakfasts stick in the memory, but this delicious one will. Presumably Qantas took it aboard fresh at Darwin. Australia's international airline should have some pull there, for it was in these parts that they originated. The peculiar name is a shortening of the early Queensland And Northern Territory Aerial Services. If I had chosen to fly straight through from London it could, incidentally, have brought me the 10,970 miles in 28 hours. But, cossetted by Qantas as I would have been, I'd have arrived mighty tired. (London-Perth by Qantas takes only 24.)

I had braced myself to face the normal sticky heat of Brisbane, but this time it was quite otherwise. Indeed in ten pleasantly warm days I saw no rain, though once in the night I heard it coming down in a way recalling the tropical storms that had scuppered England's prospects here in 1946 and again in 1950. This rain, as it turned out, though far less fierce, helped to do the same, thanks to a human error that was to set the Test series off on a highly unfortunate note. Unfortunate at least for England.

I'm running ahead a bit, though, for the first augury for the forthcoming series on the day of my arrival at Brisbane was a happy one in that MCC (having just previously beaten New South Wales down in Sydney) actually defeated Queensland. True, the margin was only 46 runs, but in seven previous games against Queensland since the war, all drawn, MCC had rarely looked like winning. And since England had also lost four Tests on the Woolloongabba pitch and won none the name Vulture Street, in which the ground was situated, had seemed sinisterly prophetic. And it was soon to seem so again.

For when Mike Denness and his side went to the ground on the Wednesday morning, two days before the First Test, the pitch to their astonishment was a morass of black mud. They left the acting-

6

curator and reigning Lord Mayor of Brisbane, Clem Jones, clad in yellow safety-helmet, flattening it, roughly speaking, with a heavy motor-roller while they went off to practise on perfect net wickets (dry because they had been adequately covered) at the Church of England Grammar School a mile down the road. The pitch at the 'Gabba, being on a bit of a slope, needs careful protection, and in this case a couple of tarpaulins were patently not enough. Clem Jones is a regular Pooh-Bah whose energies are said to have accomplished much for the city of Brisbane; but as Michael Melford put it in the *Daily Telegraph* 'civic duties and curatorship do not easily blend.'

I mention this prelude to the 1974/5 Test series, which England were about to lose 4-1, because the resultant pitch was given a ridge by the heavy rolling when it was like Plasticine, and the upshot was an overdose of bumpers on the part of Lillee and Thomson, broken English bones, and a swift moral advantage to Australia which England could not break down until the last Test of six. But the purely cricket side of the tour will be found in its chronological place.

It's the misfortune of all who travel with MCC to Australia that they are confined almost wholly to the cities and are able to see little of the out-back. I write as one who has never cast eyes on Alice Springs, or the Barrier Reef, and to whom the Snowy River scheme is only a name. We climb from city to city watching the red roofs and the green ovals recede, giving place as we reach cruising height to a huge indefinite panorama of brown and yellow splashed with green, the sun glinting now and then off blue water. It was with this vast gap in my education in mind that I planned with Thomas Cook to take the Indian Pacific train from Sydney to Perth, booking, as one needs to do, some six months ahead.

Rail travel in Australia has been hampered for generations by the variety of gauges – a strange self-inflicted disability attributable, I suppose, to early inter-state rivalry and distrust. It was only five years ago that the last stage of the standard gauge was completed and the first train made the journey right across the Continent from Sydney to Perth. The Indian Pacific now leaves three times a week each way, and the journey takes about 65 hours. One spends three nights in the train. I left Sydney on the Thursday afternoon following the Brisbane Test which had ended on the Wednesday, and got to Perth in time for breakfast on Sunday.

There is nothing scenically dramatic about the journey, but one

7

sees inevitably a cross-section of the Australian countryside from the rich pastures of New South Wales on the east, dipping briefly down to the sea at Port Pirie, across the endless Nullarbor Plain – not a tree, not a hint of moisture – to Kalgoorlie, with its romantic Gold Rush associations, and thence by night to Perth.

One can either immure oneself in one's own snug air-conditioned coupé, emerging only for meals as they are announced over the intercom, or live a more gregarious life in the bar and lounge-car with its piano and leather armchairs. My own journey is a compromise, and I emerge at the end of it relaxed and refreshed, and with a profusion of memories: of the Blue Mountains shimmering in the afternoon sunlight; of limitless gums, red-capped, as we make the twilight ascent to Broken Hill; of the frustration of a lengthy, unexplained stop outside Port Pirie which postponed the dinner-hour almost to bed-time (we made up most of the three hours lost); of times observing the social scene in the Club Car with Harold Nicolson's *Diaries,* volume one, for company – a teenage girl playing the piano passably enough and being succeeded on the stool by a nun, rendering the tunes of her youth with a wistful smile; of an old man in braces wagging his head in appreciation.

Then comes the Nullarbor and the longest utterly straight stretch of line in the world – exactly 300 miles from around Ooldea to a point east of a halt called 'Haig'. The Aboriginal word 'Ooldea' means 'a meeting-place where water is obtainable.' It is thought to come from an underground river, and it is the very last such point before one enters this featureless expanse of scrub. The illustrated map makes the most of the variety. Some apparently is myall, some mulga, and some mallee, but to the townsman's eye it is all stumpy greyish bush.

Just on the Western Australia side of the state border with South Australia is an inconspicuous halt named after the man whose courage and initiative linked the state of which he later became Premier with the rest of the continent. In 1870 John Forrest (who was ultimately made Lord Forrest of Bunbury) crossed overland above the Great Australian Bight from Perth to Port Augusta and thence to Adelaide. Horses and camels provided his transport, and the entire 1500-mile journey took five months. Forrest's object was to join these waterless tracts by rail, and this was ultimately to be achieved within his lifetime – the longest such project to be undertaken anywhere in the world. The three thousand workers proceeded yard by yard laying two and a half million sleepers, supplied by a town on wheels which followed their progress. This was the fore-runner of the 'tea and sugar train' which today caters for the needs of the railway-workers at stations which are still called camps. We passed this train from which fresh food can be bought, and which has its mobile theatre, dentistry, and facilities for 'ministers of religion'. It was in order to labour on the railways, by the way, that the Chinese were first brought down from the north – before the White Australia policy was ever considered.

The place names, as is the case all over Australia, have three main derivations. There are the Aboriginal names, euphonious and several-syllabled; Coondambo, Mundrabilla, Kingoonya, Kellerberrin, Paratoo: those imported direct from England and Scotland; Croydon, Peterborough, Penrith, Strathfield, Wimbledon, Burnley, Perth: and those commemorating people both British and colonial, from Sydney, the name of the Home Secretary at the time of the first settlement made by Captain Phillip, RN, 'dear Lord Melbourne,' and Queen Adelaide to the nineteenth-century Australian pioneers. But why Haig and Kitchener for mere specks in the desert? I asked my neighbour in the dining-car, who laughed and said, 'Well, you know, we didn't feel too good about those generals of yours.' A subtle form of revenge?

The food was good on the train, the drink likewise, though the average Australian, like most of Anglo-Saxon stock, does not exactly aim to head the field as regards grace of service. We leave the re-finements to the Asiatics and the Latins. In these egalitarian days it's rather that you, the customer, have to win your way into his regard, than vice versa. This is true except in the case of the famous Australian clubs, as I will elaborate in due course.

I had an example on the train of varying standards in this respect that makes me laugh as I recall it. Before my first lunch aboard I ordered a pink gin and was politely and correctly served, the barman first rolling the angostura bitters round the glass in the prescribed manner. A day later I approached the bar with the same request which was quite differently received.

'*Pink Gin*?' said the man indignantly, 'we don't have any pink gin.' It was as though I'd stepped into a small hotel and nonchalantly asked for pink champagne. I said, 'I think you'll find you have – I had some yesterday.'

'*Yesterday*?' he cried, 'that's got nothing to do with it. The New South Wiles blokes were on yesterday. We've got no *pink gin*.'

I remembered that the train is staffed by different state railways

9

as each border is passed – first NSW Railways, then South Australian (to which this chap belonged), then Commonwealth, and finally Western Australia. However, he was too aggressive for my taste, and so I said quietly, 'Look, you only had to say you were sorry that South Australian railways didn't carry pink gin, and I'd have understood.'

'*Sorry?*' he asked, 'I'm not sorry, I'm bloody glad.' E.W.S., fascinated by now, and puzzled at this: 'Tell me, why are you bloody glad?'

'Because it'd be more for me to bring on the train, that's why.'

I thought of telling him the size of a bottle of angostura, but, as I settled for a plain gin, delivered instead a few well-chosen (and no doubt horribly pompous) remarks about courtesy to the customer. This seemed to silence him, but when I asked my dining neighbour whether he'd heard this lively exchange he said as he was a bit deaf he hadn't caught it. 'But when I went up to order mine the bloke said "Cor, that Pom was a bit cranky, wasn't he? Reckon it was because England lost the Test!"' He'd had the last word after all.

Perth as always was delightful, apart from the cricket. As usual it had swelled in the four years since my last visit, yet there is so much space around this city astride the Swan River that life remains easy and comfortable – if expensive. (At the Parmelia Hotel $1.40 (80p) for a pot of tea for one, $5.50 (more than £3) for a haircut and shampoo.) Lake Karrinyup Golf and Country Club, where the Australian Open had just been played, was as attractive as ever and with its rebuilding even more imposing. It was here – on the fifteenth fairway, to be exact – that I saw kangaroo, almost for the only time in eight tours: three big chaps or rather, I expect, if we could have got near enough to ensure, before they hopped off into the bush, two ladies and a gentleman, or vice versa. Tom Bunning, my Australian opponent, could scarcely believe his eyes.

In Adelaide we found Sir Donald as quick and bright-eyed as ever, as indeed he had illustrated six months earlier in London when he came over to make £10,000 for cricket by a single appearance at the dinner organized jointly by the Lord's Taverners and the National Sporting Club. Also I saw again a distinguished contemporary of the Don's, just about to celebrate his 83rd birthday on Christmas Day, Clarrie Grimmett, shrivelled but spry, almost blind but with a lovely grin. Soon he was snapping his fingers and recalling old times, as we sat together at Adelaide Oval.

The best bat he ever bowled to? Warwick Armstrong. Well, he almost said that. Most of the others he could keep quiet *and* get out. Warwick was armed at all points. I made a mental reservation that Clarrie would only have bowled to Armstrong in District cricket in Melbourne when he was on his way up. He was born in New Zealand, and played first there, then in Sydney Grades, then Melbourne, and finally Adelaide, whence he made the South Australian XI! He was 33 before he won his first cap for Australia (against England at Sydney in 1925) – and with devastating effect. A mutual friend, Ian McLachlan, says that Clarrie's verdicts on batsmen are inclined nowadays to shift a bit. Generally he says that Jack Hobbs was the best bat he ever bowled at, and Charlie Macartney the most dangerous. Anyway, and oddly enough, not Don Bradman.

He's quite clear about his ideal captain – Vic Richardson. He recalls when they were stuck for a wicket Vic said, 'Boys, I'm going to switch you round': that was to say Grimmett down-wind, O'Reilly into it. 'So I came on to them a bit quicker, and Vic took all those catches.' O'Reilly said, 'Hi, that's my end,' to which the gnome answered, 'What's the matter, I'm getting them out, aren't I?'

He always fancied himself against Ponsford and one day after some difficulty persuaded Vic to give him the second over of the innings after Jack Scott had bowled the first. 'What are you doing here?' Ponny asked. 'I'm on to get you out,' was the answer: and he did, bowling him off his pads.

Clarrie remembered a bygone first encounter with an MCC team. It was the one Harold Gilligan, Arthur's brother, brought to Australia and New Zealand in 1929/30. A burly tail-ender arrived and promptly hit him for three straight sixes in a row at the River Torrens end. The second landed half-way up the slope, the third in a water-tank then situated at the top of the bank from where 5AD now broadcast. I identify the hitter as Guy Earle, and estimate the range to the foot of the tank as 130 yards at the minimum. He couldn't have any more of that so 'I rushed one through a lot quicker and bowled him out.' It's often fatal to check Wisden on such occasions, for all too soon old men forget. But there is the mention of the three sixes in an over in the 1931 edition, page 647: but the score reads 'G. F. Earle, run out 43.' Ah, well!

If there's one Australian fact of life more frequently evident than another it is the increase in the number of New Australians. On the one hand you see everywhere the perpetuation of British institutions which have lost nothing – gained rather in many cases – in the transplanting. You see how much Australian television relies on British material. *Upstairs, Downstairs* is followed as enthusiastically in Australia as at home. So are *Dad's Army* and *Morecambe and Wise.* Most of the books reviewed are published in England. A fair amount of the feature material in the newspapers derives from Fleet Street. British influence is to be found everywhere, and would take a long time to eliminate – even if there was an urge to do so, which happily seems not to be the case.

On the other hand, as one tour succeeded another one came across immigrants from every European country and beyond becoming very willingly absorbed into the Australian way of life. At Melbourne Airport on the last tour our porter was a splendid-looking fellow, a White Russian brought up in Japan. At Perth we found a regular taxi-driver who had escaped from East Germany at the second attempt. The first time when a boy he had been caught and committed to a labour camp. There was a Yugoslav airport worker who had come to Melbourne with his country's Olympic football team in 1956 and had declined to return. This had cost his father, who had gone surety for him, three months in gaol – but he thought he had since amply repaid the debt financially. Rudi Webster, a clever doctor from Barbados, was practising in Melbourne. In Rose Bay, Sydney, a Rumanian has a shop solely devoted to cheese, and one can get every English variety, Stilton included. There are Bulgarians and Greeks, 'strangers of Rome, Jews, and Proselytes, Cretes and Arabians', every man talking more or less coherently 'in our own tongue wherein we were born.' Having established that my wife and I were English, and not Australian, some of these people might have been more ready to bemoan their lot, if they were unhappy. On the contrary, neither of us met any European immigrant who was not grateful for having come to Australia, though one heard of a few British misfits.

Christmas in Melbourne meant making our Communions among a congregation of all ages spilling into every corner of every aisle at its oldest and most famous Anglican church, St Peter's, Eastern Hill, which stands on the highest point of the inner city – though now dwarfed by the Parliament Buildings, on one side, and the R.C. cathedral, both much later constructions, on the other. I never

1. Service with a smile: Thursday, 21 November 1974, 1800 hours. Qantas Jumbo flight 002 for Amsterdam, Bahrein, Singapore, Darwin, Brisbane.

Thirty years of travel: 1950 — 24 days 1974 — 24 hours

2. Three generations: on s.s. *Stratheden*, September, 1950, Neville Cardus, John Woodcock, EWS. NC was at his best aboard ship. Reminiscence flowered with time to spare.

Captains of MCC
3. W. R. Hammond, 1946/7
4. F. R. Brown, 1950/1
5. L. Hutton, 1954/5

6. P. B. H. May, 1958/9
7. E. R. Dexter, 1962/3

8. M. J. K. Smith, 1965/6
9. R. Illingworth, 1970/1
10. M. H. Denness, 1974/5

attend St Peter's without recalling my first extraordinary sight of it
on All Saints' Day, 1946. Arriving a little late I saw in solemn pro-
cession more copes and mitres than I ever cast eyes on before or
since. St Peter's still regularly attracts to its services bishops and
clergy from all over Australia and beyond, but this occasion, as it
turned out, was part of the celebration of the centenary of the church.
Looking today at the great, orderly metropolis of Melbourne it is a
striking thought that only a hundred years before this first visit of
mine to St Peter's in 1946, the letters patent of Queen Victoria creat-
ing the Anglican diocese of Melbourne and proclaiming Melbourne
a city were read from the church steps. That ceremony took place
little more than a decade after John Batman's first village settlement.

Less than a mile down the hill, enclosed within Yarra Park, lay
the object of my visit, and an institution not much less venerable
than St Peter's Church, the greatest cricket ground in the world,
held and administered in trust for the city by that other MCC, the
Melbourne Cricket Club. Its centrality and ease of communications
have much to do with the vast crowds that inhabit the MCC on
big occasions, but the fact is that comparing its population with that
of other cities Melbourne's patronage of sport must stand supreme,
whether in the Commonwealth or outside. Now on Boxing Day, 1974,
for the Test's first day there came 77,165, the largest crowd I have
ever seen at a cricket match. Of that more anon, but meanwhile let
me respectfully doff my hat to the Melbourne Cricket Club itself
for its unique service to sport. Aside from cricket, its original *raison
d'être,* its main ground is the chief focus for Australian Rules Football, the final rounds of which test the capacity (since the Olympic
Games extension) of 120,000: the club started baseball in Australia,
and it caters also for lawn tennis, bowls, lacrosse, squash, hockey
and rifle shooting: nine sports in all, for which they need to run six
grounds. There are 16,000 full members of this Australian MCC.
Strangely enough the two clubs now have just about the same membership 'ceiling'. It takes all but twenty years to attain full membership
of Melbourne, though temporary status naturally is accorded to those
who represent the club in any of its many enterprises. Quite a box of
tricks for Ian Johnson, the old Test captain, to administer as secretary,
and for Sir Albert Chadwick, President of MCC, to preside over. As
all cricket historians know, the Australian organizers of early International cricket were the Melbourne Cricket Club, on whose ground

(*The Paddock that Grew* in Keith Dunstan's evocative phrase) the first of all Tests was played in 1877. What a debt cricket owes to the two MCCs!

While MCC exercise these wider responsibilities the Victorian Cricket Association under Ray Steele, the 1972 Australian manager in England, is busy fostering the game within the state. The VCA have recently appointed Frank Tyson to a new post as state director of coaching, and they report that more cricketers than ever before are playing in Victoria. In fact there is an annual increase of 13% – which we must accept as splendid news, even if in the long term it can scarcely mean an improvement in England's prospect of holding the Ashes. Unless, of course, the National Cricket Association can report a similar swelling of the ranks at home.

Talking of Melbourne institutions it would be churlish of me, considering how often I have enjoyed the privilege and amenities of honorary membership, not to mention another even older than St Peter's or MCC, the Melbourne Club. Thanks to the good offices of Roger Kimpton the Arabs (the small cricket club I founded when young, which contains quite a few Australian members) held a celebratory dinner there on our second visit in February. I only hope this gay occasion will not prove to have prejudiced Roger's elevation to the Presidency, to which the Vice-President automatically proceeds. He will be 136th in line since the foundation of this great club in 1840.

It is part of the fascination for me of the Melbourne Club and such venerable organizations that these places, which cater for the highly civilized and sophisticated needs of their members today, were started by the hardy pioneers of Australia for whom life was rugged and perilous. The English genius for founding good and lasting clubs is nowhere better exemplified than in Australia.

There is one pilgrimage I'd have much liked to make again while in Melbourne but could not fit in, and that was to see Legh Winser and his devoted daughter, Ruth, out at Barwon Heads beyond Geelong, where he now lives in active retirement. However, at second hand I had reports of the 90th birthday dinner given for him at Royal Adelaide, his home course for all but fifty years, and of his steady golf next morning. At Barwon Heads at the age of 88 he went round in 76, *12 strokes* under his years. The *Guinness Book of Records* has a lot to say on the subject of golfers 'beating their age', but they do not make any claim as to the most strokes by which that age has been beaten. Any advance on twelve?

Legh Winser, a good cricketer in England who played with W. G. Grace and for Staffordshire, kept wicket to S. F. Barnes, and came to Australia before the first war for his health. He played cricket for South Australia, and as secretary to many successive State governors found sufficient time for golf to win the Australian Amateur, four State and ten Club titles. Now in a sense he has returned home, for of all the first-class courses in Australia none more resembles the sea-side links of Scotland and England, where the game began, than Barwon Heads.

Another pilgrimage 'on a far bigger scale' that it would have been a pleasure to make again was to New Zealand where I'd spent several happy weeks with Freddie Brown's team. I say this sincerely while believing firmly – for reasons I will put forward later – that it would be a much more satisfactory arrangement from the English point of view, and also in the long run from that of New Zealand, if MCC paid a separate and fuller visit there as the longer half of a tour also embracing Pakistan, rather than looking in when jaded after the six-Test tour of Australia.

The Third Test at Melbourne at the turn of 1974/5 – which either side could have won almost up to the last over – revived English spirits more than a little, but Sydney saw a recession, and after a game altogether too highly-charged Australia 'with a third victory' won back the Ashes. The cricket was a disappointment from my angle, and the inter-action of over-full crowds and over-demonstrative (and under-disciplined) cricketers took away much of the pleasure.

However, Sydney has much to offer the visitor apart from what in my view is the ideal Test ground. In its setting astride the harbour, sprawling over miles and miles of coast-line with views across the water almost around every other corner, Sydney for me is the finest city in the world. Sunshine and sea breezes: scenic beauty: all the cultural attractions of a great capital: where are these things more plentifully blended than in this, the first of the English settlements?

Again I must acknowledge gratitude to two clubs, the Australian and the Royal Sydney GC. The Australian Club would seem to be in clover, having demolished their own pleasant colonial-style club-house on Macquarie Street, with its wide panorama taking in the bridge, opera house and harbour, and put up on the same commanding site a modern building of which the lower floors are theirs, with twelve storeys of business premises, quite separate above. The spanking new club seems to have combined with remarkable success the traditional and the modern.

The beauty of Royal Sydney is that it is marvellously accessible, a mere ten minutes by taxi from the centre of the city. It is an ever-revolving hub of sporting and social activity with a vast club-house which has been described as 'a secular cathedral'. Viewed from the course it does have a distinctly ecclesiastical air. Built around and overlooked as it is, trespassers on the course are not infrequent and the story is told of two young lovers surprised one night by the secretary in a compromising position.

'Hey,' said he, 'you can't do that here.'

'Why not?' asked the young man.

Not expecting this riposte, the secretary hesitated before giving his verdict.

'Er, er – well, you're not members.'

I would not contradict, by the way, anyone who supposes that this crisp exchange derives from England, in or around a bunker at the Berkshire. As Maurice Tate might have said, 'It's immemorial.'

Changing the subject with a vengeance, I cannot complete this flitting about on my last sentimental journey in Australia without mentioning in deep appreciation the church at the bottom end of George Street hard by the station which has always beckoned during my visits to Sydney – Christ Church St Lawrence. It needs no words of mine to underline its excellence for its reputation is world-wide, and it has been described as the finest church in the Anglican communion. I had heard before first coming to Australia of this Catholic outpost which along with another city church, St James's in King Street, had for many years suffered ostracism and persecution from the fundamentalist hard core within the extreme Evangelical diocese of Sydney.

It was said that under the Rectorship of John Hope more ordinands to the ministry were accepted from Christ Church than from any other in the Church of England. Its services, as I first discovered in 1946, attracted a wonderfully wide cross-section of people of all ages and kinds. Fr John was evidently a spiritual powerhouse, a saintly man of extraordinary energy to whom no one came in vain. His Rectory was the refuge of 'failures' and drop-outs as much as of students, pious old ladies, and of bishops and clergy passing through.

Yet the church's very popularity was anathema to the militant Protestants who surrounded Howard Mowll, Archbishop of Sydney, and in particular to a certain Canon T. C. Hammond, who in the law-courts as well as in Synod attacked the Rector for practices of the Catholic faith which were commonplace almost anywhere else in the orbit of the Anglican church. The arch-Protestants of Sydney seemed to have, in Dean Swift's words, 'just enough religion to make us hate, but not enough to make us love one another.'

For much of his 38-year incumbency John Hope, who was inclined to over-tax his strength to the detriment of his health, had reason to believe that if the Archbishop outlived him the latter would make an appointment destined to destroy the traditions of Christ Church. In fact Archbishop Mowll died in 1958, and Fr Hope did not retire until 1964, by which time the religious climate had grown mercifully more temperate, to the extent that latterly Archbishop Mowll would visit the Rector when he was in hospital while the succeeding Archbishop, Hugh Gough, co-operated in the appointment of the present Rector, Austin Day. Fr Day was the choice of the parish as of John Hope himself, and under him Christ Church St Lawrence retains its character and influence in a community at least less bigoted than of old. In these ecumenical days it is easy to forget the struggles of such as John Hope, one of the most truly powerful men I ever met.

The last Test was naturally a nostalgic occasion for me, being the last I was destined to report – which naturally made England's innings victory, after four of the other five had been lost, even more than usually welcome. It was a joy to send good news home, belated though it was. There were many personal farewells to be made, including one on a fairly large scale. This was the last of the parties held in the state capitals which Ann and I hosted at the invitation of Thomas Cook. The idea behind the occasion was to underline the increasing involvement in sport of this, the biggest travel firm in the Commonwealth. The chairman of Thomas Cook in Australia is Sir Lincoln Hynes, by all accounts a high-class fastish left-arm bowler, who came fairly near selection to tour England with Don Bradman's 1938 side. As it was he had to be satisfied to be one of the relatively few men who got the Don out for a duck – this in a state match for New South Wales against South Australia. 'Bob' Hynes kindly proposed my health at this party, I in my reply telling the company the pink gin on the train story. Thereafter in Melbourne people were inclined to say, 'Here comes Jim. Better get him a pink gin.'

2

A Taste for Australians

Taxi-drivers the world over seem to share a basic loquacity, throwing over their shoulders, with or without encouragement, a variety of earthy comment. Those of Australia are not the most backward in this regard: there is much to be gleaned by the traveller anxious to inform himself about the country and its people. I recall fondly my first encounter with the fraternity on the journey into Perth from its port of Fremantle in the last days of September, 1946. The purpose of the visit having been established, our man proceeded to parade before my companion and me the manifold attractions and delights of Australia. We Poms naturally made occasional noises of enthusiastic interest as the recital continued. On approaching the Palace Hotel, for so long though no longer the headquarters of teams visiting Perth, he delivered the brusque summing-up:

'Yeah, it's a great country . . .' Pause. '. . . Remember it's yours as well as ours – and if you don't enjoy yourselves it'll be your own ruddy fault.'

I relished that. It smacked of the Aussies I had come to know in the POW camps of Singapore and Siam – to know and admire for their self-reliance and their readiness to help their fellows, their toughness and their laconic humour in adversity. True, there was another characteristic which one came also to expect – a sometimes exaggerated sensitivity to the attitudes of others towards Australia and Australians which is generally summed up as a chip on the shoulder. If we didn't enjoy this latter-day Eden of theirs we'd have only ourselves to blame. The best description of a well-balanced Australian, it is said, is a man who has a chip on each shoulder. (Perhaps this rude jibe was made about Yorkshiremen – they have a lot in common.) The product of the New World is inclined to be prickly in confrontation with Englishmen, at least in the early stages. He may half-expect the visitor to be reserved and unforthcoming until he gets evidence to the contrary. On his side the old colonial relationship is not yet quite dead, though it is far less evident in Australia today than it was thirty years ago.

But who cannot be accused of a chip on his shoulder where his country is concerned? However critical we may be among ourselves about the various unacceptable faces of modern Britain we do not take kindly to even the mildest reproof from outside. Australian chips have seldom worried me. Subconsciously maybe I am inclined to make an early overture, and the response is usually warm and immediate. For the average Australian is companionable and an extrovert: once the barriers are down he is a friend very well worth having.

I say I got to value the companionship of Australians while a prisoner, but, of course, I had friends among them before that, both within the teams that came to England in the thirties and outside. One of the first was Arthur Mailey whom I had first watched from the Oval pavilion playing for Warwick Armstrong's great side, spinning away with a fine philosophical detachment in utter contrast to the sound and fury of Jack Gregory and Ted McDonald. Arthur on his retirement stepped straight into the press-box bringing a fresh flavour to cricket journalism by illustrating his own articles. He was an amusing cartoonist who graduated to oils and on his later visits to England packed an easel and paints in the boot of his car.

His travels were as the whim took him, and were not always related to the whereabouts of the Australian team on whose matches he was supposed to comment. There was the day when the *Evening Standard* wired their staff cricket writer Bruce Harris in press telegraphese: 'Upshake Mailey.' To this Arthur made the crisp rejoinder: 'Tell them to upshake their accountants.' But it may have been that this was the occasion when the *Standard* were showing understandable concern that Arthur should have forecast an England Test team due to be announced, and had failed to include a wicket-keeper. Arthur's cricket philosophy was simple and clear-cut. He went for dash in batting – after Trumper his favourite was Denis Compton – and wrist-spin in bowling. The medium-pacers, now known as 'seamers', he dismissed as 'boring'. Balance and tactical niceties were beneath his notice. Wicket-keeper? With that bowling, he said, they won't need one.

Arthur was the child of poor parents living on the outskirts of Sydney in a remarkable wooden house built on land sloping from front to rear. The rooms were divided, he said, only by hessian partitions suspended from the ceiling, and as the family increased rooms were added higgledy-piggledy at the back, each requiring the support of a higher pair of stilts. On his bedroom wall hung a photograph of his beloved Victor Trumper and as the hessian wafted in the breeze so his hero swayed, back and forth, to meet the bowling. His feet, as at the crease, were never still.

Arthur's reminiscences, like those of his friend Neville Cardus, were much in demand though he never forced them. They needed to be coaxed out, and I suppose they had a reasonable artistic approximation to reality. In his early years playing for New South Wales he was a plumber employed by the water board, and one day turned up for work in his best suit beneath his overalls because of an invitation to a grand cricket lunch at a posh Sydney hotel. During the morning Arthur and his gang were called to this very hotel to attend to a fault, and he was hard put to it to finish the job in time and present himself clean and tidy at the function. When he arrived the host apologized that the meal would be a bit late, explaining that the hotel's water supply had had to be cut off. Arthur tut-tutted sympathetically. How very inconvenient, but then, of course, labour today was very different from what it used to be. Some of this and much more reflecting a whimsical picture of A. A. Mailey is to be found in his autobiography, *Ten for 66 and All That,* which can still be had, with patience, from those who traffic in second-hand cricket books. It's lovely stuff, poignant and funny.

Another rich character of a very different sort whom I met long before setting foot in Australia was Reg Bettington. Arriving at Oxford as a Rhodes scholar shortly after the first World War, Reg physically was a bull of a fellow, designed by nature as a second-row forward – he did service for the University and Middlesex in this capacity – but a natural games-player withal, light on his feet and keen of eye and brain. He spun leg-breaks and googlies with the strong fingers of a surgeon which, after graduating at Bart's, he ultimately became.

On his day he was a match for the best, and apart from winning the University Match inside two days in his year of captaincy – with due help from Greville Stevens and the weather – he once skittled the full might of Surrey, Jack Hobbs and all, on a plumb-'un at the Oval. He was the first of his countrymen to captain Oxford at cricket. All in all R.H.B. was a legendary figure in the games world of the twenties. He was a blue also for golf, and by the time he returned home had become a good enough golfer to win the Amateur Championship of Australia in the same summer as he captained New South Wales at cricket.

I heard much of him before ever we met from his great friend and contemporary, Raymond Robertson-Glasgow – including this story. One Boat Race night Reg was apprehended somewhere in the purlieus of Piccadilly and was duly marched off – possibly not without some difficulty – to Vine Street. There perhaps his mood grew reminiscent, for when after a night in the cells he appeared next morning before the bench he was confronted with a heavy catalogue of refreshment.

'Well, Mr Bettington, you seem to have made quite an evening of it, consuming apparently seven pints of beer, eight whisky-and-sodas, nine gin-and-tonics, a quantity of brandy, and two glasses of port. Have you anything to say?'

'Yes I have,' said Reg in rich Australian, as though his principles had been offended: 'Naow port!'

No Oxonian, whether games-player or not, needs to be reminded of the great contributions made in every field by the Rhodes Scholars, and none came better than Reg. Marrying into the distinguished New Zealand family of Lowry he migrated in the fifties from Sydney to Hawke's Bay. After a day's work at the hospital, where he was the chief ear, nose, and throat specialist, he was tragically killed in a car accident.

Men of the quality of Mailey and Bettington, Hone and Kimpton, did much for the good name of their country among English cricketers who knew them, and there were other cheerful outgoing figures of a wider fame who were popular between the wars with English crowds. Names such as Jack Gregory, Bertie Oldfield, Vic Richardson and Stan McCabe come readily to mind.

There were, of course, many other redoubtable Australian games-players at Oxford shortly following Reg Bettington, notably B. W. Hone, known perhaps because of his solid shape as 'Nippy', captain in 1933, and R. C. M. Kimpton, who after a year's gap followed him. Thus some of the best batting seen in The Parks in the thirties came from Australians. Brian Hone caused something of a stir in those conventional days by missing a little cricket in his year of captaincy seeking a lawn-tennis blue. However he was a staunch batsman who in 1932 took 167 at Lord's against Cambridge and in particular off Kenneth Farnes, and in the fateful year of 1933 was on the receiving end at Farnes's hands of a far from mild version of the Bodyline which had been practised with such dire effect against his countrymen down under the previous winter. This was almost the only time deliberate short fast stuff on the body with a strong leg-side field was seen at the game's headquarters. Peter Oldfield was bowled off his neck! Brian Hone became successively headmaster of two famous Australian schools, Cranbrook and Melbourne Grammar, and was knighted on his retirement from Melbourne.

Of all the cricketers known to me who from one cause or another achieved less than their deserts Roger Kimpton would top the list. Does it give an idea of his quality that at the age of 18 he made 160 for the University against the full Gloucestershire attack, the last 50 in 25 minutes: then the following year he got 101 and 106 against them in the same match, and then 102 off Lancashire in 70 minutes? This was the fastest hundred of the season from mid-May to September when Les Ames in the Folkestone Festival pipped him by two minutes, and so robbed him of the Lawrence Trophy, and, more important to an impecunious undergraduate, of the £100 cheque that went with it.

Roger was small but strong and wiry, and so remarkably quick on his feet that Tom Goddard for one could not bear the sight of him. He was 'a natural' who kept wicket one year for Oxford, bowled leg-breaks and googlies, was as good a lawn-tennis player as cricketer, more than held his own on the squash court, and for good measure also picked up a blue for golf. He would assuredly have played for Victoria in the forties and probably for Australia. As it was he went home to join the RAAF, won the DFC as a pilot and after the war found himself absorbed in the Melbourne family business. When I dug him out in 1956, years after he had played any serious cricket, to join my side in the West Indies he went darting down the pitch as of old in a way that slightly surprised our contemporary Test stars.

I was a mere hero-worshipping teenager when I first saw Gregory in violent action in the great Oval Tests of 21 and 26. But I met him after the war in Australia, and though then in his fifties he had retained every bit of the glamour and presence which too often slips away from great sportsmen in middle age. He was still a magnificent figure, and like most of the famous cricketers of his generation quiet and modest in his talk.

But by the thirties I was already writing about Test Matches, and so was on nodding terms or better with the teams brought over by Billy Woodfull and Don Bradman. In particular I recall in 1930 Vic Richardson and Stan McCabe, the latter on his first tour the youngest member of the side and obviously in proper awe of Vic who regarded him with a bluff avuncular affection. One August evening that summer I ran into them by chance in Piccadilly hot on their return from Bristol where the match with Gloucestershire had ended in a tie. Over a few glasses of beer the young reporter was afforded a blow-by-blow description of the Australian second innings including the approximate number of LBW appeals made by Charlie Parker and Tom Goddard before they got their fourth and last decision with the scores level.

Vic and Stan were a friendly, bonhomous pair who 'registered' readily with crowds. But the fact was that the average Australian cricketer between the wars was not regarded with any great warmth by the English public: rather the contrary. The vast Warwick Armstrong in his team's triumphal progress in 21 had radiated an aura of stark hostility, and he came rather to personify the Australian cricketer of imagination, a sinister unsmiling antagonist beneath the baggy green cap.

Then came Bodyline, and the acrimonious exchange of cables which seemed to confirm the impression among Englishmen that the Australians were 'squealing'. This deplorable contretemps was not, of course, just a sporting squabble but an affair involving national honour and prestige that engaged our respective governments. Heaven knows it was the Australians who were the aggrieved party in that whole shameful episode, as I have recorded at length elsewhere. The truth about Bodyline, however, took a long, long time to filter through to the English public – indeed one still comes across people with a distorted view of it all – not unnaturally perhaps since the average man was not anxious to believe that in an issue which had clear moral implications his own side were the offenders.[1]

When the Australians came to England in the year following the Bodyline tour, 1934, the atmosphere surrounding them was sometimes horribly tense, and at Nottingham, home of the chief protagonists, Larwood and Voce, outright hostile. One of the upshots of the row was that the press-boxes began to fill with the old players of both countries, sounding off according to their lights and bringing a more contentious note into the newspaper coverage as compared with the generally more restrained accounts of the old-style reporters, most of whom were great traditionalists and stuck more or less to the facts.

Among the Australians who came in the thirties and with whom I therefore became acquainted were H. L. Collins, known as 'Horseshoe,' since he was proverbially lucky, and C. G. Macartney, known, I know not why, as 'The Governor-General'. Perhaps it was because

[1]Don Bradman underlines this point in his Introduction.

he was so obviously born to command the cricket scene. Charlie Macartney's name is not often heard or read about nowadays. He was no colossal amasser of runs of the order of Bradman and Ponsford, while as for Trumper he has long since been beatified, holding a place that no one can usurp. Yet no more brilliant or exciting batsman can ever have played for Australia than Macartney. His hundred before lunch in the Leeds Test of 1926 after Australia had been put in is rightly rated among the classics, but what about his unholy devastation of Notts at Trent Bridge in 1921?

Wisden records that his 345, while including four sixes and 47 fours, was made 'in rather less than four hours' – at a rate of about 90 an hour off his own bat. It is the second fastest triple-hundred ever made. According to Crusoe, who had a mind for such faintly comical detail, Macartney favoured a line in yellow boots, and these boots were to be seen twinkling out of the ground long before close of play, bearing away their owner in high dudgeon. Not normally run-greedy, he had had in his sights the beating of A. C. MacLaren's 424, made for Lancashire against Somerset in 1895, which, incidentally, is still the highest first-class score ever made in England. Having reached to within 79 of MacLaren with some two hours of the day to go the Governor-General was adjudged LBW to Hardstaff, the seventh bowler tried! (Henceforth in these pages Crusoe, his invariable nickname, will denote my old friend Raymond Robertson-Glasgow. It derived from a remark made by Charlie McGahey, of Essex, who on being asked how he was out said 'I was bowled by a beggar I thought had been dead for hundreds of years called Robinson Crusoe.')

I cannot exactly recall Macartney's attitude to Bodyline but it would have been in character if he had been scornful of his countrymen's effort. His would probably have been a subjective judgement based on the grounds that in a phrase attributed to him in a different context, he 'could have played it with a tram-ticket.' However that may be, kindness and encouragement to the young are particular Australian characteristics, and they were certainly shown to me by Macartney and by Herby Collins. Mailey, by the way, liked Collins, the man and the captain, as much as he disliked Armstrong, whom he thought 'would have been a greater captain had he shown the toleration and sympathetic understanding that he developed later in life.' I myself had a highly enjoyable insight of Armstrong in mellow maturity at Brisbane in 1946. On the field and off Collins was at heart a gambler – which suited Arthur's bowling philosophy. His hunting-grounds, he said, were the race-courses, the dog-track, Monte Carlo and a 'two-up' school in the Flanders trenches in World War I. In his *Ten for 66 and All That* Mailey writes of Collins:

> Collins was one of the most undemonstrative yet one of the richest characters in Australian cricket, during my playing career at any rate. His faults to me were virtues. His so-called weaknesses faded away or were set in true perspective for me by the richness and fine quality of his nature.
>
> Herby never complained, never moaned. His philosophy seemed to provide an antidote for bad luck. Indeed, frowning fortune to this little possum-eyed Australian was just another incident that would be of no account when a new day dawned.

As will by now be fully apparent I have an enduring weakness for Mailey. I may however be biased, since, re-reading his book once again, I find that in discussing cricket-writers, English and Australian, he wrote 'Swanton writes in a friendly way, as to a retired Army colonel in Bombay.' An agreeable sentiment surely, even if he apparently confines me to a somewhat limited readership!

As I have written elsewhere – in this book 'elsewhere' will usually mean, as here, in *Sort of a Cricket Person* – there is no situation in my experience which sees men both metaphorically and, in our case, literally so completely in the raw as a POW camp. There I came across the residue of the AIF contingent which had fought in Johore and Singapore under Gordon Bennett, the 27th and 28th Australian Brigade groups plus such RAAF as had not been flown away under the Jap advance.

The people I first remember among the Australians are the doctors who in camps disease-ridden, verminous, and in every way generally appalling, tending men in the last stages of weakness, and with virtually no drugs or equipment save what they contrived themselves, were quite splendid. Whereas the RAMC perforce had to spend their talent over the whole vast theatre of war the flower of the Australian medical service – volunteers all, of course – were recruited for their early formations. Such names as Corlett and Kranz and Dunlop and Coates will be readily remembered by all of us who lived and worked on the Burma-Siam railway in the camps that followed the muddy waters of the river Me-Nam-Kwa-Noi. 'Bertie' Coates was the senior medical officer in captivity, and as such shouldered the permanent, infinitely depressing job of negotiating with the Japs for medical supplies which they either did not have or refused to part with. Coates was a bluff, hard-bitten fellow to whom the Japs seemed to accord a grudging respect.

'Weary' Dunlop – now Sir Edward, a leading Melbourne surgeon with an International reputation – had qualified at St Mary's Hospital in the thirties, in the great days of St Mary's rugger and had achieved the rare honour of being elected a Barbarian. 'Weary' was a legend up and down the river, to whom many, British, Australian, and Dutch owe the fact of being alive today. It was he who made the decisions when it was a question whether to amputate legs and arms that were putrefying from ulcers. If the limb in the absence of healing drugs could not be saved 'Weary' had to balance the chance of a man surviving the shock of an operation probably to be performed without an anaesthetic. Despite his nickname which derived from a deceptively languid manner and speech he was absolutely tireless, and in confronting the Japs quite without fear. That meant, of course, that he was sometimes in trouble, and I recall one day at Kinsayok, some half-way up towards the Three Pagoda Pass that formed the border between Burma and Siam, 'Weary' Dunlop, all six foot-four of him, had been set to stand out in the sun, for some imagined offence, in front of the Jap commander's hut. A Korean camp guard, seeing a chance of amusing himself, picked up a length of bamboo from a pile nearby – all construction was of bamboo, the staple jungle building material – and began beating 'Weary' with it. 'Weary's' reaction was to catch the bamboo in mid-flail and hurl it away. Another bamboo went the same way and then another and another, by which time Japs and prisoners had gathered to see the fun. The air was thick with bamboo sticks and curses.

The little Korean grew beside himself at such loss of face, and if he had found an ally or two among the guards the consequences would have been sadistic and sickening. Happily the Japs seemed to enjoy the Korean's humiliation and Dunlop was released.

Talks by experts – more or less – on every subject under the sun were the order of the evenings when railway work was done, the speaker illumined by the only oil-lamp in an otherwise dark hut in which sat or lay anything up to a hundred men. With the 1939 *Wisden* to fortify my memory I talked endlessly about cricket, chiefly of its history and about contemporary characters with special emphasis on England v Australia. There were Aussies naturally who had seen the MCC teams led by Gilligan, Chapman, Jardine, and Allen, so the information was decidedly two-way. Thus I met Rohan Rivett, keenest of students of Australian cricket who, on return home after the war, brought out the first of the POW books, *Behind Bamboo*. He became editor of the *News* of Adelaide, and is now among other things cricket writer of the *Canberra Times*. Rohan is just one of those I have looked forward to meeting on revisiting Australia.

Another Australian I encountered briefly at Changi on Singapore island after the surrender was Ben Barnett, the 1938 Australian wicket-keeper. In the lull after the battle before prisoners were set to work, Ben and I organized a few games of cricket. On a horribly low-calorie diet dominated by rice we found the Army bats awfully heavy! After the war when he came to England to live (he has only recently returned to Australia) I played MCC and other cricket with Ben and got to know him well. For many years he was the resident representative of the Australian Board of Control, now succeeded in that capacity by John Warr.

Before I get down to saying something about the first of the post-war tours to Australia, it is worth recording the account I wrote for the 1946 edition of *Wisden* of one particular game between England and Australia which we played and enjoyed at the New Year of 1945 in the only camp in Malaya and Siam which was described (laughably maybe) as a hospital.

Cricket at Nakom Patom reached its climax on New Year's Day, 1945, when a fresh, and certainly hitherto unrecorded, page was written in the saga of England v Australia. The scene is not easy to put before you, but I must try. The playing area is small, perhaps sixty yards by thirty, and the batsman's crease is right up against the spectators, with the pitch longways on. There are no runs behind the wicket, where many men squat in the shade of tall trees. The sides are flanked by long huts, with parallel ditches – one into the ditch, two over the hut. In fact all runs by boundaries, 1, 2, 4 or 6. An additional hazard is washing hung on bamboo 'lines'. Over the bowler's head are more trees, squaring the thing off, and in the distance a thick, high, mud wall – the camp bund – on which stands a bored and sulky Korean sentry. (Over the bund no runs and out, for balls are precious.) In effect, the spectators are the boundaries, many hundreds of them taking every inch of room. The dress for onlookers is fairly uniform, wooden clogs, and a scanty triangular piece of loin-cloth known (why?) as a 'Jap-Happy'. Only the swells wear patched and tattered

27

shorts. The mound at long-on is an Australian preserve, their 'Hill'. The sun beats down, as tropical suns do, on the flat beaten earth which is the wicket. At the bowler's end is a single bamboo stump, at the other five – yes, five – high ones. There is the hum of anticipation that you get on the first morning at Old Trafford or Trent Bridge, though there are no score cards, and no 'Three penn'orth of comfort' to be bought from our old friend 'Cushions'.

The story of the match is very much the story of that fantastic occasion at the Oval in August 1938. Flt-Lieut John Cocks, well-known to the cricketers of Ashtead, is our Hutton; Lieut Norman Smith, from Halifax, an even squatter Leyland. With the regulation bat – it is two and a half inches wide and a foot shorter than normal – they play beautifully down the line of the ball, forcing the length ball past cover, squeezing the leg one square off their toes. There seems little room on the field with the eight Australian fielders poised there, but a tennis ball goes quickly off wood, the gaps are found, and there are delays while it is rescued from the swill basket, or fished out from under the hut. As the runs mount up the barracking gains in volume, and in wit at the expense of the fielders. When at last the English captain declares, the score is acknowledged to be a Thailand record.

With the Australian innings comes sensation. Captain 'Fizzer' Pearson, of Sedbergh and Lincolnshire, the English fast bowler, is wearing BOOTS! No other cricketer has anything on his feet at all, the hot earth, the occasional flint being accepted as part of the game. The moral effect of these boots is tremendous. Captain Pearson bowls with shattering speed and ferocity, and as each fresh lamb arrives for the slaughter the stumps seem more vast, the bat even punier. One last defiant cheer from 'the Hill' when their captain, Lieut-Colonel E. E. Dunlop, comes in, another and bigger one from the English when his stumps go flying.

While these exciting things proceed one of the fielders anxiously asks himself whether they will brew trouble. 'Should fast bowlers wear boots? Pearson's ruse condemned – where did he get those boots? . . . boots bought from camp funds: Official denial . . . Board of Control's strong note . . .' headlines seem to grow in size. Then he remembers gratefully that here is no Press-box full of slick columnists and Test captains, no microphones for the players to run to – in fact, no papers and no broadcasting.
But it is time to move on.

. Melbourne: the world's biggest cricket
ound: 77,165 watch Australia take
e field during the third Test on Boxing
y, 1974.

ans then and now

. Free and easy, with an occasional barracker—
e first Test, Brisbane, 1946. **13.** Sun, beer,
orched flesh, comment loud and earthy:
e outer' at Melbourne, 1975.

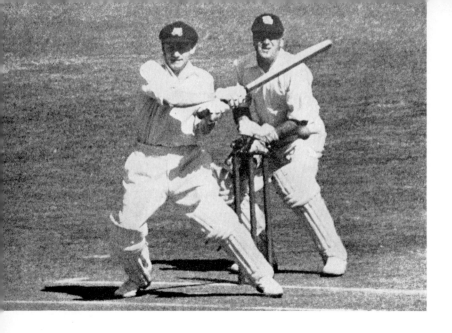

Key men, 1946/7

14. *(above)* Bradman, after years of enforced inactivity, and serious illness, played his way back to something like his old supremacy. Note the wrist-turn that keeps the hook stroke on the floor. **15.** *(below)* Lindwall, after prolonged war service in the jungles of New Guinea, returned in time to take his place in the Australian XI. Sideways on at full stretch: a splendid action, but how far is the right-foot drag going to take him? **16.** Miller — explosive bowler, dangerous attacking bat, magnificent fielder. He first came to prominence in the 'Victory Tests' in England in 1945 following a gallant war-record as a night-fighter pilot.

3

Resumption of Play

The first impression on our landing at Fremantle on 24 September 1946 of those of us who had not been previously to Australia – which was most of the press party of fourteen as well as the seventeen of the MCC team – was of its astonishing abundance: after the austerities of post-war Britain here was a land flowing with milk and honey – everything in fact except tea which we had imagined to be the staple drink. (It's not – it's beer.) There was a vast traffic in food parcels from Australians to friends and relations in the old country, and wherever we went, from Perth round the coast to Adelaide, Melbourne, Sydney and Brisbane, we added to the volume bound for home. Thus one salved one's conscience, and at least a few family larders became replenished with almost unobtainable luxuries.

Well-housed and fed, greeted with a special warmth in the light of the common experience and shared suffering of the war, and with three weeks on the true practice net pitches of Perth before the first first-class match was due, the tour of Walter Hammond's MCC side was propitiously embarked. After nearly a month at sea on a crowded ship run on austerity lines by the Government – no defined classes and no drink – there was, however, much hard training to be done.

I had cabled from the *Stirling Castle* a reasonably optimistic first despatch, noting Bill O'Reilly's retirement, announced while we were en route, and, fortified maybe by this news, rating English chances at 50-50. I thought the England Test side would go into the field with eight men capable of making a hundred, and that victory might depend very much on the success or otherwise of the all-rounders. I underlined the importance of Jim Langridge in this regard, especially as a bowler, pointing out that on all five between-the-wars MCC tours the slow left-armers – respectively Woolley, Kilner, White and Verity (twice) had been much the most economical bowlers in terms of runs per over. As it turned out Langridge never looked like fitting into the shape of Hammond's Test side, though he might have come

29   D

into the last two Tests had he been fit. Bill Edrich did some service as a fastish bowler with a slinging action while Norman Yardley's all-round skill won him a place in all the Tests. With his deceptively plain-looking medium-pace he actually took Bradman's wicket in three successive Test innings, and without help from a fielder at that. But our out-cricket was simply not good enough. Wright was the best bowler (23 at 44 runs apiece), Bedser was still an enthusiastic and tireless learner (16 at 54), but Bill Voce aged 37, in one of the hottest Australian summers, could not recapture the old magical fire. So one way and another, with Keith Miller and Ray Lindwall swiftly emerging as all-round cricketers of the highest class, the left-handed Arthur Morris establishing himself as the perfect opening partner for Sid Barnes, and Don Tallon as a wicket-keeper in the best Australian tradition, Bradman had plenty of talent to mould and encourage.

The operative word was 'encourage', and it was in this respect that Australia was to hold such a vital advantage. I had seen Hammond as a touring captain in South Africa in 1938/9, and on the evidence of that MCC tour to South Africa was more than apprehensive how he would answer the considerably more rigorous demands of this one eight years later. Like other brilliant natural sportsmen to whom success has come easily Hammond had little apparent understanding of the problems faced by less gifted mortals, nor did he seem to appreciate the value of the personal word of cheer and advice. He could be very good company when in the right vein, but there were bleak, moody spells which were apt to coincide with his own failures and those of the side. Rupert Howard, who at the age of 46 had been an exemplary manager of Gubby Allen's side to Australia ten years earlier, could not supply what the captain lacked – it was not to be expected. Wally found himself in closer rapport with his manager than with his team, and they were apt to make the many long journeys in a Jaguar, leaving the team to follow by train in the care of Yardley and of the famous old baggage-master, 'Fergie'.

But let us back to Perth, and I recall there a little incident which was, as it proved, significant – which, of course, is why after some thirty years it sticks in the mind. Denis Compton came in at an interval, not-out after some adventurous and entertaining batting against the spin of Bruce Dooland and Ian Johnson, both of whom he was seeing for the first time. In the hearing of several the captain was sarcastic about Denis's 'capering about' outside his crease, and rubbed in the point by turning to Jack Ikin and commending him for sticking in his ground. 'Let the ball come to you – that's the way to play out here.' Denis, from whom I had the story, was much deflated – he was, in fact, stumped for 98 – and throughout the tour felt that Hammond was wanting him to play in a way altogether foreign to his nature.

The fact was that Hammond on his first tour in 1928/9 had his great successes – his 902 runs in the five Tests is still the most ever made in a series in Australia – playing in a quietly determined, self-denying way quite different from his normal method at home. He decided it was safer for him to stay in his crease, and his results speak for themselves. However, genius can make its own rules, and it may be added that that Australian attack of 1928/9 was about the weakest they ever fielded. Moreover it contained no bowler who gave the ball such air as McCool, Johnson, Dooland, and Tribe, who in this first post-war series were to play so depressingly on the English reluctance to use their feet.

The oracle was listened to with vast respect, and his dictum was largely taken up by those who immediately followed him in England XIs – especially by Hutton, who was a fine enough technician to play slow bowling without coming out to meet it. To the ordinary mortal, however, it is fatal so to surrender the initiative to slow bowling. One can scarcely remember an Australian who did not aim to adjust the length of the ball by judicious footwork. The Don himself was a perfect example, and one can think of any number more – even men as different in build and temperament as Bill Pons-ford – a heavy man but marvellously nimble on his feet – and Neil Harvey.

The man on whom Hammond's tactics weighed most heavily was Compton – a genius, too, but of a different order, to whom the wiser captains gave his head. Was Hammond jealous of the popularity of the young star who threatened to dim the lustre of the old? Perhaps subconsciously he was. At all events the effect was highly unfortunate – we had come to the Fourth Test before Denis touched his best, just as Walter was bowing out of the arena for good.

From Perth MCC made the traditional progress anti-clockwise round Australia, calling first at a town of rudimentary graces (in those days at least) called Port Pirie where the opposition was terribly bad and very few people even came to watch. Hutton and Compton made their first hundreds in Australia, Denis needing only 67 minutes. After the first day I hopped on to the train, which was complete with cow-catcher in front of the engine and which, as in

Wild West films, ran down the centre of the main street. I was anxious to get an advance look at Bradman in the Adelaide nets. There had been speculation for months whether or not he would be fit to play. On what I saw I reported home that I thought he would be ready for the First Test, but that he was appearing against doctors' advice, and it would be a near thing.

Nearly everyone falls for Adelaide at first sight. Laid out by an Englishman, one Colonel Light, its first Surveyor-General, Adelaide is trim and prosperous after a more leisurely manner than the great cities of the east. The inner environs bounded by four wide Terraces named after the points of the compass, it has the advantage for strangers that they can easily find their way about. Below North Terrace the road sweeps down to the bridge over the Torrens river. Beside the river whereon swans dispute the oarsmen's sway lies a green and gracious park, and beyond that the Adelaide Oval, the chief centre of South Australian sporting activity. A little further on behind the scoreboard stands Adelaide's modern Gothic, twin-towered, Anglican cathedral.

It was in Adelaide that I had my first experience of club-life in Australia. Wherever the Union Jack has flown the traveller finds that most British of institutions, a club, and nowhere in the former colonies to my knowledge have clubs caught on so widely as in Australia. One might add that, according to hearsay for I write merely as a grateful temporary honorary member of many, nowhere are they said to be more particular whom they let in. I leave it to the psychologists to explain the paradox of a people delightedly free and easy in many ways yet unusually prone to enjoying the sound of black balls dropping into a ballot-box. Further, both inside and outside clubs, an unexpected formality has often to be observed. You must wear the right dress in restaurants, and for that matter the right cap on the cricket field.

Once inside the sacred portals of the Adelaide Club the courtesy and friendliness to visitors in disarming and completely delightful. They keep an excellent table, and you may choose the peace of library or writing-room and the sociability of smoking-room or veranda. It is sometimes unduly hot in Adelaide, and when the temperature rises on the veranda a vast blind is lowered, down which cooling water flows into the courtyard below. I have never seen this ingenious device anywhere else.

As you sit down with companions in wicker chairs one of them has pressed the bell – a signal for the prompt appearance of waiter or waitress. He or she circles the group saying quietly to each man just 'Mr Blank's compliments, sir.' You name your drink, and when the tray swiftly arrives and the drinks are served the host is presented with no chit, still less is asked for money. It merely goes down on the monthly bill. All very civilized.

None of the 'What's yours, old man?', 'No, no, have this one with me.' No such talk, and no settlement at the time by cash or signature – the latter an arrangement possible perhaps only at a club of limited size wherein the members are well known to the staff. Among the latter are some great characters, and they seem to stay on almost for ever. Australia prides itself on being a markedly democratic country but in the best clubs – the Melbourne, the Union and the Australian in Sydney, the Queensland in Brisbane, the Weld in Perth, as well as the Adelaide, and no doubt others I wot not of, they have servants the like of whom in England one generally looks for in vain. This goes, too, for the best hotels, and notably the Windsor at Melbourne where the staff of porters are remembered as friends by travellers the world over.

At the Adelaide Club there used to be two wonderful Nellies, known to avoid confusion as Upstairs Nellie and Downstairs Nellie – I wonder whether it was thus that someone thought of the title for the famous TV serial. Ian Peebles used to stay at the club, and got to know all about the upstairs lady and her family. When he came to bid goodbye he said he'd look forward to seeing her again on the next tour four years hence. She was getting on a bit, and replied briskly, 'Four years? No, that's rather too long for me. I'm afraid you won't.' When Ian returned he found she was right: she hadn't quite made it.

You cannot enjoy the hospitality of the Australian clubs without feeling a strong sense of history, for they were founded in the last century by the makers of Australia, the pioneers, and they stand as monuments to the qualities of courage and resource of those settlers whose descendants enjoy the fruits of their work today.

Another illustration of the Australian addiction to clubs or such-like institutions was soon evident on this first visit to Australia in the activity of the RSL, which being interpreted is the Returned Servicemen's League. The operative word here is 'Returned': in other words, men were required to have served overseas in order to wear the coveted white enamel badge with the Australian coat-of-arms in the coat button-hole. The RSL is a great power in the land. There is an RSL hall in every community, and the league gives positive help to its members in the way of loans at low interest rates, the issuing of business qualifying certificates, and so on.

Only volunteers were sent abroad. The conscripts and others who served only on the home front wore a bronze badge of distinctive shape. There were, and still are, also United Services' Clubs with excellent amenities to which honorary membership was accorded us: likewise sporting clubs complete with pools and saunas, supported chiefly by the racing men, such as Tattersalls in Sydney.

Opposite the Adelaide Club, and flanked by University, Museum, and National Gallery, stands in ample grounds Government House, a late Georgian mansion of suitably vice-regal proportions which was inhabited by Sir Willoughby Norrie, one of Auchinleck's desert generals. Here I found installed as ADC Michael Farebrother, one of our band of Arab cricketers, son of Felix, vicar of Wareham, hard by Horsham, birthplace of the George Coxes, father and son. Michael was completing his military service in this highly congenial way before turning to his chosen vocation of schoolmastering. (He has been for many years now headmaster of St Peter's, at Seaford.) So I got to know the Norries, and when at the end of our first stay in Adelaide the MCC party, players and press, found problems in getting to Melbourne, the next stop, because of a rail strike, the Governor kindly offered Vivian Jenkins and me seats in his small aircraft which was taking over his daughter and a friend for the Melbourne Cup. Our colleagues, condemned to a long journey by coach, were not enraptured at this preferential treatment, but surely a Governor's invitation is a command!

Willoughby Norrie looked every inch a gubernatorial figure, yet that he and his wife managed to avoid the impression of stuffiness which Australians are inclined to look for in the English (and to resent not unnaturally when they find it) is evidenced by his being invited for a second term of office in South Australia, after which he set sail south-east to become Governor General of New Zealand. So his tour of duty in the Antipodes lasted thirteen years, at the end of which, returning home, his conventional yet well-merited reward was a seat in the House of Lords.

As to MCC's cricket at Adelaide it did not live up to the setting of the most gracious and satisfying of the great grounds of Australia. Hammond's safety-first axiom was to be seen in the partnership between Hutton and Washbrook that in five hours' play on the easiest of pitches produced only 235 runs. I reminded readers at home:

This present visit has taken place specifically because an Australian statesman pleaded that after six years of war his countrymen might enjoy the game they love best in all the glory and excitement of a Test Series. Many more days like today will make the under- taking one of more than doubtful value.

Some middle way must be evolved by the MCC cricketers which does not include the eternal pushing of half-volleys and the gentle nudging of longhops from noon until dark. Hutton and Washbrook are too good to prod about like a pair of mediocre county batsmen playing for a draw.

The most interesting aspect was naturally Bradman's first major innings since the early days of the war. He made 76 and 3 in the manner of a man carefully plotting his bearings. He played easily for the most part, though his legs, unsurprisingly, were not working as quickly as his brain. Dick Pollard had him missed in the first innings and took his wicket in the second. Pollard was no bat, and no great mover in the field, but I always felt that he was unlucky not to have had his chance in a Test on this tour.

The Oval of Adelaide is, as I say, the pleasantest of grounds and among other things the most sociable. The one long, crescent-shaped stand stretches round from behind the wicket at the city end almost to the sight-screen at the other. So one watches from a square position which while not ideal has its advantages. If the cricket is dull you may lift up your eyes unto the hills of Mount Lofty on the skyline, or drop them to observe the parade of youth and beauty passing below the stand in the Members' Friends enclosure.

And so, with a moral victory to sustain them, to Melbourne, where MCC surpassed themselves by beating Victoria, reputedly the strong- est state, by 224 runs. Hutton and Compton both made hundreds, having been rapturously greeted on first appearance on the world's largest cricket arena by the world's largest cricket community: Yardley got 70 and Wright took ten wickets. But MCC had won an almost conclusive advantage by batting first, since the pitch — as sometimes happens early in the Australian summer and close on the finish of the Australian Rules Football season — altogether failed to last. MCC missed chances innumerable, and, looking back over one's cuttings, it comes as a surprise to read how poor the English fielding, and especially the catching, was on this tour. This weakness had something at least to do with the fact that this was the first and, it proved, the only first-class victory of the tour.

From now on it was the younger Australians whose development came on apace, while Bradman prepared himself with ominous concentration for a return to Test cricket. The Japanese war had not ended until mid-August, 1945, and in the previous season (of 1945/6) there had been no Sheffield Shield, though an Australian Services side had played all five states, and there had been a dozen other inter-state games, most of them three-day affairs. To this extent Australian cricket was less well prepared for a return to Test cricket than England. When the first Australian team was announced it contained only three men who had ever previously played in a Test Match – Bradman, Hassett and Barnes. However, the young Australian is a notoriously quick developer, and although they had mostly had little cricket for a while the new team was physically mature enough: notably a dashing 27-year-old airman named Miller who had flown Mosquito night-fighters over Europe and his fellow opening bowler, Lindwall, two years younger, back from some three years in the jungles of New Guinea and the Solomons. The average age of the first post-war Australian side was 28, while England's was quite a bit older at 32.

As it turned out, the teams that faced each other at Brisbane continued to do so with little amendment throughout the series, though for the First Test Hammond preferred Paul Gibb to Godfrey Evans as wicket-keeper. The captain rarely consulted anyone, but one morning when we were breakfasting together at Brisbane he said he was finding it hard to decide between these two. What did I think? I said that though Gibb was a better bat Doug Wright was our trump card as a bowler, and that Godfrey was better at keeping to him, having regular practice in doing so with Kent. Yes, I had a point, said Wally, but both of them had missed chances – Evans in fact had let Bradman off at Adelaide early in his come-back innings. I wasn't surprised at the decision in Gibb's favour because Hammond was remembering the South African tour of 1938/9 when Paul had batted for ever and a day (Test average 59.12). However, the Australians had soon detected in him a weakness against wrist-spin, and played on it incessantly. As soon as he came in the spinners began to flick their fingers, and the fielders closed in like bees round a honey-pot. Gibb made few runs on this tour, and by the end of it Evans had secured the position which (apart from two Tests in South Africa in 1948/9 when Billy Griffith was preferred to him) he held without challenge for twelve years.

My other pre-Test memory of Brisbane is of a belated and short-lived effort to improve the fitness of the MCC party with some PT before breakfast, under the supervision of the captain, who had been involved with this sort of training in his RAF days. All performed on the lawn of our hotel, the traditional resting-place apparently of teams visiting Brisbane. However, it had plainly seen better days, and when we soon moved into the plusher Lennon's in the middle of the city the PT fell by the wayside.

The first controversies surrounding the tour, which post-war goodwill was powerless to still, was a purely English matter. It blew up on the eve of the First Test in the form of some blunt Yorkshire criticism of Wally Hammond by Brian Sellers, who was in Australia writing for the *Yorkshire Evening Post*. Sellers couldn't follow Hammond's field-placings and also thought the captain should smile a bit and give some encouragement to the team when they did something good. There was nothing particularly violent about such stigmas; they had also been voiced by others including myself. But the point was that Sellers had been one of the MCC selectors who, under the chairmanship of a fellow-Yorkshireman, Sir Stanley Jackson, had appointed the captain. More than that, Sellers was among those who had promptly chosen Hammond as England's captain against Australia the moment he turned amateur in 1938, and who named him again in 1946 against India in the series which was the prelude to this tour. So there was much indignation, official and otherwise, duly recorded by Peterborough in the *Daily Telegraph* who thought 'there is something to be said for straightforward reporting by journalists.' He went on: 'I cannot help recalling the compliments which have been made to Mr Swanton's reporting by such judges as Mr C. B. Fry, Sir Pelham Warner and others.' I still felt myself to some extent on trial, and was duly gratified by this.

I can do no more within the space of this book than to provide some sort of brief commentary on each of the forty-two Test Matches embraced by the period, but some were both more interesting and had greater significance than others, and of course this first one set the pattern of almost unchallenged Australian dominance that was to last for all too long.

Maybe, man for man, the Australian sides of this early post-war period were intrinsically stronger than England's. They were certainly much better in bowling, and equally they were far better led. Yet if the luck had gone England's way at Brisbane rather than Australia's the picture would have emerged very differently. In the first place Bradman won the crucial first toss, in the second place he survived, when 28 what those close to the bat thought was a fair catch, and went on to score 187, and in the third place England's first innings had barely begun when the heavens opened to unleash the first of two thunderstorms which turned the pitch for the remainder of the match into the most treacherous imaginable.

As to the 'catch', which, of course, has been endlessly written about, almost exclusively from the English angle, the question was whether in trying to run down the gully a well-pitched ball from Voce Bradman hit it into the ground immediately upon impact or whether he hit the ground with his bat as the ball flew off the upper edge. The Don waited for the decision, confident that it was a bump ball, and the umpire, Borwick, ruled 'not out'. At the end of the over the captain of England remarked to the captain of Australia that that was a fine way to start a Test series, and the gloves were off, even though on reflection Hammond went on record saying, 'I thought it was a catch but the umpire may have been right, and I may have been wrong.'

Bradman after the shakiest of starts now called on all his resources of resolution and stamina, and gradually, surely fought his way from doubt to certainty, and latterly to command. Before the game, on the front page of the *Daily Telegraph,* I went on record as saying:

Above all the speculations and chatter surrounding the occasion one name surmounts all others, the name of Bradman.

Were Australia's captain only half the man he was before, and that would be a vastly rash prediction, the fall of Bradman's wicket would call forth a stress of emotion, whether exultation or despair, that would dwarf all else.

Psychologically and technically, Bradman is the key to the match, just as he has been since his slow stride to the crease was first seen on an Australian field nearly 20 years ago.

Imagine English feelings as he came in now at close of play not out 162, he and Hassett having already added 246. Some of us recalled the last meeting between England and Australia when Hammond continued the England first innings away past the 800 mark with Hutton at last back in the pavilion having eclipsed Bradman's record Test score. If it was in our minds the Don was unlikely to have forgotten it.

English apprehensions of retaliation by the little man, lively indeed overnight, were stilled on the second morning when in trying to force Edrich to the on-side off his back foot he was bowled off his pads. However, he continued the Australian innings on the third morning until they were all out for 645, the highest they had ever made on their own pitches. In the next Test at Sydney Bradman batted until they had exceeded even that, finally declaring at 659 for eight. He was remembering not only the Oval in 1938 but his very first Test in 1928/9 when England batted again although 399 ahead on first innings – England 521, Australia 122. The captain who ordained this was the debonair, carefree Percy Chapman. In a timeless Test Chapman's decision was the way that pointed to victory without a scintilla of doubt: but I have always believed that this initial Test experience of the Don's helped to formulate later attitudes, and that England had no profit from it in the long run.

If England had held even half their chances the Australian score might not have been out of reach, while if Bradman had gone for 28, making Australia 74 for three, it could have been they in their second innings who were caught on the rain-ruined pitch. As it was England were snared, one by one, the only extraordinary thing being the time needed for their dispatch. At its worst the pitch was utterly unplayable. Yet such defensive skill was shown, especially by Edrich, Compton, Hammond and Yardley, so inaccurate was the Australian bowling that in nearly three hours on the fourth day only four wickets were lost. Before the game was continued on the fifth and last day Bradman took his slow-medium left-arm bowler, Ernie Toshack, the ideal man for the job, out on to the pitch and in front of everyone showed him where to bowl. Toshack belatedly responded by taking nine of the last fifteen wickets that fell.

Incidentally Australia in 1946 had not arrived at the stage of complete wicket-covering in Test Matches, but at Brisbane the point made no practical difference since no covering devised by man could have withstood the tempest wherein the tarpaulin crease covers were blown about like handkerchiefs, hailstones fell the size of golf-balls, and the trim field was swiftly reduced to a lake whereon floated the stumps. What was equally extraordinary was the strength of the tropical Queensland sun which next morning sucked away the moisture, so that against all prediction, and thanks also to the sandy soil perfect for drainage, play was possible sharp to time. I recall broadcasting home from the ground at 8 a.m. on Wednesday, 5 December 1946, which was 10 p.m., Tuesday, in London, describing a scene of desolation with part of the playing arena still under a foot of water. I quoted the curator as thinking there could be no cricket that day. English listeners who had gone to bed with this comforting information had to be told when they woke up next morning that fifteen English wickets had fallen and the game was over.

39

England had been cruelly used at Brisbane – though their poor fielding had contributed to their undoing. At Sydney they could offer no excuses since they won the toss on a perfect wicket, and were bowled out cheaply after a palsied exhibition of batting against the Australian spin. Here was the captain's 'stay at home' policy reaping its due reward. The game was all but decided on the first afternoon when in an evil hour Hutton, Compton and Hammond himself – the flower of England's batting – went one by one to the high, slow, teasing spin of McCool and Johnson, each giving the ball more and more air as though trying to discover whether there was any parabola they could not describe without impelling the forward step that would have allowed the ball to be met on the full-pitch or the half-volley. In *Farewell to Cricket* Bradman wrote in wonderment about this episode: 'I was even allowed the luxury of playing two short-legs with no outfield to a slow off-spin bowler, Ian Johnson. With such a field on a plumb wicket in his initial spell Johnson delivered 11 overs and took 1 wicket for 3 runs. This meant that 85 balls out of 88 were not scored from. It was incredible.' To English eyes it was also deeply depressing as, with scarcely an offensive gesture, the innings ended for 255 – Johnson six for 42!

The vast Australian reply took 11 hours 40 minutes to make, the slowness enforced by Doug Wright who bowled beautifully with the most wretched luck. What one chiefly recalls is the contrast between Barnes and Bradman who made 405 together, the highest-ever Test stand in Australia. Bradman had pulled a thigh muscle and therefore demoted himself, arriving to join Barnes at No. 6 when Australia were still 96 runs behind. Both scored 234, Barnes in ten hours 40 minutes, Bradman in six and a half hours. Though Bradman had to play almost entirely off the back foot he always seemed to have two or three strokes to Barnes's one. I referred in my report to the 'disparity in class' between them. Sid Barnes was a fine player, especially of the strokes that suited his strong, thick frame – the hook and the cut. His record against England (average 70 in nine Tests) is second arithmetically only to the Don's (average 89 in 37 Tests), but it has to be remembered that he played at a time when our attack was at its weakest. He could have been assessed with greater certainty if he had stayed on in the game to face the much more formidable bowling of the middle fifties. Barnes, the great showman, maintained afterwards that he got out on purpose (in the next over after Bradman went) not wanting to overtake his score: which could well have been so for he was a man of quixotic mood and temperament. As has so often happened to England in my time England batted far better in trying to save the game than they had done initially: better, but not sufficiently well to stave off defeat.

So they went two down to Melbourne where over the New Year there assembled the largest crowds I ever saw at a game (346,675 was the official figure, some four thousand fewer than the world's record that still stands, also at Melbourne, in 1936/7). England now made a far better fight of it, and at times held narrow advantage, but the younger Australians were quickly finding their feet in the Test arena. Their three centurions were all fresh to it in this series: Morris, the opener, McCool (No. 7) and Lindwall (No. 9). The lower batting could now be seen as remarkably strong. When their seventh second innings wicket fell they led by 355, and with the pitch remaining as plumb as plumb the game was still open. But now Tallon (92) and Lindwall (100) added 154 in an hour and a half as Hammond allowed the English effort to slip. Well as these two played, there were too many cheap runs to be had as the captain, sphinx-like, marched from slip at one end to slip at the other, apparently, as Plum Warner wrote of him, just 'letting the game go on'.

England needed to bat seven hours to save the match, and with threequarters of an hour's respite for the weather they did so with three wickets remaining. Nearly everyone accomplished something on the English side, as the score proclaims, but none more than Yardley, who scored 114 for once out and took five good wickets including that of the great man himself in each innings. Once the Don played on, once he was caught and bowled, and of his six Tests against England at Melbourne this was the only one in which he failed to make a hundred.

A final memory of Melbourne, 1947 is the generosity of the crowd towards Hammond's team. The English press had come under attack for certain loud assertions about umpiring mistakes. If I remember rightly the sobriquet 'E. M. Wailings' dates from about this time. But this unpopularity had not rubbed off on the players. No point at this distance in saying more than that the rumpus was blown up out of proportion. A bad decision by general agreement was given against Bill Edrich when he made 89, but if the unmpiring had been indifferent Hammond could have petitioned for the removal of the old firm of Borwick and Scott, who stood in all five Tests, as they had done on Gubby Allen's tour ten years earlier.

The drawn match meant Australia's retention of the Ashes – which had scarcely been in doubt since things had gone so auspiciously for them at Brisbane. 'Cricketers of talent and strong fibre seem to fall from trees in this country,' sighed the *Daily Telegraph* correspondent. The Australians had attuned themselves to the highest class of cricket more quickly than England, though the England batting at the start was far the more experienced. It was herein that the chief disappointment lay, and it was the brightest stars which had failed to sparkle. Edrich, Yardley and Washbrook had scored twice as many runs as Hammond, Hutton and Compton. This illustrious trio had made only one fifty between them in eighteen innings. However, from Len and Denis at least far better performances were on the way.

My abiding memory of the Adelaide Test is of the stifling, almost insufferable heat. This was the game wherein Arthur Morris and Denis Compton both had hundreds in each innings, an unprecedented achievement. The bat was on top from the start. Even so it needed a long stand between Compton and Evans to extract England from danger in their second innings. Godfrey took 95 minutes to make his first run, the pair of them running with wit and wisdom to give Denis most of the bowling. The key to this lay in their beginning to look for the single off the fifth ball of each eight-ball over, leaving the tail-ender at most three to play but never a whole over. The Mount Lofties on the skyline shimmered in heat which on four days out of the six topped the hundred mark.

Denis at least cast off his shackles and after a very slow start, in which for one of the few times in his life he was barracked, 'it was grand to see him in the afternoon and early evening gradually get atop of Australia's persevering and skilful attack, and finally dominate it completely with all manner of lovely strokes to the extent of a run a minute off his own bat.' I thought that 'Compton's innings, judged from every angle, stands with Bradman's at Sydney as the best played in this series so far.' Altogether Saturday, 1 February 1947, was no mean red-letter day since over the weekend the scoreboard read Australia 24 for two in answer to England's 460. I was dining that Saturday evening chez Bradman, and with Jessie Bradman and her son John was escaping the rush by leaving an over before the close. We were beneath the stand when there was a tremendous uproar from above. 'That'll be Dad,' said John, and he was right. It was.

Bradman, b. Bedser 0

So I cannot give an eye-witness account. But the victim has done so in *Farewell to Cricket*. Hear what the Don says: 'The ball with which he bowled me in the Adelaide Test Match was, I think, the finest ever to take my wicket. It must have come three-quarters of the way straight on my off-stump, then suddenly dipped to pitch on the leg stump, only to turn off the pitch and hit the middle and off stumps.'

Alec had not perfected the leg-cutter by 1946/7 though he had by 1950/1, his peak period. His body action gave him a natural tendency to in-swing however he held the ball, and on this tour he began experimenting with a grip across the seam in order to get movement from leg off the pitch. When swing and cut worked to perfection on the blind length the answer was the almost unplayable ball, of which this at Adelaide was a prime example. I was sorry, of course, not to have seen it, though from sideways on (as one watches at Adelaide) the trajectory could only have been deduced.

It is passing strange that although of his 63 Test innings against England he made top score 21 times, and scored 19 hundreds, Bradman also had half-a-dozen ducks. Bedser, by the way, took his wickets six times in Tests – only Hedley Verity (eight) had it more frequently.

On the face of it, it could be held that since Hammond needed to win the last two Tests to square the rubber he should have given his bowlers longer in which to bowl out Australia on the last day. The fact is, though, that as the pitch was playing the hope was really infinitesimal and the prospect of a third defeat correspondingly probable. What really ruined England's chances of retaining their grasp on the game was, in the first place, a superb forcing innings by Miller – he was the seventh and, mercifully, last Australian to make a hundred in this series – and in the second the Playing Regulation that allowed the pitch to be rolled after rain if in the curator's opinion he could improve it by doing so. There was a sharp storm after the fourth day – which did not temper the heat for long – and the subsequent rolling simply bound the pitch just when it was beginning to wear.

It was also the case that Hammond, in what proved to be his last Australian Test, was in great discomfort from fibrositis. He dosed himself in an effort to get relief, but was much incommoded, and did not play again on the tour of Australia, though he did in New Zealand. Walter, past his best physically at 43, just did not have the properties for leadership of a touring party, but he must have made

43

a better job of it if he had not been dogged with such consistent ill-luck. His very last stroke in Australia, a swinging leg-hit, looked worth four runs but was marvellously caught by Lindwall 20 yards from the bat.

By promptly following his first Test hundred at Melbourne with two more at Adelaide Arthur Morris set himself up as a No. 1 for Australia for a while to come. He played indeed until the end of the 1954/5 series before retiring with an average against England of 50. Arthur at his best looked out of the top drawer, a left-hander with all the strokes, and only one (much-publicized) weakness against certain bowling and in particular Bedser's. He miscalculated sometimes in his estimate of the relative positions of his feet and the leg-stump which he was apt to leave uncovered, and so was bowled behind his pads. Yet his record speaks for itself, and what the figures do not say is that few more charming men have ever played for Australia, and I cannot name one who was more popular with his opponents. There are any number of cricketers whose manner and appearance have belied with particular emphasis the modern rubbish which proclaims that to reach the top at games it is best to be aggressive, abrasive and generally bloody-minded. Some but not so many seem to be infected with this idea, and sport is infinitely the worse for them, just as it is the better for the Morrises who go round the world acting, unconsciously, as the best ambassadors for their countries.

Morris was still in form in the Fifth and last Test which was the most closely fought game, from first to last, in the series. Sydney had seen a lot of rain, which meant that the pitch was always giving the bowler something, England's opening 280 being the highest innings. Clearly, as the score shows, England might well have won a consolatory victory. Under Yardley's leadership they might have done so especially if Hutton after batting through the first day unbeaten for 122 had not then been obliged to retire from the match with tonsillitis. On the last day, too, when Australia had to get only 214 to win on a rough pitch, Bradman had made 2 when he edged one of Wright's leg-breaks to slip. Edrich could not take the chance, whereupon the Don stayed until the issue was almost decided. Broadly speaking the England batsmen lost a match which Wright and Bedser deserved to win. The *Daily Telegraph* correspondent thought that there was a 'spendthrift casting away of English wickets' in contrast to the Australians who were hanging on by their teeth. He also thought a good deal of Yardley's leadership. 'The general positioning of the field and the blocking of the batsmen's known strokes were admirable, and his placing was responsible for at least three of the catches made. He certainly has the knack of keeping his men equable and happy. If there were just a little more punch or bite in his make-up one could regard Yardley as a thoroughly satisfactory England captain of the near future.'

So in fact he proved in following home series against South Africa, Australia, and the West Indies – with that proviso about punch and bite still relevant when it came to confronting Don Bradman once again. What a contrary race these Yorkshiremen can be – either too much belligerence or, very occasionally, not enough! Seriously, Norman would have made a good touring captain, as was recognized at Lord's, for he was first choice for South Africa in 1948/9 and again in Australia in 1950/51. MCC were lucky in the men that they finally turned to, George Mann and Freddie Brown respectively, just as Yardley was unlucky that business claims prevented his again going abroad. It is a great achievement to captain England anywhere against anybody, but among cricketers the ultimate honour is the MCC tour of Australia.

As MCC after the Fifth Test departed by flying-boat for a relaxing and successful short tour of New Zealand I secured for my paper the Don's thoughts on the series and on some immediate cricket issues. He considered that, despite the result, England had only one or two gaps to fill; that Wright was the best of his type sent to Australia 'for at least thirty-five years', presumably (though he turned the wrist) since Barnes; that Bedser was an even finer bowler than Tate in 1928/9, though not necessarily than in 1924/5, which was before his time; also that Evans was in the highest class. We needed a truly fast bowler – not to be forthcoming for another five years – and a man like Verity, for whom it might be said England are still waiting.

He thought before the series started that Australia would be strong but they had turned out better than he hoped with batting to meet all demands, well-varied bowling, with almost everyone capable of making a hundred, including Tallon, the keeper. Moreover there was a 'natural aggressive spirit' about the side that heightened their attraction. (I didn't need to be told that!) He spoke of 'the sheer artistry, the classical style and power of an innings by Miller.' The quick resumption of Anglo-Australian Tests had justified itself in every way, psychologically, technically, financially.

Don said he still wanted what he had advocated in the 1939

Wisden, a further extension of LBW on the off-side so that the batsman would be out even if his pads were outside the off-stump – as, of course, now obtains if the batsman attempts no stroke. The most vital consideration in cricket was the mental attitude of the player 'who can if he chooses spoil any game by his interpretation of its character.' Too often pitches were too good; they should be true, but reasonably natural. Personally he preferred to bat on English pitches, though most batsmen did not. It was at Lord's that he had played the best innings of his life, the 254 against England in 1930.

What about his own future? As to that he was very doubtful though it would be premature to say he would not consider coming over in 1948. It was obvious he had had to husband his strength carefully. He would love to go to England again, but on the whole thought it unlikely. (In the event he did come.) A side-swipe at a few jealous critics who had seen nothing satisfactory in anything he had done – whose intent was 'so obvious as to be laughable', and that was about it.

So much for those who thought of Don as withdrawn, uncommunicative, unhelpful. I have always found him completely the opposite. And so much for the first of my tours in Australia. All have had their points of attraction, but about the initial discovery there was something altogether special and unrepeatable.

4

Too Tough for Brown and Co.

The mood of the second post-war party to tour Australia with MCC was very different at the outset from that surrounding the first. However things turned out in 1946/7, the great thing at the start was relief, now the war was over, that the old battle was to be resumed in friendly rivalry. How good the Australians were likely to be was at first a secondary consideration that would be resolved in good time.

Resolved it was, and now four years later it was clear enough that Australian cricket stood at the pinnacle with England still vainly trying to fill the gaps caused by the loss of a generation. Since the last tour to Australia England had not only been crushed by Don Bradman's great team of 1948 but had lost two series to the West Indies and halved a rubber of four drawn games against New Zealand. Against this were home and away victories over South Africa. It was impossible then to be sanguine about any great success attending Freddie Brown's side which was an unusual if inevitable mix of the pre-war young and the newly-fledged. Nine were 32 or more, six were 26 or less. Only two were in what one might call the prime age bracket between the two extremes – Godfrey Evans and Reg Simpson. In the last two pre-war teams to Australia Jardine had ten men in this ideal age category, Allen nine. The 26 to 32 group would have been 15 to 21 when war broke out, and if they survived had certainly been deprived of cricket during their formative years. I do not intend in any way to minimize the Australian war effort by stressing England's difficulty in this regard: it was splendid. The fact is, though, that while the Sheffield Shield was suspended after 1940 the Grade and District cricket, which is the staple source of supply, continued. Again, in his more favourable climate the average young Australian matures more quickly than the average young Englishman.

In the result the English batting in the Tests was absolutely carried by Hutton (aged 34), with assistance of any substance only from Simpson (aged 30) and Brown himself who celebrated his fortieth birthday just after the First Test. The bowling was carried by Bedser (aged 32), Bailey (aged 26), Wright (aged 35) and, of course, Brown. The youthful half-dozen achieved depressingly little.

Yet in spite of all the failures, and in particular the extraordinary eclipse of Denis Compton – who averaged 7.5 in the Tests and in the other first-class games 92 – England put up a surprisingly good fight. It is even possible to maintain that if they had not been so cruelly robbed by the weather at Brisbane – in an even worse way than Hammond's side had been because Brown had established a definite advantage before the rain came – the rubber might perhaps have been halved.

But I'm running ahead of the story, and must at least mention the long heart-searching and indecision that preceded the choice of Brown as captain and then the announcement of his team, which came out in four instalments. First the selectors chose Bailey, Dewes, Bedser, Compton, Evans, Hollies, Hutton, Parkhouse, Simpson, Wright and Washbrook. At the same meeting they also picked Close but the announcement came later as he had to be released from National Service. At the same time we heard that Washbrook had withdrawn. The next batch consisted of Sheppard, McIntyre and Berry. Lastly Warr came in and also again Washbrook, who after some persuasion had changed his mind.

It was Freddie Brown's magnificent hundred at Lord's for the Gentlemen that clinched his appointment – going in No. 8 he made 122 out of 131 in an hour and fifty minutes, and then bore the brunt of the bowling, taking four wickets. Retrospectively he seems to have been the obvious man – certainly once Yardley and Mann had declined. But several were palpably lucky to have got the preference in a low-quality field, while it is hard to expiate the omissions of Edrich, Laker and Wardle, these last two easily the biggest wicket-takers of the English season.

MCC this time provided two managers of comparable seniority, and both county secretaries, Brigadier M. A. Green, of Worcestershire, and John Nash, of Yorkshire, and we travelled out, with even more cricket writers than before, comfortably and congenially on the P & O ship, *Stratheden,* relaxing in that unique way possible, alas! no more. There is no longer a regular eastward run by Orient – P & O, and even if there were fares would be too exorbitant to be borne. Also the players, while enjoying the sea journey, prefer the longer time at home which air travel allows.

One of the benefits for MCC teams of going by sea was the chance of meeting Australians returning after spending holidays in Europe, getting to know them, and renewing friendships as we later progressed around the country from Perth to Brisbane. The *Stratheden* was full of Barr-Smiths, and Prells, and Haywards, and Hoskinses and Robinsons, and the atmosphere was of the utmost bonhomie only momentarily threatened when King Farouk (myself) underwent assault and battery at the hands of an Arabian chief (F.R.B.) at the Fancy Dress Ball. 'All a young man can want, sir, sun, sea, and sweat,' Gerry Weigall used to observe on a former MCC voyage, and for some at least, including me, it made a blissful holiday.

The Australian press and public took a quick liking to Freddie Brown, and being weary of their team's unbroken run of post-war success were more than well disposed to his side, who for their part wanted all the encouragement they could get. Apart from a terrible mauling at Sydney where MCC under Compton, the vice-captain, were hit for 509 for three by New South Wales the early form was reasonable enough, considering how much progress was affected by rain (this was one of the wettest Australian summers) and numerous injuries. Even so no one was quite prepared for the happenings of the first day of the Brisbane Test wherein England bowled out Australia for 228. There was nothing wrong with the pitch, and at 116 for two the Australian batting list looked horribly long, England's bowling resources dangerously slender. However Bedser and Bailey, Brown and Wright kept admirably at it, Doug trying manfully to disguise that he had been kept idle for the past three weeks with fibrositis.

This should have been a match-winning start, but what happened? On Saturday (the second day) rain prevented a ball being bowled. After an unsettled weekend England went in on Monday on a glue-pot. In the day 20 wickets fell, and 13 of them were English wickets. Brown declared the England first innings 160 runs behind at 68 for seven; but Hassett did likewise when Australia were 32 for seven, leaving England 70 minutes' batting in their second innings. Brown this time ordered the heavy roller, no doubt to the embarrassment of the ground-staff since it had to be pulled by the famous Wool-loongabba horse. After each journey down the pitch the horse had to be unhitched and persuaded back into the shafts. Only four return trips were possible, though if the England captain had insisted on his rights of seven minutes' actual rolling proceedings would then have been so shortened as to save the fall in dubious light of three of the six wickets that succumbed in this last fatal phase of a preposterous day.

An Australian sticky (now seen in major cricket only by mis-adventure since full covering is universal) was like the old-fashioned England version only more so, in that the ball's lift and turn were even more abrupt. Survival, granted some luck, was not exactly impossible, as we had seen on this ground four years earlier, but the odds in the bowlers' favour were hopelessly weighted. Further, the fact that the ball cut such extraordinary capers tempted the bats-men – on the principle of a short life and a gay one – to indiscretions which they would not normally commit. It all made fascinating, agonized watching.

There was some batting of high quality, especially on the part of Washbrook, Simpson and Hutton in the first innings when the pitch was at its worst. Generally speaking England acquitted themselves with the utmost credit until the final half-hour when foolish strokes were made and McIntyre (brought in as a batsman in the last place in preference to Close) with Evans his partner was actually run out off a fourth run when everything depended on survival.

Next morning, because of the regulation allowing early morning rolling, the pitch was restored to normal: the Plasticine was flattened at dawn, and morning sun did the rest. I recorded how after the end of the game a man on crutches stumped down the pitch without leaving a mark. England needed 163 to win with Hutton and Compton held back. Hutton played with memorable skill, cheered on by a crowd very much on England's side, but Compton failed, and for the rest the task was too heavy. 'Never mind the result – we won't forget Len Hutton,' said an old man to me as I returned from the broadcast box, and certainly the brilliance of those off-side strokes softened the bitterness of an undeserved defeat.

It was probably the happenings of this match that led to Test pitches on succeeding tours being wholly covered in Australia, as was the case already in all other first-class cricket. It was reckoned that the lack of covering cost £7,000 in gate-money – not a negligible factor in the argument.

The luck of Brown's side did not change for the better. Compton had had a cartilage removed in London in the spring of 1950, and so missed most of the season. Now, following Brisbane, in making a hundred against an Australian XI at Sydney he so jarred the knee that he had to stand down from the Melbourne Test at the New Year. England's batting, brittle at best, was that much the weaker.

This second Test is one that is still clear in the mind a quarter of a century later. I remember it for England's marvellously good out-cricket, inspired as it was especially by Bedser and Evans; for the weakness of the batting which finally undid all the heroics in the field; for Freddie Brown's 62, the highest innings of the game, and in particular for the magnificent six he hit to the longest corner of 'the outer' over long-on soon after he came in at the grisly score of 54 for five; most of all, the extraordinary reaction of the crowd who to a degree one never experienced in any other Test abroad were willing England to win. All in vain. In the end the margin was 28 runs to Australia, who came in, with Lindsay Hassett at their head in the home state in which he was such a popular figure, to a deafening, disappointed silence. It was eerie.

Much of the match I watched from behind the bowler's arm, from the top of the pavilion. With me was Jim Cassels, then UK Liaison Officer with the Australian forces whose headquarters were in Melbourne, later to become a Field-Marshal. (I nearly wrote he must be the senior officer among Army cricketers but, of course, Field-Marshal 'Alex' was also pretty useful.) The General had been a good Army bat, and we both felt even we might have played with a bit more 'savvy' than was shown by some of England's young blood. Together in a crowd of fifty thousand we sweated out the agony of the last day which began with England's score 28 for two, with only 151 more to win. With Compton unfit Hutton at this stage of the tour was coming in at No. 4, on the theory that with two other high-class opening bats in Washbrook and Simpson the quality was thereby spread rather more evenly through England's fragile batting. So he had arrived overnight to join Simpson at 21 for two, with the destiny of the game clearly in his hands.

Simpson lasted awhile on the final morning before being succeeded by Dewes, who had spent the previous day in bed with a temperature of 103°. Now like Paynter in 33 he rose, weak, from his couch, but unhappily not with similarly heroic results. With the other end be-calmed the load on Hutton's back, in face of uniformly excellent bowling by Lindwall, Miller and Johnston, Iverson and Johnson, grew even heavier. (We did not then speak of 'the pressures', but no modern cricketer has been asked to bear quite so heavy a burden as Len was in this series.) At last Hutton, his off-side strokes blocked on a lush field which made cutting-off easy to brilliant fielders such

as Harvey, Archer, Miller and company, aimed quite uncharacteristic-
ally to hit the fastish left-arm Johnston across the flight and his
natural turn from leg, and lobbed a catch to mid-wicket. That was
92 for five and for the England tail to double the score in such
circumstances was more than could be expected. Thus our hopes
were dashed. There was never a Test among all the many in which
I had longed so deeply for victory.

The humid atmosphere enabled the ball to swing a good deal,
especially in the Australian first innings, and Bedser used the conditions like a master, his performance helped vastly by some of the
best wicket-keeping I ever saw. Evans's taking of the in-swingers,
standing up to him as usual on this fast wicket, touched the heights.
Bailey was admirable in support and likewise the captain. With
Wright to bowl leg-breaks he turned largely to medium-pace in this
and the succeeding Tests, with great effect. This series should always
be quoted, of course, when it is foolishly stated that only extremes
of speed are effective in Australia. Had not Barnes and Tate
brilliantly shown the way?

At the end one of the great Australians remarked that no side can
win a Test Match without making strokes. Johnny (A. G.) Moyes,
then the doyen of Australian critics, thought that if England had
had only three hours instead of three days to bat they would have
got the runs. It is true that in only one innings before or since have
I seen a side bat so slowly (the English rate was 31 per hundred
balls), and this despite Brown needing only two hours for his 62
and Evans wasting no time over his 49. Gilbert Parkhouse earned
credit in the second innings, but generally the occasion was too much
for the young stars, the biggest disappointment being Close, who
substituted for Compton, and so became the only cricketer under 20
ever to play for England against Australia.

In this his only Test in Australia Close arrived at the crease in
the last over before lunch at 54 for four to face a few balls from
Iverson, the new googly bowler, about whom more anon. Play down
the line? Not a bit of it. His third ball, of good length around off-
stump or outside, he crudely smeared at, and the ball lobbed gently
to backward short-leg about 15 yards from the wicket. Jack Fingleton
called it an 'awful stroke', and all in all I never saw a worse played
in a Test by a reputable batsman at such a moment. It was not easy
at the time to accept Brian's youth as an excuse.

Several rubbers later in what should have been his years of dis-
cretion he was doing the same sort of thing again to another Aus-

tralian spinner, Benaud, at Old Trafford with a similar result. Close
in fact has won his reputation as a courageous and determined
cricketer outside the Test arena: yet he has at least one monument
to his credit as an England cricketer, the gallant 70 wherewith he
brought his side to the brink of victory against the West Indies at
Lord's in '63. And, having noted his failures against Australia, I
should mention that as lately as 1972, aged 41, he was brought back
(Illingworth being hurt) to lead England in the three one-day Inter-
nationals against them and narrowly won the decisive match. But
it is reasonable to suppose, notwithstanding later disappointments,
that if Compton had played at Melbourne instead of Close England
would probably have gone up to Sydney all square instead of two
down.

In my reports I suggested that Freddie Brown might just have
tilted the balance by revising the batting order to the extent of promoting himself and Evans, and in his admirable *Brown and Company*
Fingleton makes the same point. However, there it was, and Fate
soon knocked the final nail in the coffin.

Not quite at once, because MCC had to engage in the return New
South Wales match in advance of the Third Test, and did their
stock untold good by making 553 for eight and coming close to
beating the Sheffield Shield holders by an innings. Hutton enjoyed
himself against his old adversaries, Lindwall and Miller, making 150,
while Reg Simpson, very, very slowly (in almost nine hours) compiled
259, the highest score at Sydney by an Englishman since R. E.
Foster's immortal 287 in 1903/4. So with Compton now fit again
the omens were more propitious than hitherto.

Brown won the toss (for the one and only time in the series) and
England struggled to 290, but in so doing sustained two casualties
which made the result a foregone conclusion. First Lindwall broke
Bailey's thumb, then the innings was brought to a melancholy end
when Wright ran himself out and at the same time pulled a muscle
in the groin. So on a plumb pitch England were reduced from the
normal complement of five bowlers to three. These three, Bedser,
Brown, and Warr (in his first Test) stuck to the job nobly, keeping
everyone struggling, but by slowly wearing them down in a way far
from pleasing to their own critics Australia achieved a long lead.
Whereupon Iverson came into his own.

The pitch by now was dusting slightly, but there was nothing in
it to explain and excuse such a collapse as England's. The batting
was tentative with little or no attempt to counter, spin and flight by

footwork. Someone recalled the old Scottish battle-cry on the rugger field and thought it could be adapted to inspire our batsmen: 'Feet, England, feet!' It was all a thoroughly depressing anti-climax. But there was no doubting the quality of Iverson's performance. Never was there a more unlikely hero, a tall, shambling fellow, clumsy and unathletic in all he did, then 35, who after having retired from club cricket some years before suddenly discovered a new grip that he first practised with a ping-pong ball. Somehow he tucked his index finger underneath the ball, and so flipped it out. He certainly spun the googly, occasionally turned the leg-break a bit, and was usually very accurate. His fielding was a joke, and his bat looked about as old as he was. He was Nature's No. 11. But his best was formidable enough. In 19.4 overs he had six for 27, and Fingleton thought that 'Iverson bowled as well on this day as I have seen an Australian spinner bowl.'

Consider this comment in the light of the greatness of O'Reilly, and the vast admiration 'Fingo' had for him, and the measure of Iverson's menace here at Sydney needs no further emphasis. His success was short-lived, for after this season he popped back into retirement. But Iverson's influence on this rubber was one of the chief factors in Australia's success. It was said he had never seen a Test Match until he found himself playing in one.

This book is unashamedly written from the English viewpoint by one who hoped and prayed – more often than not without avail – for English victories. But let Australia's merits not be brushed aside. The truth was that in 1950/51 they missed the batting not only of Bradman but of the two other Bs, Sid Barnes and Billy Brown. They also lacked under Hassett some of the aggression and self-confidence that Bradman in his maturity inspired in the young men he moulded and led. Strangely perhaps Lindsay Hassett's impish humour stopped short at the pavilion gate. His tactics generally – and this Third Test was a fair example – were safely unexciting. 'Subdue and penetrate' was his axiom. Australia, however, were to a man a marvellous fielding side (apart from Iverson and perhaps Bill Johnston), while their bowling had inspiration and rich variety in Lindwall, Miller, Johnston, Iverson and Johnson. Loxton was not required. The great advantage they possessed, of course, was in the number of their all-rounders. Australia had at least ten potential hundred-makers among the fourteen who played in this series, and it was to the credit of Brown and Co. that only Morris, Miller and Burke got one apiece.

In this abnormally low-scoring series Adelaide, as usual about that time, produced the highest temperatures, the slowest wicket, the most runs – and Australia's fourth victory. This should not have been. Despite another of Hutton's bravest and best the most England could ever have hoped for, once they ended their first innings 99 behind, was a draw. But draws are abundantly worth fighting for – especially when ten Tests out of the last thirteen against the chief enemy have been lost. England began their second innings needing to bat for 7¾ hours and with 503 runs, no less, between them and victory. At the end of more than four hours only three wickets were down, and Australia, lacking Iverson's bowling (he had trodden on a ball in the nets and turned his ankle), were looking well cooked in a temperature of 100°. Now, however, there was a prodigal throwing-away of wickets, as though the runs might almost have been obtained, which was plainly impossible. Evans was the chief culprit, with Bedser, of all people, not far behind. Readers of the *Daily Telegraph* read that these two had shown unmistakable skill as batsmen, 'but this was not the first occasion when they have seemed to regard batting as a sort of voluntary overtime.' Neville Cardus thought that Jardine would have greeted Bedser's return after his airy stroke 'with a countenance Caledonian, stern and wild'. O'Reilly was caustic, while from Yorkshire Herbert Sutcliffe – who would have died rather than give his wicket to any Australian – told England in effect to get in there and fight.

Once more England suffered a stroke of ill-luck in that Freddie Brown and Mike Green, the manager, after dining at Government House on the fourth evening, were involved in what might have been a fatal car accident, and the captain, badly bruised and battered, was able to bat only in an extremity. As the last five wickets toppled in no time, and there being only Wright left with two hours still to go, he did not do so.

David Sheppard, aged 21 and in his first Test against Australia, batted 3¼ hours, while Simpson also stayed a long while. Otherwise Hutton, with 201 runs in the match, was a Titan among the minnows. Poor Compton, o and 5! For Australia Jimmy Burke, aged 20, made a hundred in his first Test – as Neil Harvey, equally youthful, had done at Headingley three years before. Burke had few strokes but vast composure, and I'm sorry that the chief memory of him is that he was the worst chucker I ever saw bowl, bracketed equal with Meckiff and the South African, Griffin: that and the memory of his piano-playing – off the field in fact no one was better company.

We have waited a long, long while, one way and another, but now at last, at the fifth time of asking – the fifteenth in post-war Tests between England and Australia – the 'elusive victory' that gave me the title for my book on the series is just coming up. The scene was Melbourne, and up to a point the game took the familiar pattern with the bowlers coming up trumps yet again and the batting threatening to throw all their good work to the winds. When Roy Tattersall – who with young Brian Statham, two Lancashire lads, had been sent out as reinforcements following the injuries to Bailey and Wright at Sydney – came in No. 11 to join Simpson England were only 246 for nine against Australia's first innings of 217. Simpson was 92, and he now proceeded to let the bat go with a classical poise and power that was a hint of paradise to English eyes. Tattersall stuck there with a fine Northern phlegm, a figure of more than ordinary interest to me since, as his feet had swollen on the air journey, he was wearing my boots. (With four wickets, too, at Adelaide they did a good job.) Simpson at his best was a lovely, graceful player and this was his hour, as he took out his bat for 156 with England now 103 to the good.

The pitch was still perfect, but again Bedser showed his fondness for Melbourne; Brown, who had had five for 49 in the first innings, caught and bowled Miller, Australia's most dangerous bat, for the second time in the match; while Wright ended Hassett's stay of more than three hours with a perfectly-pitched leg-break. In the end England needed only 95 to win, and it was utterly fitting that Len Hutton should have been undefeated with 60 of them. Thus the heroes of the tour from the English viewpoint – Bedser, Hutton, Brown and Bailey – had the consolation that meant so much to everyone concerned – and to the immediate future of Test cricket.

This was the tenth MCC tour of Australia, and only twice had England won the last Test. By then they usually seemed past their peak, and Adelaide had strongly suggested 1950/51 was no exception. So the success had the added savour that it was quite unexpected. For Australia 28 February 1951 marked the end of an era – the period of unbroken success enjoyed by the great team that had come together under Don Bradman at Brisbane in November 1946. Twenty-four Tests they had played without defeat, fourteen of them against England. They had been a magnificent side, comparable with the best in any age, whose play had in no mean way rekindled interest in cricket in Australia, England and also South Africa where Hassett had taken them in 1949/50. Now the first post-war cycle was over: England's turn was coming up.

There had been three outstanding cricketers in the series, Hutton, the batsman, Bedser, the bowler, and Miller the all-rounder supreme. As to Len, scarcely a batsman in Test history has ever so dominated a series, never certainly in a losing cause. He averaged 88.8, more than double anyone on either side. Simpson's average was 38, and Brown's 26. The captain also took 18 wickets at 21 runs each. Weigh how you will the playing efforts of MCC's fifteen captains in Australia, and none can be found to better this record: and he was 40!

The MCC captain, as may have been gathered, achieved also an intangible though very real success in his and his team's relationships with the Australians. Lindsay Hassett was a charming, whimsical fellow, and the friendship existing between the captains was reflected throughout their teams which fraternized in a way not known since before the Bodyline series. 'Fergie', the Australian baggage-master to every MCC and Australian side since 1905, thought that this was the 'easiest' and most contented side with which he had travelled.

A popular Australian magazine had for its cover a full-page picture of Freddie complete with grin and a pipe. The caption said: 'Perhaps we are sticking our necks out by naming England's captain, Freddie Brown, our Cricketer of the Year? We don't think so. When he was first chosen to lead England, all of Australia wondered why. Since then he has inspired his team by his own refusal ever to give up a losing fight. That, for our money, is what makes a real cricketer.'

To the Australians the England captain was not only a good fighter but a friendly fellow, as also was a more eminent English visitor whose tour coincided with ours, the Archbishop of Canterbury, Dr Fisher. I have a memory of him preaching to a congregation chiefly of women on a mid-week morning in Perth Cathedral, and afterwards moving about, beaming with good fellowship, visible intermittently amid a rippling multi-coloured sea of hats. There was little love lost in those days between Anglicans and Roman Catholics in Australia, and especially in Sydney, but the little Archbishop bridged all gaps, and it was said that no visitor had ever made a deeper impression.

Another Englishman outstandingly popular then – and still – in Australia is Arthur Gilligan, captain of the 1924/5 MCC side, and in the fifties one of the two experts on the broadcast panel of commentators. The other was Vic Richardson, of whom I have already said something in an earlier chapter.

'What do you think, Vic?'

'I dunno. What do you think, Arthur?'

became something of a national joke. But it was a joke affectionately based, for here were two characters who came across as sportsmen with a sense of humour and a down-to-earth turn of speech which didn't confuse the listener with too many technicalities. They knew the game, but forbore to force their knowledge down people's throats. Above all, as cricketers themselves, they gave due credit to both sides, indeed generally erred by being over-generous to 'the enemy'. The atmosphere they created was a salutary antidote to the caustic tone sounded at times by the press critics of both camps.

Arthur Gilligan's face and voice were known all over Australia – which worked to his advantage once when he took a long taxi journey into the suburbs of Adelaide. When he got to his destination the driver declined to accept payment saying 'Let a dinkum Aussie stand a dinkum Pommie a ride.' The dinkum Pom knew better than to argue the toss after that.

Jack Fingleton recalls another more astringent Anglo-Australian exchange involving Eric Hollies – though the Aussie element was said also to have more than a hint of Eric's own unmistakable Birmingham accent. Not exactly the fleetest member of the side, Hollies on the pickets under the Sydney 'Hill' was dashing this way and that, always just failing to cut off the four, as Miller and Morris for New South Wales made hay against the MCC attack.

'Eh, Hollies, don't tha bury tha dead in Brummagem nah?' To which the victim, in no mood for such pleasantries, replied, 'Nah, tha stuff 'em and send 'em to Australia.'

Eric Hollies must be added to a long list of English leg-breakers whose spin hasn't been quite fierce enough for Australian pitches. He would certainly have had a more successful tour, as well as a more comfortable one, had he not found himself utterly allergic to airplanes. As he had never flown before landing in Australia it was not to be foreseen that flying made him horribly air-sick. In time Eric discovered that a generous dose of alcohol was the only remedy but, of course, that also had its after-effects: so the result was unfortunate either way.

As I've said, this 1950/51 side were a popular and amusing bunch of people, and none contributed more to the general atmosphere than John Warr, who had squeaked into the last place. Warr was no doubt a better bowler a couple of years after this tour than when he was picked, yet he earned a place in two Tests and, strange to relate, had actually contested the last bowling place at Brisbane with

Alec Bedser, who had been much under the weather with 'flu and had been quite off-form. As it was, John's baptism of fire came at Sydney when England were reduced to three bowlers, and he did very well without getting a wicket. Then came the dead Adelaide pitch, and more hard but fruitless toil until at last after 72 Test overs Ian Johnson edged a catch off him to Evans. The umpire seemed doubtful, but Johnson settled the matter by 'walking' – which, by the way, I'm glad to say has never been an Australian habit.

John in fact in these two Tests took one for 281, which caused a few of us thereafter childishly to hum in his presence the Ancient and Modern Hymn number 281, 'Lead us Heavenly Father, lead us,' with emphasis on the lines

> Lone and Dreary, Faint and Weary,
> Through the Desert thou did'st go.

In fact, of course, it was J. J. Warr's prime virtue that he never seemed either faint or weary, on the field or off. Laughter was seldom far away when he was about, and the value to a touring side of someone of such communicable cheerfulness is not to be measured in figures – which show, incidentally, that he bowled more overs on the tour than anyone except Bedser, for a return of 23 wickets. His presence was not the least reason why the 1950/51 tour is remembered with such nostalgic pleasure by those who took part or followed it.

These, too, were days when I considered myself still young enough to enjoy the night-life now and then and yet fulfil the requirements of the *Daily Telegraph* and the BBC. Sydney in particular was always a favourite spot to which to return. There were always old friends with whom to enjoy the old jokes – one of which may illustrate the atmosphere of that time. Two fellow POWs on the Burma-Siam railway simultaneously received letters from their wives after the Japs had ordained a maximum length for all letters of 25 words. The first chap, whom we may call Dick, was delighted to find that his wife had made maximum use of the words allowed after this fashion:

Children fine Mary engaged Tim won cricket colours gran cheerful spinner has litter of eight hibiscus flourishing house painted broke as usual much love Pauline.

When Dick proudly showed his letter to his pal – let us call him

Claude – the latter was plainly envious, as he passed on his 25 words from – well, let's say Jean.

Dear Claude, since writing to you last we are now only allowed to send 25 words so fear this will be brief much love Jean.

The Jap reason for limiting the wordage to 25, by the way, was that they couldn't be bothered to censor long letters – which in view of their mentality one could understand might take a long time. Let me illustrate. A prisoner was sent a letter wherein it was said that 'the old battle-axe' – probably a mother-in-law – was still going strong. This was returned to the sender because it was forbidden to mention instruments of war.

When I first struck Sydney in late 1946 the war was still fresh in all our minds, and one heard how dutifully the grass-widows of Sydney had extended hospitality to servicemen passing through: first to the Americans and later the Royal Navy. It was a shock to see the contrasting physical forms of their husbands when after the defeat of the Japs they were drafted home. The tale is told of one beautiful Sydney girl who, on first spotting her emaciated husband at the quayside, grasped her neighbour's arm saying 'Oh, dear! Is malnutrition catching?'

The Australian tour finished, I continued this time with the team to New Zealand where they were due to play two provincial games and two Tests, the visit lasting all but a month. One travelled in those days by flying-boat, slowly but comfortably and with ample room. Lifted as though with the utmost effort we scudded and hummed our way over the black waters of Rose Bay, Sydney – a slightly eerie experience at night – finally arriving in Auckland, where we landed in the harbour at breakfast-time. Brown and his men had spent a full twenty weeks in Australia, and though fortified by their Fifth Test victory they were inevitably somewhat jaded.

We found sub-tropical heat at Auckland and a multi-purpose arena (like all others in Australasia) whereon both the Empire Games and a rugger International against the British side (not by then christened Lions) had recently been fought. The New Zealand religion of rugby football came into most of the talk, and we had graphic descriptions of a wonderful try engineered by those great Welshmen, Ken and Lewis Jones. But the success of Walter Hadlee's 1949 New Zealanders in England – they won 14 matches, lost only to the University at Oxford, and drew all four Tests, a record never bettered by a New

Moments of leisure

17. County cricket at Camden Park, New South Wales, the home of Quentyn Stanham. One of the few private grounds in Australia — and what better?

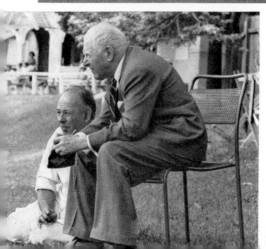

18. *(above)* Golf at Christmas, 1962: Crawford White, Ken Barrington, Billy Griffith, John Woodcock, Tom Graveney, Sir Donald Bradman, Alec Bedser, Ted Dexter and Colin Cowdrey. At Kooyonga, Adelaide.
19. *(left)* Old friends: of mine and of one another. Jack Fingleton sits at the feet of Ben Travers, the famous playwright and follower of cricket tours. At Cranbrook School, Sydney.

20. Morris b. Bedser 155 at Melbourne, 1946/7. One of ten times in Tests when Morris either moved across too far and was bowled behind his legs or was LBW to Bedser—who had his wicket eighteen times in forty Test innings.

21. The catch that started the rot. Harvey c. Evans b. Tyson 11. At Melbourne 1954/5. Australia's last eight fell for 36 (Tyson six for 16). Evans thinks this his 'best ever'.

Zealand side in England – had vastly stimulated interest in cricket, and the household names such as Hutton and Compton were greeted as heroes. The grounds were full wherever we went.

At Dunedin we were transported to a countryside not unreminiscent of Scotland and with temperatures to match. Otago were Plunket Shield champions that season, their star being none other than Bert Sutcliffe, arguably the best batsman produced by New Zealand (though Martin Donnelly presses him hard while such men as John Reid and Bevan Congdon have made even greater contributions, and Glenn Turner has the best record). Unhappily for Otago a violent storm over the weekend was too much for the covering system after MCC had made plenty on a plumb pitch on the Saturday, and they had no chance of doing themselves justice.

Christchurch with its cathedral and university and quiet walks by the riverside reminded me of Cambridge. The ground at Lancaster Park with its backcloth of rolling hills makes a worthy scene for a Test Match, the only snag on this occasion being a lifeless pitch from which no bowler could extract anything. After Australia the crowd of some 18,000 seemed marvellously sedate and quietly mannered – rather as though one were home at Worcester. Unfortunately the cricket was quiet, too, with a draw soon writ large on the horizon. The New Zealand side – much the same as had played in the 1949 Tests – had had rather too little preparation while their opponents had had rather too much. One realized at first hand the practical difficulties of the cricketers of a small country keeping match-fit when their own domestic competition allowed them only four first-class games a season. The left-handed Sutcliffe made a polished hundred, but even the polite watchers were sorely tried by Trevor Bailey, who in making his first Test hundred needed 4½ hours to reach fifty. He bucked up later, but I called it at the time 'a joyless burlesque of the art of batting,' and could not think that the occasion had won many new adherents for the game. My chief memory of the match is of Hadlee arranging with the umpire for the return to the wicket of Cyril Washbrook who on being given out LBW was making a very leisurely return to the pavilion. He had edged the ball on to his pads.

The tour ended in bitter cold at Wellington where, after a game of low and slow scoring on a turning wicket, England ended a sequence of eight draws against New Zealand, winning by six wickets with only quarter of an hour to spare. The central figures had been mostly those chiefly in the limelight in Australia, Hutton,

Bailey, Wright and not least Brown, who fittingly made the winning hit. But there was also a new hero in Roy Tattersall, who with six for 44 – still in my boots – had most to do with the victory. I always enjoyed seeing Roy bowl, for he brought a lively mind and many subtle variations to the off-spinner's art.

Likewise on the New Zealand side it was good to see Tom Burtt, whose slow left-arm bowling, flighty and teasing, was the mainstay of the attack as it had been in England. Wallace was an attractive player, Scott a hard man to dislodge, while the promise of Reid was there for all to see. Mooney was a high-class keeper, young Hayes looked a likely bowler, and Hadlee guided his ship with a steady hand – and with no little humour behind his glinting specs.

Apart from the inconvenience – even the impossibility sometimes after a day's cricket – of having to dine at six-thirty sharp I greatly enjoyed New Zealand and the necessarily brief look at a green and gracious country. This was my only visit, as things turned out, not so much by my own choice as because in the fifties I was needed to cover the tail-end of the football season at home. Latterly Australia has left me eager for a rest, and I have been only too happy to hand over to Ron Roberts or Michael Melford.

This visit, however, was enough to convince me that from the MCC point of view it asks too much after the major campaign is completed to put the necessary zest into a visit to another country. The last four MCC sides, from Dexter's to Denness's inclusive, have had to contest eight Tests inside three and a half months. It is really more than flesh and blood can stand, and I was sorry to read that my old friend Walter Hadlee, and Bevan Congdon were openly critical of the approach of the 1974/5 side. A cloud shrouded the outcome of the First Test since the end came with the near-fatal injury to Ewen Chatfield, but the fact that England made 593 for six and won by an innings does not suggest lack of effort. Rain was the victor in the Second Test, and though the England over-rate was indefensible it seems that by the end they were thoroughly disenchanted with the umpiring. There were niggles on both sides.

New Zealand have always pleaded for MCC to come on from Australia rather than at some other time, partly because it involves less expense and therefore a bigger profit and partly because the Australian series gives the New Zealand visit such a good publicity build-up, and thus heightens the interest. It was harder to resist this line of argument when New Zealand cricket had such negligible encouragement from Australia, but this is not now the case, and it must grow in strength and maturity from the more frequent contact.

The obvious arrangement in the English interest is to couple Pakistan and New Zealand in a tour containing three Tests in each country and spread over, say, three and a half months. On balance New Zealand should likewise find this a happier alternative to the present plan, for MCC could then play all the Plunket Shield sides, flying the flag of cricket in more places, and should be fresh and keen for a three-Test series at the chief strongholds of Auckland, Wellington and Christchurch.

After nearly six months of fairly continuous travel a few days on a warm beach beckoned invitingly, and so I broke the air journey home – it was too near the start of the English season to go by sea – enjoying for a few days the luxury of the Royal Hawaiian Hotel, Honolulu, and surfing in the long boats at Waikiki Beach, and inspecting the upturned wrecks of Pearl Harbor, and meeting the Sheriff and king-pin of the island, a superb physical specimen still though getting on in years, called Duke Kohanemoku. At least I think so. Duke had started life as a beachboy at Waikiki, living in and by the surf, and had come to fame representing USA in the Olympics as a swimmer, Honolulu being of course one of, and the furthermost of, the States of the Union. 'There's American democracy for you,' my friends seemed to be saying as I was warmly received by the great man.

A brief stop-off in San Francisco, another in New York, and on 6 April 1951 I was home, after 204 nights away: it was my longest trip, the war excepted, and in its scope and variety one of the most memorable.

5

Speed Does it

The MCC Australian tour of 1954/5 had many points of difference when compared with its two immediate predecessors. In the first place it was led for the first time by a professional, Len Hutton. Secondly England came as holders of the Ashes which it was up to Australia to snatch back if they could. Third, the number of the press party was almost double that of the team, and we sailed in a correspondingly larger vessel, *Orsova*, flagship of the Orient fleet. It seemed that much more prestigious an expedition, and I ventured some comment on current attitudes in an article on the *Daily Telegraph* leader page before departure.

Percy Chapman's tour of 1928/9 had strong parallels with Hutton's in that following the war Australian cricket had enjoyed a long spell of dominance until the tide at last had turned, in both cases at the Oval. Hutton and Chapman both left home as defenders of the Ashes – and incidentally history was about to be repeated in that they both succeeded in the job. But whereas Chapman was accompanied by two cricket writers to report the play, one from Reuter's, one from Exchange Telegraph, Hutton had a whole corps to keep happy. Even on board ship he found himself involved in press conferences, although there was really nothing to say. The captain was extremely conscientious, let me add, in all his public relations work, and developed the art when it suited him of delivering with much gravity Delphic utterances which his hearers could interpret however they pleased.

Geoffrey Howard, then the Lancashire secretary, managed the team with good-natured efficiency, while Fergie's place was filled by none other than George Duckworth. His official post was 'scorer and baggage-master', but George was not to be confined by labels. He was guide, philosopher and friend to all who had the sense to see the worth of his experience of cricket and Australia. George also formed a valuable bridge between the players and the press.

After Hutton had captained the MCC in the West Indies the previous winter – a tour which at best could be rated only a qualified success – I thought that 'the tour will be a searching test for modern professionalism's powers of leadership and example'. The game in Australia had been losing ground – partly because of the lack of challenge. 'The public will be weaned back only by cricket that has a proper degree of action and positive purpose.' (The old refrain!) I'm sorry to see that I thought that although Australian batting was unsound by the old standards the presence of more all-rounders gave them slightly the better chance. That seemed a good enough prophecy up to Christmas – until it was falsified in a few hectic weeks by Frank Tyson.

It is true that Hutton was poorly off for batsmen who could bowl and vice versa – apart from Trevor Bailey, whose batting, limited though it was in strokes and aggressive intent, had come on since 1950/51. There just was not the quality around. However, in one respect at least Hutton was more fortunate probably than any captain to Australia before or since. Consider his bowlers: Tyson, Statham and Loader for speed, Bedser and Bailey also to use the ball early, Appleyard, Wardle and McConnon for spin. Observe indeed those who had to be left behind: Trueman, Laker and Lock in the forefront, to say nothing of such capable fellows as Tattersall, Jackson of Derbyshire, Shackleton and others. Modern English bowling was at its peak at this time, even if that was far from true of the batting. (Only four Australian hundreds were destined to be made on the tour against the English bowlers – an unprecedented scarcity that argued much for the bowlers' skill, just as it also suggested a falling-away in Australian batting standards.)

With the leadership telling on Hutton's own play, as it had done with nearly all his predecessors, England all too often had to struggle for runs. However, without very often enthusing the crowds, in the end they just about managed enough. This time the two young ones chosen for their batting, May and Cowdrey, covered themselves with credit. Now, too, Compton – though hampered by 'the knee' and less brilliant than in his golden years – played his full part. Those who wrote him off after the last tour had to swallow the fact that he topped the tour averages.

The tour opened at Bunbury, a town on the sea some hundred miles south of Perth which is (or was) something of a timber port and a bit of a seaside resort, with long, rolling surf and alongside the Indian Ocean a showground on which MCC disported themselves in a fairly light-hearted manner. No one seeing Frank Tyson churning up spouts of sand as he charged over an uneven surface to the wicket, and firing his thunderbolts in every direction but the right one, could have imagined him as the destroyer of Australian hopes in the Test series. There was a great barbecue under the stars, and much hearty hospitality, and a pretty primitive hotel of which Ian Peebles, obliged to share a room, observed with distaste, as he remarked resignedly, 'Ah well, a day's march nearer home.' This within a day or two of the tour's beginning.

The tour was made much the more enjoyable for me by the presence for the first time of my old friend, who with the late King George V was inclined to think that, generally speaking, 'Abroad was bloody'. It was fun to introduce him, as we progressed, to the delights of Australia, and I need hardly say that he succumbed to the country and its people, and four years later he returned to cover Peter May's tour, like this one, for the *Sunday Times*. The discomforts of out-back Australian hotels – which were fairly basic places on these earlier tours – have now given place to the standard cleanliness and convenience of motels which of recent years have sprung up everywhere.

There was one and only one clue to coming events in the early stages of the tour, supplied by Brian Statham who flew away from Perth with a dozen cheap wickets, the chief architect of two wholesale victories. The pitch at the WACA, an unlovely name for that spacious, agreeable ground by the Swan River, was truly quick, and seven English bowlers tasted blood: all in fact save Bedser who had gone down with a lowering attack of shingles.

Compton turned up to join the party at Adelaide, and announced himself on his favourite Australian ground with a hundred. As a safeguard against his recurring trouble the team had been augmented to 18 by the late choice of the Yorkshireman, Vic Wilson: there could be no more congenial tourist, but so long as Compton was fit eight specialist batsmen is one surplus to establishment. Partly because of the shortage of opportunity with eighteen men to be accommodated, the MCC batting struggled until at Sydney in the fifth match the situation was immeasurably brightened by Cowdrey. At 21 the youngest member of the party and still an Oxford undergraduate, he made a hundred in each innings against the Sheffield Shield holders, New South Wales. Before this match the evidence suggested that the captain saw Colin's presence in the team primarily as an investment for the future. (I happen to know that he made a modest bet backing Wilson to get more runs than Cowdrey in the Tests – a reasonable enough attitude considering their relative experience. Promise was a poor substitute for experience in the mind of the average professional cricketer, then as now.) At Sydney Cowdrey came in after Wilson to join Hutton at the grim score of 38 for four. Four hours later maturity and youth both had three figures against their names on the giant scoreboard, and from this auspicious moment of arrival it could be said that Cowdrey has never looked back. When in the second innings he made his second hundred the selectors at home who had insisted on backing 'class' must have been shaking hands with themselves. They were, by the way, a more select and perhaps a more prescient bunch than those who had chosen the two previous sides, as these names will indicate: Altham, Wyatt, Ames and Allen – plus, of course, the captain. (Profiting by the 1950 experience they had chosen the lot, Wilson apart, at one sitting.)

Len Hutton was converted so completely by Cowdrey's soundness of method that he sent him in first in the second innings – though he had never batted there – and also in the Queensland match preceding the Test. In this game he failed, and for a while the idea was put aside, to be resurrected with success in later series after Hutton had retired. It was easy to see Hutton's reasoning, for he distrusted Reg Simpson's technique against speed and in fact never found himself a stable partner in this, his last Test series.

What a nightmare that Brisbane Test was to English eyes! One's foreboding came with the picking, two days before the match, of an attack containing four bowlers of whom Bedser was the slowest. Apart from Melbourne 1932/3 (when England were beaten) this is the only instance in history of our going into a Test without a spin bowler. Here surely were the fruits of the captain's obsession with speed. By plumping for pace so unequivocally he had practically committed himself to putting Australia in if he won the toss, as duly happened. The pitch was utterly dry and easy, and – well, Australia made 601 for eight, keeping England in the field until lunch on the third day. Numerous chances were missed, most of them difficult. With the years and the publication of several memoirs the number has increased even beyond the twelve decreed by *Wisden*. To add to England's troubles, Compton, after a vain attempt to save a four, heedlessly braked his run by clutching at the pickets, slipped and fractured the fourth finger of his left hand. England's double failure with the bat – not inevitable, certainly, but always likely in the light of the fatigue and demoralization induced by those eleven and a half long, grilling hours – needs no special documenting, though if anyone wonders why Compton was sent in to bat No. 10 with a finger in plaster in the second innings when, with more than six hours to go, his side were still nearly 200 behind, I fear I cannot enlighten them. In brutal truth the game had been bungled by England from start to finish.

Now between the First and Second Tests the crucial event took place. Against Victoria at Melbourne Tyson cut down his run from the strength-sapping length we had seen all the way from Bunbury. Frank explained that he made his decision in the light of his experience at Brisbane – one for 160 in 29 eight-ball overs – but that it was not something new for him, rather a reversion to the 18-20 yards he had bowled from in Staffordshire league cricket with Knypersley. His mentor Alf Gover had suggested a shorter run before the Australian tour. At Melbourne Tyson, bowling in three-over bursts, took six for 68, clean bowling five, and so ensured that whoever gave way to a spinner at Sydney it would not be him.

In the event it was Alec Bedser, scourge of the Australians with his record 69 wickets in two series, and England chose not one spinner but two – Appleyard and Wardle. On the face of it, the resting of Bedser was understandable in that it had taken him a long time to throw off the effects of shingles, and he was still groping for his old fizz and accuracy. But the Sydney pitch after much rain turned out a fast green-top that would have been after Alec's heart. The faster bowlers, Tyson, Statham and Bailey, bowled 82 overs for 19 wickets, the slow ones 17 overs for the odd one. Altogether it is hard to think that if Bedser had been preferred on this pitch to either Wardle or Appleyard the Australians would not have been more cheaply bowled out. But this is only supposition, and the hard unlikely fact is that though they did little as bowlers the two spinners and Statham made crucial contributions with the bat. In the first innings the last wicket put on 43, the longest partnership in an innings of 154, with Wardle's 35 top score, and in the second the last wicket put on 46 (Statham 25, Appleyard 19 not out) which meant that Australia needed 223 to win. Wardle was an outrageously unorthodox hitter with a good eye, but who could ever have foreseen these two stands which together settled the match?

Seldom has fortune swayed as it did in this game. I have two abiding memories of it without the slightest recourse to cuttings except to check the figures. One was the second innings stand of 116 for the fourth wicket between May and Cowdrey which took England from 29 behind to 97 in front, every run a precious inch of ground won back at a moment when the Ashes seemed to have receded almost out of sight. This was the first decisive impact made by either against Australia, and for all their several triumphs ahead none exceeded in value this redeeming partnership. Naturally to English eyes it heightened the relief and pleasure that the recovery was shaped by batsmanship of a classic method executed by two young men, May just coming up to 25, Cowdrey to 22, both of whom had learned the game at such traditional homes of amateur cricket as, respectively, Charterhouse and Fenner's, Tonbridge and the Oxford Parks.

Late in the day Cowdrey advanced to drive Benaud straight and was caught at deep mid-off, and his mortification in the dressing-room when he came in is still remembered by those who were there. However, Edrich helped May to his hundred, and the extraordinary tail-end flourish finally set Australia a target that they just could not reach.

The concluding memory, of course, is of Australia being put to rout by the speed and fury of Tyson, marvellously well supported by Statham holding the up-wind end over after over till it seemed he could give no more. For what a wind it was, half a gale in fact, blowing pretty well straight down the field at Tyson's back: and what speed he engendered, unaffected seemingly – or perhaps urged on – by a bump the size of an egg on the back of his head. This was a scar of war at Lindwall's hands sustained while batting the day before. Harvey played exceptionally, taking out his bat for 92 in an innings wherein the next highest score was 16. When Bill Johnston joined Harvey at 145 for nine Australia needed 76 more – which on paper meant that the result was now almost surely ordained: but it scarcely seemed that way on the spot, partly because Harvey was in such devastating form, and equally because the fast bowlers were almost burst.

Harvey kept almost all the strike, helped by England's slowness in the field, while Johnston who on less momentous occasions openly derided his own batting, was not nearly such a duffer as he pretended. Between them these two got half-way to the target when, in what would probably have had to be Tyson's last over, Johnston swished on the leg-side and was caught by Evans.

Now, of course, the rubber was truly made, but it was early yet for complete optimism – one narrow win set against defeat by an innings, and Australia at that weakened by the absence of both Johnson, the captain, and Miller. Australia had tried to bolster their batting by bringing back the ultra-quiet, determined Burke, who had batted so slowly in the first innings as to elicit this from the Hill:

'Hi, Burkey, you're so like a statue I wish I was a pigeon.' I have an idea that Douglas Jardine might also have been subjected to this witticism. He was fair game for anything – including the shout when, whilst batting, he swatted at flies that had been pestering him:

'Nah then, Jardine, just you leave our flies alone. They're the only friends you've got.'

Happily now Australia had a greater liking and respect for Len Hutton than for his predecessor of 20-odd years earlier, and more so after this Second Test in which he had shown much wise generalship in the handling of his attack. The burden of my post-mortem on this historic match was that the game had been won for Hutton by four young men under 25, Tyson and Statham, May and Cowdrey, two of whom (Tyson and Cowdrey) would never have been in the team if the matter had been left to popular choice.

I thought that England would only retain the Ashes if some of the burden could be lifted from the captain's shoulders on the cricket side, the better organization of practice, for instance, and of training generally, to keep all 18 players at their peak. Again, all teams except Test teams were chosen by him alone. I wanted the cricket to be more of a planned exercise with the senior men playing their part, and the captain left as free as possible to recover his batting form. (I had regretted when the MCC team was chosen the lack of a distinguished cricketer to assist Geoffrey Howard in the managership.)

When the Third Test came up at the New Year Hutton was so obsessed with the strain of events that on the morning of the match he could only with difficulty be persuaded to play – a fact not publicized at the time but disclosed in subsequent autobiographies. What also remained undisclosed for a time is that at Sydney Bedser was only told in front of the team and immediately before the toss that he was to be left out: at Melbourne Denis Compton has recalled how he was asked to take Alec to look at the pitch in full view of the crowd to get his opinion of it. Alec, whose greatest successes had been at Melbourne (22 wickets in three Tests!), said he thought it looked very much as usual. Yet this time his only intimation of exclusion was when the team was pinned up in the dressing-room without his name. These things are indications of stress at the top, for Len Hutton was always a considerate person, sensitive of other people's feelings.

Incidentally, Bedser's estimate of the pitch did not turn out to be

wholly accurate, but the strange goings-on connected with it lay, of
course in the near future. On the first morning it was merely sweating
and accordingly lively to bowl on, and Miller, having at first said
he didn't think his back would stand the strain of bowling at all,
returned to the ranks with what one might call a 72-gun salute. His
90-minute pre-lunch spell is enshrined for ever on the tablets:
9.8.5.3. The three were Hutton, Edrich, and Compton, while Lindwall
at the other end accounted for May. At England's worst pass the
score read 41 for four.

But this, of course, was Cowdrey's day – 102 out of 191 all out,
a chanceless innings, and for the youngest Englishman to have made
a hundred against Australia in forty years, astonishingly mature. In
my report I remarked how, though deep concentration is at the very
root of his batting, Colin has the happy knack of being able to switch
it on and off, as required. He was passing the time of day with his
opponents and seemed 'to have the art of playing hard without
looking grim and unhappy about it all.' It is a knack which, thank
goodness, he has never lost.

I also quoted a reader writing from home who said:

'It is a matter of some amusement here that when we are bowled
out for 150 it is miserable, spineless batting, and when they are
bowled out for the same it is magnificent bowling. Don't the
Australians ever bowl well or bat badly?'

I hope this correspondent was not particularly referring to me, but,
of course, making a fair division of the credit is often extraordinarily
difficult. Yet sometimes, as now, figures spoke for themselves.

The Third Test never relapsed from its absorbing start – it was
a dog-fight all the way. The only complaint when England were in
the field was that, apart from the flight of the ball down the pitch,
it was played in slow motion. This second was the evil day when
they bowled only 54 8-ball overs in five hours. (Australia on the
first day had bowled 67.6.) It was murderously hot – and it was
known that Harvey, now Australia's most dangerous bat, fretted if
he was kept inactive. The dilatoriness was in part at least tactical,
and this suspicion was soon voiced angrily by the crowd. I never
remember noticing until this day in any game that the action was
being decelerated of malice aforethought, but the sorry truth is that
the habit has since been so generally followed that a rate which then
was deplored as exceptional is now common practice.

In this respect a stigma attaches to this Melbourne Test. However, for sustained drama it rates with the best. On the second day the variability of the bounce kept Australia enchained just as England had been – bowlers on top all through and Australia having to be thankful chiefly to Len Maddocks, the Victorian wicket-keeper playing in his first Test Match, who made top score of 36 not out. Australia at Saturday's close of play were 3 runs behind with the last two wickets left. Then over the weekend the hot north wind blew, and the heat grew utterly intolerable, and after Melbourne had experienced the hottest night in its history England, going out to field on Monday morning, were amazed to find evidence of moisture in the pitch. They had left it desiccated and friable: now the sprigs on their boots which had slid over the baked, shiny surface cut lines on the turf.

I fear I have little now to add to this story of the watered pitch. The curator announced it had 'sweated', and University professors burst into print to say that in these climatic conditions this is just what they would have expected! Percy Beames, however, cricket writer of *The Age,* and a former Victorian captain, wrote categorically that the pitch had been watered, and though this was strenuously denied by Vernon Ransford on behalf of the Melbourne Cricket Club, *The Age* stuck to their guns. No doubt the curator or who-ever did the job was concerned for his reputation without any particular thought as to which side was likely to benefit. In fact the artificial refreshment of the pitch suited England well, for it gave them the truest surface of the match for their second innings. It was rumoured that the Australian Board were considering whether, if their side had won, they should offer to play the match again. What MCC's reaction would have been to this I have no idea, but it would have been a vast embarrassment all round with outbursts from 'certain sections' of the English press which, even at this range of time, scarcely bear thinking about.

Melbourne had been troubled with their square at this time, and had brought in one Jack House from their No. 2 ground, known as the Albert, to prepare the Test pitch. According to the principal actor in the last stages of the drama, Frank Tyson, 'had he not acted there can be little doubt that there would have been hardly any wicket left on the Monday.'

As it was young May on that third day played fully as well even as he had batted at Sydney, and on the fourth England struggled to 279. At the close that night Australia, 75 for two, needed 165 runs more: with both openers gone the position bore an extraordinary resemblance to that at Sydney where from their last eight wickets Australia needed 151. Clearly each game might have gone either way. At Sydney it went England's, and now . . .

Australia's headlong rout on this extraordinary morning began with a phenomenal piece of cricket on the part of Godfrey Evans which disposed of Neil Harvey, around this time their best bat and also the most dangerous. Talking only recently to Godfrey I discovered he thought this almost the best catch, from a genuine fine glance, he had ever taken when standing back. He moved across to the leg side not by pre-arranged plan but on a hunch that Harvey would play the stroke, and he took the ball after the most prodigious leap at fullest stretch. I underline the catch now in belated justice to Godfrey, since in my match report I described it in prosaic terms and can only assume that for some reason I did not see it.

England, given such a start to the day, raced resistlessly to victory on the broad back of Frank Tyson. From the far end he thundered up, apparently putting every ounce into every ball as though conscious that everything was synchronizing perfectly and the sooner the business was wrapped up the better. He was very fast, and the pitch was his ally in that no one knew how high the bounce would be, or indeed whether there would be any. Miller stopped four shooters running (from Statham), 'and from the fourth earned one of the only two boundaries of the morning off the oilhole of the bat by way of the space between his pads and the leg stump.' No doubt some of the Australian strokes, as the critics sharply observed, were altogether too flowery, but I wonder now who would have withstood Tyson as he was on this pitch on this January morning. Six for 16 he took in 6.2 overs (to make his figures for the innings seven for 27), and in little more than an hour fifty thousand people were applauding him in and then wending their way home, chattering adjectivally, I expect, in profane disbelief.

Australia's cricketers were very much under a cloud after Melbourne, Johnson, as captain, and the selectors, Bradman, Ryder and Seddon not least. I wrote that a famous old Australian cricketer had called 'for the dropping to a lower place in the order of no fewer than six batsmen, Morris, Favell, Harvey, Miller, Benaud, and Archer, with the sacking of Lindwall thrown in. I don't see how you can demote six batsmen except by putting a couple of rabbits in first.' No doubt after Brisbane the shock was not easily absorbed. Also the country was divided as to the rightful captain – Keith Miller, glamorous as ever and now leading New South Wales, the strongest state, having at least as many supporters as Ian Johnson. All sorts of heads were demanded on chargers – the lot indeed, Miller and Harvey excepted. Lindwall in fact was hurt, so Alan Davidson came in for his first cap against England. Colin McDonald was blooded likewise.

The game at Adelaide was akin to those at Melbourne and Sydney in that up to the last hour or two either side could have won, and as before English speed in the end carried the day. It took place in 'blinding, breathless weather', and began with Australia taking all day to score 161 for four. No one could remember their making fewer. Instead of hazardous strokes as before now there were almost none. This tempo predominated throughout the match, apart from a brave flurry on the part of Maddocks and Johnson in Australia's first innings. In the heat the spinners were called on to play a larger part, and did so with distinction, Appleyard and Johnson especially so.

In Australia's second innings Appleyard took the first three wickets. His part in this series was subsidiary but highly important. I can scarcely remember an English bowler in Australia who picked up so well the art of pace-change. He let go from his full height at speeds ranging from slow to medium, and bowled a wonderfully good line, with always the hint of turn from the off. If he had had just a few more seasons in the game before illness forced his retirement my belief is he would be rated at least in the same top bracket as Jim Laker.

The captain and also Denis Compton played their important innings here, the latter keeping the ship steady when England were stumbling appallingly after being set only 94 to win. It was 18 for three with Miller bowling like a demon when Denis arrived to see England to the victory that meant the retention of the Ashes. For the third time our relief and thankfulness were redoubled by the knowledge that the verdict might so easily have gone the other way.

With the strain removed the last Test was something of an English celebration. It was delayed by torrential rains until after lunch on the fourth day, by which time only 13 hours remained. Hutton even so came close to winning by an innings, though he never looked quite like doing so. There was no doubt which way the moral balance tilted now – yet Brisbane was still only a bare three months behind us!

Graveney, replacing Edrich once the tour's object had been achieved, made a rapid, graceful hundred which sent the Australian critics into superlatives. Why hadn't we seen more of him? they asked, reasonably enough. But of course the old hands among them knew well that when it came to the pinch England always distrusted brilliance, and settled for grim, brave, unwearying defence. Tom would have played more often for Australia than he did for England – of course!

There was even room for a warming instance of *noblesse oblige*. When the game began Lindwall in what everyone assumed (though wrongly) would be his last Test needed three for his hundred wickets against England: no fast bowler of either side had achieved this, nor has done so since. Coming up to the tea interval on the fifth day, the natural point for Hutton's declaration, Lindwall had bagged only two. However, at the last possible moment Trevor Bailey – scarcely perhaps the popular idea of a Sir Galahad – contrived to miss a straight one, and everyone naturally was delighted. He 'at one stroke achieved heights of Australian popularity – to which he could scarcely have aspired.'

Wardle bowled chinamen and googlies well enough in this match to make clear what he might have achieved by this method if it did not go so much against the grain, in Yorkshire and England circles. The final ironic touch was provided by Hutton coming on – not quite for the first time against Australia – with wrist-spinners and with the last ball of the series clean bowling Benaud.

England had not been so conclusively on top at the end of a Test against Australia since the Oval in 38. It was a pleasure to cable my last thoughts on the tour the day after it ended:

The historian of the 11th tour of MCC in Australia which ended yesterday knocks his toes at every step against paradox, apparent contradiction and surprise.

Len Hutton's team scored fewer runs than any of their ten predecessors in half a century: but they finished with a better record than any side since 1932-3 when victory was won only at the expense of a quarrel, the scars from which are scarcely healed yet.

England won the rubber by three wins to one and had a moral win in the remaining match: yet the runs-per-wicket average of the two sides is identical.

England began the series by being completely outplayed in the First Test. They ended it by completely outplaying Australia in the Fifth.

All-rounders are said to hold the key to Test Matches. Australia had four or five to England's one; but it availed them nothing.

'Fielding wins matches' is the oldest of maxims. Australia were much the better fielding side; but they were beaten just the same.

England's batting is Hutton, their bowling is Bedser. So it has been for years. But six batsmen stand higher in the averages than Hutton; and in four Tests out of the five Bedser was not needed.

So one might elaborate. But too close an analysis is merely confusing, and where old principles have been upset it can be described without extravagant sophistry as a case of the exception proving the rule.

Further, there is one maxim, not perhaps as well appreciated as it might be, that has been amply fulfilled, and it is this: fast bowlers are apt to win modern Test Matches. McDonald and Gregory, Larwood, Voce and Allen, Lindwall and Miller, these are the bowlers and partnerships that have settled most of the series since the first war. In these last few months while Lindwall and Miller have each bowled brilliantly in spasms England's younger pair, Tyson and Statham, have gone at it day after day, maintaining their speed and control, admirably willing always, shrewdly used by their captain, never since the Brisbane Test really collared.

Statham, of course, one knew from the Tests in West Indies as a winner. Tyson's success is a triumph of intelligence and character, the credit for which as also in Cowdrey's case belongs in the first place to the selectors who picked him out of the blue. It would have seemed ludicrous to have suggested when one saw him ploughing away at Bunbury in the first match that Tyson would emulate the only two English bowlers since the war to have taken fifty wickets in an Australian season, Wright and Bedser.

Tyson and Statham, with a superb effort of skill and fortitude, pulled England's chestnuts from the fire at Sydney in the Second Test and thereafter never looked back. But had it not been for the partnership between May and Cowdrey which held up the Australian bowlers at the last ditch when the position looked practically hopeless, England must have been as good as beaten in three days. The Ashes then would have gone up in smoke and Hutton's captaincy been popularly written off as a failure. It was as close as that.

The tide in this extraordinary rubber first began to turn that

22. *(above)* Statham applauded in after his seven for 57 at Melbourne in the second Test, New Year, 1959. The 'straightest' of fast bowlers: if they missed, he hit. From the left: Graveney, May, Loader, Richardson, Bailey, Watson. 23. *(below)* Careful appraisals, 1954/5. Len Hutton, captain of England, and Don Bradman, knighted six years earlier, chairman of the Australian selectors.

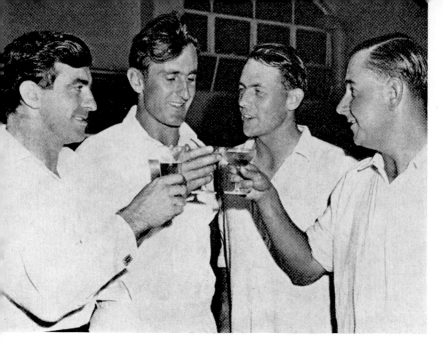

24. *(above)* Moment of elation after Melbourne, 1962/3: Trueman, Dexter, Sheppard, Cowdrey. Fred seems to be assessing the contribution of the future Bishop of Woolwich and of Liverpool. 'Tha's spilled some catches, but tha' made a hundred.'

25. *(below)* Men at work: from left the 1962/3 selectors, Cowdrey, Dexter, the Duke of Norfolk, Sheppard, Statham, Bedser. In the Sydney dressing-room before the last, drawn Test. The pitch, the square and the outfield combined to frustrate them.

Monday afternoon. Thereafter England took ever-increasing confidence from success and Hutton, having got on top, was not the
man to be loosed from his grip. Gradually the fielding improved;
more men, Appleyard, Wardle, Graveney, found parts to play,
Bailey as ever was usually contributing something timely, Compton
on his recovery from injury improved the batting while Evans's
wicket-keeping maintained an excellence scarcely less than it had
reached four years earlier.

The *esprit* naturally nourished by success was greatly helped
by May's conception of the job of vice-captain. On the field
Hutton was always the skilful, calculating tactician; off it within
the party May played his part to perfection and gave his captain
all possible co-operation. The harmony of their partnership was
a considerable factor in the victory.

While England were building up, everything from the Australian
viewpoint proceeded to distintegrate alarmingly. The older players
went down with injuries and lost their form, the young ones,
lacking much in the way of steadfast example from their seniors,
disappointed one after another. The critics ranted against the
selectors – without producing much in the way of constructive
alternatives. Melbourne and Sydney stood in two camps violently
opposed on the question of the captaincy.

Even the Australian wickets seemed suddenly to deteriorate and
there is no doubt that the moment the batsmen had cause to be
doubtful what the ball would do after pitching England were
greatly helped. Even more than English the Australian wickets
are affected by weather both in the winter and spring and in the
few days immediately preceding the match. One wondered more
than once whether the quality of groundsmanship was quite what it
used to be.

Australian cricket is not so impoverished as it looked in the
Tests just ended. But it does stand in immediate need of strong
leadership at all levels, not least administratively. It is not perhaps
realized in England that the breeding-ground of Australian teams
is largely contained in the 30 grade and district clubs of Sydney
and Melbourne. Temporarily at least Australia's disadvantage
in numbers is telling against them. There is a distinct shortage of
class.

From many aspects it had been a successful tour. The series
has been on the whole amiably fought (even in print): the umpiring has been thoroughly satisfactory, rather better than in recent

series in England: the crowds have been appreciative of good cricket more or less irrespective of nationality; and, above all, our tough, blunt, hospitable cousins have not lost their humour. The current joke concerns the Italian immigrant waiter who observed 'We losea da Ashes. We no winna them back till we getta the New Australian Team.'

My diary in those more spacious days merely hints at the pleasure that followed the tour's end. There was a week to be spent enjoying the delights of hospitality in Sydney, of golf at Royal Sydney, and the sophisticated pleasures of dining at the old Prince's and Romano's, of a barbecue on a moonlit beach, and picnic sailing parties in the harbour: all this waiting for the friendly *Orsova* to work up steam for the homeward journey. And, drinking deep of the heady wine of success, basking in the reflected glory of the English victory, how much more pleasant and relaxed was that voyage! Out through the Heads we sailed in the sun of late afternoon, with calls to make and acquaintances briefly to renew at Melbourne, Adelaide, and Perth; a dinner at Colombo with the remarkable family of de Soysa; Aden, Port Said, Naples; then a final hop by air to reach home in time for Easter. For me there was no happier prospect than three or four weeks at sea on a good ship in the company of friends. Alas, that the old mail-boats on regular services are no more: only cruises at exorbitant prices and the doubtful pleasure of rubbing shoulders with the very rich. And in some ways the Jumbo, with the facility of 'stopping off' here, there and everywhere in places where no ship can penetrate, is no mean alternative.

6

The Great Eclipse

England were very much cock of the walk when in 1958 the time came for MCC to set sail again for Australia. It was seven years since a major series had been lost. Australia had been beaten three rubbers running. On the surface too the signs for MCC's 12th visit to Australia were encouraging enough, as in a horribly wet summer England waltzed through five Tests against New Zealand.

By now the routine for picking touring teams had become established. The four Tests selectors did the job plus the appointed captain and manager plus one or two men co-opted for special qualifications. In this case the party met in the rural seclusion of Roger Allen's hotel at Lymm on the Sunday of the Old Trafford Test: Gubby Allen (chairman), Les Ames, Wilfred Wooller, and Tom Dollery, who had been picking the summer's England teams, with Peter May, the automatic choice as captain, Freddie Brown, who had been named as manager, and two others, Brian Sellers, perhaps to improve the North's representation, and Doug Insole, captain of Essex.

They chose 17 ranging in age from Roy Swetman at 24 to Willie Watson, who was 38. There were seven batsmen – May, Cowdrey, Graveney, Milton, Richardson, Subba Row and Watson; only one all-rounder – Bailey; two keepers – Evans and Swetman; and seven bowlers – Statham, Tyson, Trueman, Loader, Laker, Lock and Wardle. I wrote that a *fourth* fast bowler was one too many (remember there was also Bailey), and that Ted Dexter, aged 23, just down from Cambridge and currently playing in his first Test, would have been a better bet. The selectors, I said, should have backed class in the same way as they had done so successfully with Cowdrey four years earlier. As ill-luck had it the Manchester weather had deprived Dexter of a chance to show his paces before the choice was made. I thought they should have waited and seen, and was fortified when on the Monday he batted better than anyone – apart from his captain – for 52 on an awkward pitch.

As it happened Dexter in mid-tour had to be hurriedly sent for and arrived fresh from a job in Paris. Though chosen for two of the Tests he scarcely justified his belated choice, but his subsequent career at least suggests things might have run differently for him in Australia if he had been an original choice, able to acclimatize himself gradually anti-clockwise round the coast from Perth. I had been a fan of Dexter's ever since seeing him as a second year under-graduate reaching his hundred before lunch against Lancashire at Fenner's and going on to get 185.

This perhaps is why after so long I recall a snatch of talk about Dexter's merits with Wilf Wooller earlier in the summer of 1958. The captain of Glamorgan said he'd want a lot of convincing that the young man was ready for Australia, but added: 'Anyway, Sussex are coming down to Pontypridd, let's see what he does down there.' Indeed, said I, but the Tests were to be played at Sydney and Melbourne, not at Pontypridd.

However, academic points of this sort were soon lost in a rare explosion of feeling revolving around Johnny Wardle. Within a few days of the MCC side being announced the Yorkshire committee sat and decided to sack Wardle in the interests of discipline and team unity. May promptly said that irrespective of this he still needed Wardle in Australia. However, Wardle now proceeded to put himself out of court with the cricket world generally by giving his name to an outrageous series of articles in the *Daily Mail,* strongly critical of the Yorkshire captain, J. R. Burnet, his fellow-players, and not least the Yorkshire committee: all this under headings a mile high such as 'We're carrying the Captain', 'By gum, I warn Yorkshire', and so on. Cheque-book journalism with a vengeance, and, of course, ghosted at that.

What these outbursts achieved was to convince even the most forthright critics of the establishment that Yorkshire were well rid of the fellow, and that MCC must support authority by withdrawing the invitation to tour – which they duly did. When the verdict was announced even Wardle, who had been brought before the MCC committee, said 'I asked for it.' There was another aspect which I never heard satisfactorily explained – that the tour selectors were apparently given no inkling of what was in the wind up in Yorkshire.

It was all a great pity, and as one looks at the old cuttings and recalls the furore, now almost forgotten, it is impossible to avoid the impression that with different handling by the county the break might have been avoided. At all events May was deprived of the man who, on the evidence of the tour to South Africa the previous winter, was his most valuable bowler on overseas pitches. The culmination was as unsatisfactory as the rest of the business, for the selectors failed to replace Wardle, the party being thus reduced to 16. This meant that only when Laker and Lock were both playing could MCC field a reasonably balanced attack.

In the event there were more potent reasons for the non-success of May's side, but the absence of Wardle and the fact that he was not replaced before the team left was certainly one adverse factor. Incidentally, I had been on three tours with Wardle and had never seen or heard of him stepping seriously out of line.

On the eve of our sailing on the P & O liner *Iberia* the head-line over my prospect piece was 'Future of Australian Cricket at Stake', followed by 'MCC Sail tomorrow for Tour that is Mission as well'. The Australian public, it seemed, had to be re-enchanted for cricket against various competing attractions. 'The average young Australian is inclined to spend most of his weekends under water, studying the varieties of marine nature, spearing fish, and caring for his lady-friend. There are many other things to do in the sun-shine than watch cricket.' The poor record of the 1956 team in England – the worst ever by an Australian team – was what had chiefly disenchanted their countrymen. So MCC had to provide the glamour. Nevertheless I added that 'if pressed for a forecast I would say that the proper odds at this stage must be just a shade in Australia's favour.' This was far from the average Fleet Street view, and it was the general idea of the team as one of the strongest ever to leave home that exacerbated the post-mortems when failure had to be accounted for.

'All journeys by sea in good ships and congenial company are happy times,' I cabled from Aden, 'and this one not least.' However, the next of all the team's misfortunes had already struck, for Watson had injured his knee, of all innocent things in getting out of a deck-chair. Should he be sent home, and a replacement called for at once? Retrospectively that would have been the better course, for poor Willy missed the first couple of months of playing-in. But, of course, there is a human side in these matters, and no one could foresee that when Milton and Richardson failed to find form Subba Row would then fall out just before the First Test with a fractured thumb that took two months to heal.

By this time Mortimore had been sent for as a belated replacement for Wardle. Then Dexter arrived to make up for the loss of Subba Row. Some of this chopping and changing was avoidable, some not. In any case it was all thoroughly unsettling. The rhythm of a tour, once upset, is difficult to recapture. As for the replacements, John Mortimore looked in the Fifth Test the highly useful all-rounder he has always been. Dexter, turning up at Brisbane after a long and hateful air-journey, showed scarcely a glimpse of his true self, and I imagine his troubles may even have caused Crusoe to ponder the validity of his judgement. After the original selection he thought the omission of Dexter 'the biggest clanger I have ever known selectors anywhere commit . . . a child of six who'd played one season's cricket on the lawn with his mother could surely have seen Dexter's genius . . . He is a possible Trumper or Macartney, and all his critics can do is to say "he has much to learn about slow bowling." Well, if it comes to that Harry Vardon had much to learn about putting to the end of his life and won six Open Championships. Gibbering dolts! Thanks, I feel better now!'

Strong stuff, and I'm glad that Crusoe lived to see his prophecy come reasonably close to fulfilment – he was at least at Lord's that glorious day in 1963 when Ted cut Hall and Griffith to ribbons.

But I've jumped ahead of MCC's progress round the states, which on the whole was reasonably satisfactory. At Melbourne we had a first look at Meckiff, whose fastish left-arm stuff had been picked out for special scrutiny in advance. Meckiff in the match took five for 85, and the batsmen were strongly inclined to think he threw. However, it was said that he didn't throw particularly well, and no official comment or complaint was made. This, as things turned out, looks to have been an important and misguided decision.

There was a marvellous interlude at Sydney against the Australian XI when May made 131 and 114 of the best runs imaginable on this, his favourite ground, and MCC won by 345 runs – a gigantic victory which caused much local gloom. Laker and Lock played havoc on a pitch that took spin towards the end, but May's cricket overshadowed everything. He won £A500, incidentally, offered by the *Sydney Daily Telegraph* for scoring 100 in a session of play.

From the Australian viewpoint the preliminaries to the series were significant in two respects. One was the emergence of Norman O'Neill as a new and exciting batsman: his style was classically based, and he hit the ball mighty hard. In short, he was precisely what his countrymen were praying for. Then there was the struggle for the captaincy. At the tender age of 24 Ian Craig had led the Australians successfully in South Africa a year previously, but had made few runs. Favourite at the start of the season, he dropped out of the captaincy when he declined, for health reasons, to lead the

Australian XI at Sydney in the usual dress-rehearsal. Harvey took his place, but when Australia announced their side for Brisbane they named as captain not Harvey but Benaud, who after three indifferent series against England had excelled himself as an all-rounder in South Africa. Of first-class captaincy experience he had none – not yet! It was a historic decision, and retrospectively not the least of Don Bradman's contributions to Australian cricket.

Benaud, once he had recovered from the surprise of his appointment, began to put a keen mind to the job. He instituted team dinners before Tests (such as England always have) and encouraged everyone to voice their ideas. On the field he recalled his French ancestry by a positively Gallic reaction to success. The idea was to crowd these Englishmen, who had been top dogs over a spell of fourteen Tests, in the field. When Australia batted they would aim to snatch the initiative, and especially to show up English fielding slowness by quick running. With Harvey, O'Neill, Davidson and the captain outstanding, Australia under Benaud developed into a superb fielding side, beside which England were inclined to look slow and unathletic.

The first Test was, I honestly think, the dullest and most depressing I have ever watched. There was some excuse for England's failure in the first innings on a fresh pitch – the sort which Hutton was hoping for when he had put Australia in four years earlier. And the bowlers then did a worthy best to keep their side in the game by restricting Australia's lead to 52. Now came the deadly tedium of what is almost but not quite the slowest innings ever played in a Test Match. On a pitch now plumb perfect England batted 8½ hours for 198, Bailey (68) batting, according to *Wisden,* for 7 hours 38 minutes. Even at this range of time one finds the gorge rising at the recollection of a piece of cricket for which according to my report there was no tactical or technical justification whatever.

Did England think the pitch was going to 'go'? Did they hope to bat out a draw? The answer is that the pitch at the end was perfect, and Australia's eight wicket win was gained with a day and a bit to spare. Bailey against the best bowling was always a batsman limited to front-foot play, apart from the dab to third man and nudges down to long-leg. He could be an awkward man to get out, but to promote him to No. 3 which meant May himself, the best player, batting at No. 5 and Cowdrey, the next best, as low as 6, was something that I'm sure the captain would scarcely now defend. The truth was that at this stage of his career Trevor was apt to enjoy playing a character part. 'Barnacle Bailey' as a sobriquet had stuck all too firmly, to the detriment at such times as this of his side (Durban a year earlier was another sickening example), and to the infinite frustration of the crowds – which here at Brisbane showed their feeling by simply staying away.

My mind turns now and then, when I listen to Trevor's admirably crisp and balanced comments over the air during Test Matches, to this parody of a stone-waller's innings at Brisbane. Out of 426 balls received he scored off only 40: he made 23 singles, ten twos, three threes – yes, and four fours. Even this is not all, for he compounded his long-drawn-out offence by sending back Tom Graveney (36 at the time) when he was half-away down the wicket and engaged on what would have been a comfortable single and ran him out. Later in the day Cowdrey was given out to a catch by Kline at short-leg about which there were the gravest doubts. 'So the malign afternoon pursued its interminable course,' I wrote in a report which questioned 'whether victory, if it should come, is worth the cost in terms of sterile, boring play that made one sick at heart to watch.'

Victory, of course, did not come. When Australia went in to make 147 with all the time in the world Burke even outdid Bailey in slowness, but with the difference that his partners kept going briskly. It was O'Neill in his first Test who redeemed the game by making 71 not out quite beautifully in less than two hours – so nailing conclusively the nonsense so often on these occasions emerging from dressing-rooms that strokes were impossible because the ball was not 'coming on to the bat'. This innings confirmed O'Neill as the white hope of Australian cricket. Everything was in his favour as a popular hero, including good looks. He fielded, too, like a great natural athlete. It seemed as though New South Wales had produced another prime stroke-maker in descent from Trumper, Macartney and McCabe.

Notice, by the way, that chucking had not come into prominence as a major issue at Brisbane, though Meckiff had May's wicket in both innings and Cowdrey's in one. But the storm was due to break soon enough. It was preceded by a good deal of criticism of the MCC team from English writers on the grounds that they were taking the tour too easily. Hard words from the professional cricket-writers were cabled back to Australia, while Len Hutton (now knighted) and Johnny Wardle were with us, providing comment – with ghostly aid – for papers in both countries. Australian readers like their comment earthy and to the point, and are unimpressed by literary flourishes – though they took greatly to Neville Cardus, whom they had come to know first as a music broadcaster from Sydney during the war. Cardus was missing, though, from this tour, a fact lamented by a tough taxi-driver, as I remember. However, said this worthy, brightening up, he enjoyed the writing of his successor with the *Sydney Morning Herald*, W. J. O'Reilly. He thought he could detect in the latter a distinct imitation of style. I had much pleasure in passing on this pleasantry to Bill O'Reilly.

Talking of Neville Cardus (knighted likewise, of course, but subsequent to this) I remember Sid Barnes once in the press-box, having sought in vain for inspiration for his column 'Like it or lump it', calling out: 'Hi, Neville, put a black (carbon) in for me, will you? Our styles are much the same.' This at least was more complimentary than the accusation made against the best of all cricket-writers of the romantic school by one B. J. Evans of the London *Star* (both journalist and newspaper long since dead), whose English in print and talk alike was almost more basic than anything I remember: 'Cardus? He's the – who pinches my – ing epigrams.'

The events of the Melbourne Test at the New Year would have tested the philosophical detachment of any cricket writer, of whatever school. I'm glad to see that in my preview before the game I noted that the increase in doubtful actions had been the most remarkable aspect of Australian cricket on the tour, and I named three suspects – Meckiff, Slater and Burke. I said that both Slater and Burke had been no-balled, once in each case, for throwing, and that I hoped the Australian umpires would do their unpleasant duty if they 'be not entirely satisfied', as the Law ordains.

Vain hope! Peter May redeemed another terribly slow start by England, making the first hundred by an England captain in Australia since Archie MacLaren in 1901/2. (Denness has since followed him.) When he had 113 against his name on the board May went vaguely back to a ball from Meckiff and was clean bowled. The sun was shining, and May was batting beautifully at the time. Yet he explained later that he had completely lost the ball from the instant it left the hand. It is characteristic of the chuckers that the flight of the ball is far harder to pick up. Meckiff also had the wickets of Bailey and Evans in this first innings, but this was nothing compared with what was to come.

Neil Harvey (167) played almost his best innings for Australia, and on a working day – though certainly it was during the holiday period – seventy-one thousand turned up to acclaim his hundred with the echoing roar that is peculiar to the vast Melbourne arena.

Yet Australia's lead was only 49 when England went in again after lunch of a fine Saturday afternoon before another vast crowd. Talk about Christians being thrown to the lions! The English innings began disastrously, Australia caught just about every snick that flew above ground, May and Cowdrey again came in as low as 5 and 6, and before close of play the rout was complete: all out 87, the lowest score made by England in Australia since 1903/4.

I never saw anything so blatant as Meckiff's action as, with the swell of the crowd in his ears, he came up that afternoon full pelt from the bottom end towards the pavilion – unless it was the action of Griffin, the young South African, in England in the following year. Meckiff took six for 38, and the batsmen were undone, I suppose, by feelings of indignation and resentment as much as by the intrinsic difficulties caused by a fastish left-arm bowler letting fly with his tail up in this highly unorthodox manner. The cables home from the English press camp were outspoken to a degree, and at least one Australian, Jack Fingleton, writing in the *Sunday Times,* said he thought Meckiff should have been called. But he also added he thought the English batting was poor both technically and in spirit.

England had a grievance, without a doubt. Yet this defeat, the manner of which, following Brisbane, more or less assured the rubber to Benaud's young side, underlined the batting weaknesses which even in the years of victory the bowlers had only counterbalanced with difficulty. Even two years before when on paper England had such a resounding success on their own pitches against Ian Johnson's side it could be argued that they might not have won the rubber unless they had bolstered the batting by bringing back Cyril Washbrook after five years' absence from Test Matches, and calling David Sheppard away from an East End parish after he had given up serious cricket.

There is precious little in the story of the last three Tests to make happy reading to English eyes. The batting continued insubstantial, and the bowlers with so few runs behind them were, not surprisingly, mastered by degrees. May and Cowdrey both did their best, mostly in an inhibited style, while Graveney was consistent up to a point without ever contributing a big innings. England tried four opening bats, and only once did the first wicket raise more than 30. Injuries were never-ending, with Milton, Evans, Statham and Loader all out of action at times in the second half of the tour. One way and another the dice seemed most unfairly loaded.

The Third Test at Sydney was drawn after much rain delay, but

England were fighting an uphill battle most of the way and only a long partnership of 182 between May and Cowdrey saved a third successive defeat and so kept the Ashes in suspense. The pitch this time was friendly to the spinners, and for the only time in Australia Laker and Lock in harness must have evoked for Australian survivors of 1956, a few unwelcome memories. However, Benaud in Australia was more than their equal, and when Slater's off-breaks failed to come off Burke came pinging in to break the May-Cowdrey stand. This was on the sixth day, and by then the game was just about saved. I wrote 'after lunch Benaud for the first time employed Burke, whom I had too hurriedly supposed he might not have used yesterday on grounds of conscience.' Like beauty chucking exists in the eyes of the beholder.

Meckiff had been hurt at Sydney, and so for the Fourth Test at Adelaide Australia fortified themselves by bringing back Ray Lindwall, at the age of 37, plus Gordon Rorke, the very tall 20-year-old, of New South Wales, whose action MCC also thought dubious. He was very wayward in direction, but was certainly the fastest bowler in Australia, and had an even more phenomenal drag than Lindwall.

Little had gone right for poor May – apart from his own batting – since the start of the tour, and at Adelaide the course of events on the first day meant that his prospect of keeping the Ashes practically disappeared. The weather was baking hot, and the pitch brown and tinder-dry. England, of course needed to win to keep both the rubber and their Ashes hopes alive, and their best prospect seemed to be to bat first, make a tall score, and hope that, as the match progressed, Laker and Lock might find enough purchase for their spin to do the job. However, before the captains tossed word came that Laker was unfit with a sore, stiff spinning finger and would not play. Thereupon May, on calling right but deprived of his trump card, thought he must take the slim chance of the fast men breaking through on the first day and sent Australia in.

Jim Laker recently told me that for some days there had been doubt whether when the moment came he would be able to bend the top joint, but this possibility was kept quiet. Having bowled for twenty minutes in a net he decided he couldn't play – and that, as one realized with a sickening certainty at the time, put the lid firmly on English hopes. Statham, Trueman, Tyson and Bailey stuck admirably to the job, but by close of play McDonald, competent, cautious, composed, had made his first hundred against England, who had taken just one wicket. It was a slow, slogging day, but just before the close Harvey hit Lock for six to the longest straight boundary in the world at the Cathedral end, and so 'directed our eyes to the towers and pinnacles – with the underlying suggestion, perhaps, that prayer would not be out of place.'

England were kept grilling after lunch on the third day, where-upon on the plumbest of plumb pitches six batsmen made only 14 runs between them and of the batting as a whole I must have been stretching charity to write of 'a certain worthy doggedness'. The fact is that England followed on, and lost by ten wickets, with an hour or so to spare, and it was left to some dejected Englishman to answer the manager of the American Davis Cup team then in Australia who earnestly enquired: 'What precisely is an ash?'

And so, after a few days in the country at places with colourful Aboriginal names (Wangaratta and Wagga Wagga), for a brief rest before the final examination in Melbourne.

There are several amenities in Australia for which Melbourne is best. One is the Windsor Hotel, where the service, and especially that of the staff of porters, is world-renowned. The Windsor epito-mizes Victoria's prosperity and respectability. It would be an ana-chronism in Sydney – it's exactly right where it stands, solid and four-square facing the Parliament Buildings above and aloof from the clamour of the city.

Another attraction is the golf. Royal Melbourne with its courses in the middle of the sandbelt that encircles Melbourne to the south-ward is one of the world's great golf clubs, and it is surrounded by all but a dozen others in more or less the same class. Not much further out lies the Peninsula Country Club, also with 36 holes in splendid golfing country; away down the Mornington Peninsula one comes upon Sorrento which is a bit hilly for old legs but provides good, amusing holiday golf.

I associate Sorrento with the names of Baillieu and Guest, Gilder and Grimwade, and there is a story of Fred Gilder and Geoff Grim-wade (the latter now dead) which illustrates as well as anything the Australian keenness for a wager. One day after lunch they sat in the bar discussing the terms of their forthcoming match. They left at length for the first tee and were there seen for some while deep in animated conversation. But they never hit off. Still talking they returned to the clubhouse. They had simply been unable to agree on the strokes and the stake. Would such a story be credible of any others than Australians? I rather doubt it.

Talking of Royal Melbourne I recall playing there, either on this tour or the next, with Gilder and Ted Dexter. Fred had watched all the greats there at one time or another. Yet twice on the round, if not three times, he said when we reached Ted's ball, 'You know, I've never seen anyone get to within thirty yards of this.' If there was a finer example of harnessed, classic power than Dexter hitting a cricket ball it was Dexter hitting a golf ball. Peter May, of course, matched Dexter as striker of a cricket ball, and though his golf was not of anything like comparable quality he has always played pretty well off about 9. On this tour when briefly out of action on the cricket field he took exercise playing golf with Ann, my wife – at her best handicap 4.

Golf is a lovely relaxer on cricket tours, but I must get back to completing the disappointing saga of the 1958/9 series which had, so far as England were concerned, no consolatory ending. At Melbourne they found a pitch which the groundsman had had to keep fresh until the last minute to counteract the deadly north wind and another temperature around the hundred mark. There was sure to be moisture on the surface, and, sure enough, Australia announced four fast bowlers, won their first toss of the series, and put England in and out for 205. The biggest stand was of 63 for the eighth wicket between Trueman and Mortimore, playing in his first Test to the exclusion of Lock. On his home pitch McDonald obliged with another hundred, and Australia never looked remotely like losing their grip. Thus with a day to spare ended the last Test, and we had to take some comfort from a truly perfect piece of batting from Cowdrey, who had made 56 in 50 minutes, showing every stroke in the book, when he and Richardson got into a muddle over a run, as a result of which Colin was 'adjudged' run-out – a mighty near thing. Richardson at the eleventh hour showed something much more like his normal English form.

This was not the best of tours from the umpiring standpoint, largely because Mel McInnes, who had been hailed as a model four years earlier, progressively lost the players' confidence and with this, naturally, his own. Too much was written on the subject, needless to say, but there were surprising decisions about which some comment was inevitable. The culmination came at Adelaide when, at the bowler's end, he moved the wrong way to judge a run-out with the result that Burke, acting as runner for McDonald, passed behind his back. He was a yard from home when the wicket was broken, but McInnes, after momentarily and as though by instinct raising the finger, swiftly signalled not out. McDonald saw just what had happened, promptly swung his bat and got himself out.

Earlier in the same innings Mackay had started to walk after snicking to the keeper, then stopped when he noticed McInnes immobile, and waited several seconds until at last the finger was raised. 'Walking' was then almost unknown in Australia, though the next MCC team introduced Australians to a practice which goes all against their instincts – and, if it comes to that, mine also. I mention these incidents to underline that though there was much controversy on this tour both sides observed well enough the chivalries of combat.

As I've said, I always thought that England would be hard pressed to win the series. Yet the margin of the result made this the most surprising rubber of all I've seen. The extraordinary truth was that not after a single day of any of the five Tests could it be said that England enjoyed an advantage. Sometimes they fought back to somewhere near equality, only to suffer a further set-back the next day.

It was a tour which saw all sorts of perverse happenings – from an injury list that never stopped (and culminated in only 12 out of the 18 being fit to fly on to New Zealand), to the dissatisfaction with umpiring and bowlers' actions that so undermined morale. From various causes England gave below their best against a side, as I wrote, 'incontestably better in batting and bowling, and with the more positive tactical plan: one might add also, with the fresher and more zestful approach to the game.' It was the end of the road, or thereabouts, for quite a few of May's side – of the more seasoned men Bailey, Evans, Laker, Loader, Tyson and Watson were all making, as it proved, their last tours.

7
Measure for Measure

The English prelude to the 1962/3 MCC tour of Australia contained rather more than the usual quota of drama and surprise. The first significant event was the appointment of Walter Robins as chairman of selectors instead of Gubby Allen who decided during the winter that 'seven years hard' was enough. The perennial feeling that the game in England needed 'brightening' was specially strong at this time, and no one personified the idea of cricket as an attacking game in quite the same way as Walter. It had been his watchword ever since he took over the leadership of Middlesex in 1935. In proclaiming his gospel he had ruffled certain feathers, not least when he was managing MCC in the West Indies a couple of years before. But for him the cause had to come before the feelings of individuals, however distinguished. Doug Insole stayed on from Allen's committee, while Alec Bedser and Willie Watson came on – Alec, of course, as it turned out, to begin a span of record length.

The first and most important question to be faced was who was to lead England. Peter May, who had done so over an uninterrupted span (apart from illness) of 41 Tests, announced that he could no longer spare time for tours – which meant that the new leader for Australia would have to emerge from the home series against Pakistan. There were two clear candidates, Colin Cowdrey – May's regular deputy – and Ted Dexter, who had led MCC in India and Pakistan the previous winter. There was also the prospect of David Sheppard claiming a Sabbatical leave from his East End Mission and so making himself available. Everyone remembered his qualities as a captain: indeed he too had also led England against Pakistan at home in 54.

The selectors did not make up their minds in a hurry, for after naming Dexter for the first two Tests, both of which England won easily, they reverted to Cowdrey who with equal ease won the Third. Then Cowdrey was named captain of the Gentlemen against the Players, in preference to Dexter, with Sheppard also included. Between Cowdrey and Sheppard then? We shall perhaps never exactly know – unless the selectors' meetings were closely minuted and cricket's secret papers are disclosed in the fulness of time. However, Cowdrey at this juncture was laid low, retiring to hospital with stones in the kidney. Dexter accordingly led the Gents, Sheppard made a classic hundred – and Dexter was promptly given the job. Cowdrey on his recovery was named vice-captain as in 58 – and as he was destined to be also in 65 and 70. Sheppard won his place as an opening batsman. Not often have there been three candidates with better credentials lined up in competition for English cricket's most coveted honour.

In passing I should add a valedictory word about Gentlemen and Players, often known as 'the G and P', if only for the benefit of young Australian readers who must find the title utterly baffling. The fixture was the second oldest on the Lord's calendar, dating from 1806, only a year after the Battle of Trafalgar and the first match between Eton and Harrow! Cricket in England – unlike Australia – had always been compounded of the two strains, amateur and professional, independent and dependent, and in the last century the title of this classic event of the summer, established long before Test Matches were thought of, must have seemed natural enough. Latterly it was regarded by most people as an amusing anachronism though it attracted many a cheap dig from the popular press. It was a game, to repeat the old tag, where all the Players were gentlemen and all the Gentlemen players.

Since the distinction was dropped by the Advisory County Cricket Committee in the autumn of 1962 this proved to be the last fixture between them. Held at Lord's, it produced big crowds and some of the best cricketer of the summer. Fred Trueman proved an able captain of the Players, and the 137th game of the series ended in an honourable draw. It was the 28th draw, the amateurs having won 41 times, the pros 68. Incidentally the counties only came to their decision to abolish by ten votes to seven, and as in those days their committee was only 'advisory' to MCC the latter could have declined to accept the verdict. In practice they left the counties to run their own affairs: looking back it was a pity they didn't at least fulfil a delaying function, for more mature consideration, rather in the manner of the House of Lords. All sorts of stunts were cooked up by 'the Advisory', including the abolition of the Follow-on in English cricket. Was there ever such nonsense?

Talking of the Lords, the really big surprise preceding the tour followed, for the manager was now named as none other than the Earl Marshal of England and premier duke, His Grace of Norfolk.

Some leading batsmen — English . . .

26. *(above)* Compton sweeping. Productive as played by this great batsman, this stroke, slavishly imitated by lesser players, is the bane of English batting quarter of a century on. **27.** *(right)* Stroke of authority: Peter May was one of the four architects of England's victory in 1954/5, and with Colin Cowdrey supplied the backbone to the batting in 1958/9. The best purely post-war English batsman. **28.** *(below)* Barrington (2,111 runs v. Australia, average 63.96), though not normally a forceful player, reached four of his Test hundreds with a six. This one was at Adelaide in 1962/3. Grout is the 'keeper. **29.** Balance, control, concentration: Boycott hitting square off the back foot.

. . . And Australian

30. *(above)* Morris, one of the post-war greats. Only six Australians have made more runs than his 2080 (average 50.73) against England. **31.** Harvey v. Laker, and perhaps the best stroke in the book. Note the footwork and position of the head. He made 167 here at Melbourne in the second Test, 1958/9, the highest of his six Test hundreds against England. **32.** *(below)* Lawry in a characteristic pose: the most disheartening Australian to bowl at over the 1946/75 period. **33.** Greg Chappell, following through from a hook stroke, eyes still focussed on the ball. Australia's finest batsman of the 'seventies.

Dexter had been known by his contemporaries since his schooldays as Lord Ted, no doubt from a certain aloof dignity of bearing – I wonder, by the way, what Dexter's generation would have made of an earlier Sussex captain named C. B. Fry – so the popular joke was that it needed a duke to bring him to heel.

But how came the Duke to be appointed right out of the blue? Well, when the MCC committee met to make the decision a long debate centred on Billy Griffith, assistant secretary of the Club who was due to succeed Ronny Aird as secretary on 1 October 1962. After the troubles of the last MCC Australian tour, and the contrasting triumphs of the intervening Australian-West Indies series, it was argued that the best man must go, and he was Griffith. However, those who thought he could not be spared from Lord's immediately on his new appointment won the day. Over drinks after the meeting one of the younger members said, 'You know, Ted's not the easiest chap to handle.'

Duke: 'I could handle him.'

Y.M.: 'Yes, but you're not going to be manager.'

Duke: 'No one's ever asked me.'

It was Lord Nugent, president-designate, who followed up this remark, and after due consideration the offer was made and accepted. The question which with his death must remain unanswered is whether the job was a long-cherished ambition or the result of a sudden inspiration.

Knowing the Duke pretty well, as I came to do, my guess is that he had greatly enjoyed the company of first-class cricketers, and felt he understood them, when he took his own team to Jamaica a few years earlier. At some point during the 1962 summer therefore it may well have occurred to him that if Billy were required at Lord's he would like to try and do a service to MCC and to cricket by tackling this tricky assignment in his own way. He was intrigued perhaps by the challenge of something so far removed from his normal orbit. At all events the MCC tour in no way disillusioned him, for six years later at my suggestion he took on the tour to the West Indies which remains among the fondest memories of Colin Cowdrey, our captain, and of all of us who took part.

Billy Griffith believes that in going to Australia as manager Bernard Norfolk was fulfilling an ambition; he also thinks that the Duke may well have stipulated the necessity of coming home for a month in mid-tour on affairs of state in order to give Griffith, the new secretary, the chance of replacing him over this period, and so getting the feel of a modern tour and familiarizing himself with the

Australian authorities on their own ground. This is what happened, and it would be completely characteristic of his thoughtfulness.

Alec Bedser was chosen as assistant-manager, both to keep an eye on the cricket and to deal with the financial side of the tour, and a very successful and harmonious combination it turned out to be.

The side that Robins and his colleagues named seemed powerful in batting, and though the bowling gave less confidence most judges accorded them a sporting chance of winning back the Ashes, but no more. The weakness of the bowling was its sameness: six fast or fastish bowlers, all right-arm and including two all-rounders, and three off-spinners. That was the attack. For the only time in history MCC set off for Australia without a left-arm bowler of any kind, nor even a right-arm leg-breaker to spin the ball away from the bat. Nor again was there a medium-pacer of the stock variety.

For the first time MCC did not sail all the way to Australia. Instead they flew to Aden and then boarded the *Canberra* on its maiden voyage. I had jumped a bit ahead, having flown to Naples, which was the first port of call. The Duke joined us four days after Aden at Colombo.

One way and another, and not a little due to the identity of our manager, as well as the presence of an unusually gifted set of English batsmen, there was rather more glamour to this tour than most. The Australians go for youth and colour and personality, and Dexter had all three – in fact he was, at 27, and is still the youngest captain to lead MCC in Australia. They had taken to Cowdrey when he had first come as a 21-year-old with Len Hutton. Tom Graveney, Fred Trueman and Brian Statham were old favourites. They were intrigued by the return of the parson.

Also they had no mean stars of their own, headed by Richie Benaud, who having snatched the Ashes back in 1959 had held on to them by winning one of the most pulsating of all Test Matches, at Old Trafford in 1961. Neil Harvey and Alan Davidson were still on the scene – though due to retire at the end of the series – and Norman O'Neill was a young and glamorous figure. The omens in fact were good from the start, and, apart from the anti-climax of the final Test Match, expectations were generally realized, even if Dexter's side could not live up to the resounding impact they made in their first big match, the traditional one (in those days) against an Australian XI.

The captain strode on to the great Melbourne bowl on the first morning when after 45 minutes MCC had rather tentatively reached 26 for one. When he departed an hour and three-quarters later (183 for three) he had made 102 of the most majestic runs imaginable, and the hands of the bowlers and the fielders in front of the wicket were bruised and burning. I have seen Walter Hammond in full spate, and Clyde Walcott, but I never saw the ball driven harder than it was by Dexter on this November Friday in Melbourne. Thanks to this marvellous example MCC ended the day with 458 for five, and next day went on to 633 for seven.

Altogether this was a notable week since those of us not on duty at Adelaide in the previous game were able to fly over in time to see the greatest of all Australian spectacles, the Melbourne Cup. Nothing 'gets' the Aussies like the Cup. They have an insatiable taste for a gamble, and being perhaps countrymen at heart – even though millions may seldom leave the great sprawling suburbs that hug the coastlines on either side of each of the five capital cities – they venerate the horse.

Everyone seems to be an expert: your air hostess will declare confidentially that the favourite is not a good back runner. It's nothing out of the ordinary if an evening paper devotes its whole front page to the report of a secret dawn trial. The general state of knowledge being so professional, all the listener wants from a race broadcast is fact. The position of every horse must be reiterated as often as possible. When many years ago now Raymond Glendenning's description of the Derby was broadcast in Australia his much slower pace and off-beat comments in the then approved BBC style was a national joke. For myself the quick-fire Australian commentary might as well be spoken in Greek.

Altogether the first Tuesday in November is to the Australian almost as the Fourth of July to the American and the feast of St Patrick to the Irish. There are remarkable similarities with Ascot, the gay luncheon parties in the car parks, the spacious lawns, the Viceregal splendour, the feminine high fashion. In this particular year with the Queen's Ascot representative on parade the resemblance was even heightened. There were 100,000 of us at Flemington, and the other 9,900,000 Australians were listening. The New Zealand horses, they say, are the best stayers, and not infrequently win the Cup which is an all-age handicap over two miles to which the Cesarewitch, I believe, is the nearest English equivalent. The winner, Even Stevens, duly came from New Zealand, and it was said that five million pounds changed hands over the race – ten shillings in the old money for every man, woman, and child in Australia. Quite a solemn thought!

The first Test at Brisbane began with Australia favourites, fielding exactly the side that had retained the Ashes at Old Trafford except for the substitution of Jarman for Grout, the keeper, who had had his jaw broken standing back to Wes Hall, who was then bowling for Queensland. As can be deduced from the scores this was an evenly-contested game wherein the chief protagonists were the respective captains. England at this time were said to have a 'Benaud complex', and he certainly bowled his wrist-spin beautifully and with more success than subsequently. But Australia were likewise near to getting a 'Dexter complex'. Having made 70 in the first innings he came in on the last day after lunch clearly interested in the possibility of England reaching the 376 in six hours which Benaud's overnight declaration had set them. He was bowled hitting over a yorker for 99 made in 2¾ hours: a superb innings worth more than most of the Test hundreds ever made. In the end England did not achieve a draw without some anxiety – but at least the spirit had shown willing. Trueman bowled very well, as did McKenzie for Australia, but altogether the batting on both sides looked rather better than the bowling.

Nevertheless the two following Tests were both brought to a conclusion. The New Year Test at Melbourne is the one that sticks most clearly in my mind, naturally enough, since there's nothing to compare with the spectacle of Melbourne when the big crowds come – and also because England won a handsome victory by seven wickets. Since I've seen only nine English Test wins on eight tours and eighteen defeats who will be surprised that it is the former which are the more memorable? Again it was Dexter, this time with Cowdrey's aid, who first tilted the game towards his side in a handsome stand of 175 for the third wicket, made in only 3¼ hours: this was in contrast to Australia's pawky batting all through. I see that in welcoming this contrast from the usual run of things I remarked that in eleven of the last twelve series between the two countries Australia had scored the faster. The 1956 summer in England was the only exception. As it happened England ended the series a solitary run behind Australia over-all, 39 per hundred balls as against 40, but at least it could be said that this was the fastest English rate in Australia since 1924/5. (It has been once beaten since, by Mike Smith's side in the tour following.)

There was some fine bowling by Trueman, used in short spurts in the heat, a lovely run-out by Harvey in the covers that cut short an auspicious innings by Graveney, some inexpressibly dull batting by Bill Lawry, and a hundred by Brian Booth, that model of a man and of a batsman who tends to be under-rated and forgotten because both he and his cricket were so blamelessly self-effacing. Tall, upright, correct in method, ever-patient, he repeated the hundred he had got at Brisbane, and so gave England a target to go for while all around him were failing. And who could forget the chequered fortunes of Sheppard?

When he and Geoff Pullar opened England's second innings with 235 needed to win 'the Rev' had behind him a duck in the first and was it a couple of dropped catches or three? There were various versions of Fred Trueman's comments on these serious lapses from grace, but the general drift was that they were extraordinary in one who should have so much more practice in keeping his hands together than the rest of them.

However, redemption was now at hand, first with Dexter for company and finally with Cowdrey. The scores were level when David, having exactly repeated the 113 he had made as a young cleric against Australia at Old Trafford seven years earlier, ran himself out. This was England's second win only in the last 13 Tests against Australia. It was watched by all but quarter of a million, and of course it 'made' the series.

We had reached half-way on the tour or thereabouts, and in my half-term review I wrote back that the English victory had gone down well in Australia because the party had made a very good general impression.

As has been mentioned already the manager has identified himself in the friendliest way with many sides of Australian life while in the past month the secretary of MCC, Mr Griffith, has fully maintained the example that the Duke of Norfolk set in his relations with cricket officialdom and with the Press.

More than one English side out here in my experience has given an impression of aloofness which has been inclined to keep Australians at arm's length and tended in consequence to put up a barrier against their own enjoyment.

Dexter's team have been seen and met in schools, clubs and other institutions as well as at formal gatherings and, of course, privately.

In this connection must be mentioned the church-going population of Australia. The presence in the pulpit of David Sheppard, the centurion of Melbourne, has filled the Anglican cathedral of every state capital from Perth round to Brisbane.

The captain himself appeals too as a tough, cheerful, challenging figure for whose own cricket they have a tremendous admiration. Dexter is taking in his stride an aspect of his duties about which not everyone was confident when appointed.

Nowadays the captains are expected to be prepared to talk before the cameras or for publication at any hour of the day or night and Benaud, a journalist himself, is a past-master at all comment both for and off the record.

Of late Dexter has not lost a trick in this phase of operations. He manages to make a good balance between confidence in his own side and generosity towards the enemy.

After the second Test the two captains spoke briefly to an expectant throng from above the dressing-rooms. Watching them in admiration one wondered what sort of job some of their famous predecessors still sweating from their efforts in the field would have made of a similar situation. Armstrong and Douglas for instance.

I would not suggest we are exactly witnessing the perfectly-run tour. Apart from obvious flaws in the itinerary and the fact of MCC having too many players, the best has scarcely always been made of the material on the field partly because the captain's tactical sense is having to be acquired the hard way.

He has the good general's gift of self-confidence and personality but as will probably have been gathered at home he could not be described as a natural schemer.

So far so good in fact, but as things turned out we had seen the best.

It was one of the misfortunes of this tour that it was Sydney's turn to stage two Tests rather than Melbourne's because for once the playing conditions at Sydney were far from satisfactory. The pitch was slow and uneven in bounce, and like the rest of the square unevenly grassed. Where the middle had too little covering the outfield had too much. Even the strongest strikers found it hard to find the boundary in these circumstances, and the scoring both in the Third Test and the Fifth was turgid compared with elsewhere. Australia, whose cricket so far had not excited their countrymen, made a concession to public feeling by dropping Ken Mackay (after 30 successive Test matches) in favour of a burly West Australian left-hander, Barry Shepherd, who promptly justified his place. England disappointed me – according to my pre-match preview – by preferring Len Coldwell again to David Allen whom I thought England's most dangerous spinner, despite Fred Titmus's all-round utility. How often have England, faced with the choice of spinner or 'seamer' of recent years, plumped for the latter and been proved wrong!

Whereas the English faster bowlers could bang nothing out of the pitch Titmus held the attack together in an admirably-sustained spell from the Randwick end, floating the ball away with the help of a long-leg wind and turning it at times almost sharply. Looking back I'll make bold to say that if Allen had had the chance of bowling with Titmus in partnership the result could very well have gone the other way.

However, it was a superb spell by Alan Davidson with the new ball in England's second innings that turned a hitherto evenly-poised game towards Australia. 'Davo', with his late swing and cut, was a superb bowler at his best, and this was about it. What he had started the Australian spinners completed, and all England could point to in extenuation was that John Murray – preferred in this one match of the five to Alan Smith as keeper – had so injured himself making a catch at the start of Australia's first innings that he could only bat defensively while Parfitt had to take over the gloves for the remainder of the game. Soon after lunch on the fourth day it was all over, and England had gone – oh, so mildly!

And so to Adelaide where the pitch's ease and the January heat have tended over the years to make the bowlers' task more onerous and less rewarding than almost anywhere in the world, Barbados perhaps excepted. Ian McLachlan, of South Australia, had been named among Australia's twelve but was appointed twelfth man, which was interesting in that – strange but true – this is the nearest any Australian from Oxford or Cambridge has ever got to a Test place since the 1888 side in England fortified themselves by picking up Sammy Woods when he was a Cambridge freshman. (He played in all three Tests for Australia that summer, then settled in Somerset for whom he performed legendary deeds, and also represented England in South Africa.) Many worse batsmen have played for Australia than the McLachlan we saw in Australia in 1962.

A more significant choice for the future though it scarcely seemed so at the time was that of Ray Illingworth for his first Test in Australia. His figures look none too good in the score-book, but bowling analyses all too rarely do the bowler justice. Here on the first morning Illingworth not only bowled out Lawry in his first over but had Harvey missed off successive balls in his next. There was a strange epidemic in this series among the England side and it wasn't catching. Harvey, whose 154 on the first day greatly tightened Australia's defence of the Ashes, was missed four times in his first 26 runs. There had been talk of dropping Norman O'Neill before this game, but unluckily for England he was given another chance and took a hundred. O'Neill was missed when 2, one of two catches let drop, I thought, because short-leg was too close, three yards distant instead of five. Nor did the off-spinners ever bowl to a man in the deep while batsmen of the skill and temper of Harvey and O'Neill were making 194 together, and the cricket correspondent of the *Daily Telegraph* got a bit steamed up about it. Listen to this:

> One of the things present cricketers are inclined to announce – without apologies for their immodesty as a rule – is that modern field-placing is more 'scientific' than it used to be. My own watching experience goes back little more than thirty years and I can only offer the view, which today's events may certainly have made slightly more acute that geometrically, arithmetically, psychologically, geographically, and from every other conceivable point of view, the setting of modern English fields often seems completely haywire. That is an unscientific word by which I mean illogical and devoid of principle.

So there!

But the team came under more distinguished displeasure than this, for I had to report home that the Duke had had them all on the carpet for disturbing the other guests at the Pier Hotel, Glenelg by undue noise at night. The manager's rebuke, I thought, had come none too soon.

Australia had the ill-luck early in the England first innings to lose Davidson with a thigh strain. Thereafter Benaud seemed, not unnaturally, more interested in saving the game than winning it. England were the thrusters, and if their catching had not continued to let them down Australia might have been out early on the last day, so giving Dexter and company a fair chance of victory against an attack reduced to McKenzie, Mackay, and three leg-spinners. As it was, Ken Barrington made the first of his hundreds against Australia, and in so doing kept at arm's length any serious fears of a collapse.

All then turned on the last Test at Sydney, but before it happened a greatly heightened interest was given to the annual match against the Prime Minister's XI at Canberra by the astonishing news that at the age of 54 Sir Donald Bradman had agreed to play. Of course many men have still batted well in their fifties. Of the only two batsmen in history of comparable stature to the Don W. G. Grace had played his last important innings on his 58th birthday for Gentlemen against Players at the Oval and made 74, throwing his bat on the table as he came in, saying, 'That's enough. I'll not play any more.' Jack Hobbs was in his 52nd year when he finished his days with Surrey. But these two had played continuously whereas Don had not had a serious innings for 14 years, and for most of them had not so much as touched a bat.

All agreed that it was a great sporting gesture, and no one wanted to see him bat more than Dexter and his side – especially perhaps the captain, than whom there was and is no keener theorist. Report came that the great man was getting down to regular practice – which, of course, was completely in character – and that he was seeing and timing the ball beautifully. In he came at No. 5 followed all the way to the wicket by photographers, and applauded at such length that Tom Graveney, the bowler, had to wait before he could deliver a friendly straight full-pitch which was duly driven for four.

What MCC wanted to do was to give the greatest run-getter in history a few overs to find his bearings before aiming to get him out. But contrivance at cricket is seldom easy, and at the other end the Don played a shade late at Statham, the ball, struck firmly, somehow squeezing between his pads and rolling back with just sufficient momentum to dislodge a bail. In the shilling sweep on his score in the press-box the lowest guess was 19, the highest a hundred: such is fame.

But we must come back from nostalgia and pathos to grim business, and at Sydney 'grim' was the word. It was the first time since 1936/7 that a series in Australia had come to the last Test with the Ashes to play for, and since Adelaide there had been a fortnight to build up to the great event. England's advance estimate of the pitch was shown when they picked all three off-spinners. Australia chose for the first time Neil Hawke, destined to become a fine bowler but whose role here was soon seen to be defensive. He was generally short of a length, a livelier version of Mackay.

By taking nine and a half hours to make their 321 on winning the toss England could point to the difficulty of forcing the ball away from so turgid a pitch and so dusty an in-field and finally across a slow, lush, green carpet. Naturally suspicious of players' alibis, I was very much on their side this time – up to a point. Granted the difficulties, the onus was on England to take the initiative, Australia's attitude being 'what we have we hold.' Far from taking risks, there was more than a suggestion that England were prepared to grind it out because they thought the pitch might go. Only *three* fours came on the first day.

Of all the Tests I've watched the number of times I've seen a pitch really disintegrate – apart from interference by rain – can almost be counted on one hand: Headingley and Old Trafford in 1956, Melbourne in 1955 (temporarily rectified by the watering-can) are the notorious instances. On the other hand, how many times have predictions that pitches would dust proved false?

Australia when their turn came were extremely wary of the off-spinners; Titmus and Allen bowled 90 overs in the innings, taking seven for 190, while Illingworth was given only five; but O'Neill and Burke raised the tempo appreciably, ensuring their side of a narrow lead. By now, bad light and drizzle having made inroads into the time available, it was very nearly lunch on the fourth day. England mended their pace somehow now, as they were bound to do, but it scarcely smacked of attack to send Illingworth in first instead of Cowdrey, who had an infected, swollen eye. Why not Graveney? Again, why not Dexter, much the most forceful bat on either side, at No. 3, however much Barrington might like batting there? Sheppard's last Test innings (68) was a worthy one, but Dexter, when he eventually arrived, impatience in every movement, in bad light with only three-quarters of an hour to go on the fourth evening, was soon snared by Benaud, who thus had his rival's wicket once in every Test of the series.

Leading by only 137 on the last morning with seven wickets left England needed to bat until lunch at which they were bound to declare, come what may, and Barrington and Cowdrey, with all Benaud's resources deployed in defence, saw to it that the runs were safely gathered in. The vice-captain's 53 took two hours, Barrington's 94, following his safe, sedate 101 in the first innings, nearly four and a half.

The declaration left Australia to make 241 at precisely a run a minute and England four hours in which to bowl them out and bring home the Ashes. Benaud was committed by all he had said since the tour's beginning and before – and in his daily press conferences after play he had said plenty – to make some sort of effort to achieve the target. Simpson being bowled off his pads for a duck, Harvey, affectionately greeted on his last appearance, was promoted

to his old place at No. 3, O'Neill following. Both were clearly disposed to press along with a sort of discreet enterprise, preparing
the ground if possible for hitters like Benaud and Davidson to do
their stuff after tea. Lawry, however, obviously the tactical anchor,
was slow even by his own standards. When Allen had not only
Harvey and O'Neill but also Burge out with 70 on the board and
with some two and a half hours remaining Australia gave up all
pretence and shut up shop. If Burge had succumbed to his first ball
from Allen instead of snicking it perilously past slip Australia would
have been 72 for five, and England might have achieved the improbable. As it was, no further wicket fell and anti-climax was complete.

The verdict of press and public was highly unflattering, and MCC
accordingly flew off to New Zealand with their bright image sadly
tarnished. It could easily have been so much better. The pitch and
indeed the whole field were to blame, attitudes at crucial times were
to blame, the over-importance of the Ashes was to blame. Yet if only
the game had been arranged over six days instead of five – as
happens now with last Tests if the rubber is still in contention –
how different the end would have been. It needed further frustrations,
though, notably at the Oval in 1964 and at Melbourne in 1966, to
bring this about.

Looking at the tour in perspective afterwards one had to recog-
nize that Dexter's side had halved the series, which most people had
thought beforehand was beyond them. They had been watched by
more than a million people, a figure only once exceeded, in 1936/7,
and had brought home a record profit of £24,000. There had been
no major upsets, and the atmosphere surrounding the two teams had
been keen but amiable. As to individuals Barrington, thanks to his
great spurt at the end, had emerged with a better record than any
English batsman in Australia since Walter Hammond's first visit.
Fred Titmus had been the find of the tour. What England chiefly
needed straight away was an opening pair of batsmen, a new ball
bowler, and not least some safe catchers round the bat. Statham was
as game, philosophical and uncomplaining as ever, but on his fourth
tour of Australia something of the fine edge had gone.

For Australia, with the retirement of Benaud as well as Harvey,
Davidson and Mackay, it was the end of an era. No doubt Richie
would have liked to go out on a higher note, but he had a record
against England second only to Bradman's: won 7, lost 2, drawn 6.
With the material available no one could have achieved more: he
must go down as one of the great captains.

8

Runs Galore

Shortly before Mike Smith's MCC team of 1965/6 flew off to Perth
– they were the first to do the whole trip by air – I had a line from
his prospective opposite number, Bobby Simpson, who had led his
country in England the previous year and also, though unsuccessfully,
between then and now in the West Indies. He wrote, 'I was pleased
that Mike was appointed skipper. It will be nice to be on the same
wave-length, and I'm sure that we can get together to make this a
wonderful series.' These, need I say, were the sentiments commonly
exchanged before Test series, spiced by the clear implication that
Australia's captain had not been exactly 'on net' with Smith's predecessor, Ted Dexter.

I never heard of anyone having a row with Ted, but it was true of
him, I think, that he often found himself more *en rapport* with older
people than with his contemporaries. The sad thing was not so much
that he would not be available to lead as that he would not be
available to play. First England lost Peter May to the City at 32,
and now Dexter at 30, in his case to 'the media': magnificent players
both of them.

Personality, as well as great talent, departed with Dexter, but the
new captain impressed himself firmly enough though in a quieter
way. On the field Smith was inclined to undue caution, according
to the fashion of the day, and it was in the light of this, and in view
of Australia's particular request for a positive approach on the part
of their side, that MCC accompanied the announcement of Billy
Griffith, their secretary, as tour manager with a statement according
him over-all control of the cricket.

This was an experiment that has not been repeated – which is not
to say it was necessarily inexpedient at the time, considering the
characters involved. Even though his control was visualized as
strategic rather than his having any tactical say on the field, it needed
someone of Griffith's tact as well as prestige to fill the bill. The
presence as assistant-manager of Jack Ikin, the young Lancashire

tourist of 1946/7, completed as amiable a trio as can ever have directed a touring side.

Retrospectively Billy does not think today that the addition to his rôle made much, if any, practical difference though he recalls 'getting on at them' repeatedly about the overrate. He remembers with a laugh the captain in the first match at Perth asking him when he thought he should declare. 'Now,' said the manager. After a thrilling game MCC won on the stroke of time by 9 runs, whereupon M.J.K. observed, with one of his dead-pan looks, 'that's the last time I take the ruddy manager's advice on a declaration.' I suspect that sub-consciously Griffith's extra powers did have a certain effect. At all events the cricket generally was as enterprising as Smith and his team could make it, considering the weakness in bowling. In fact this 1965/6 series was the only one of the eight I saw in Australia wherein England's scoring rate was not slower than their opponents'. It was faster in fact by two runs per hundred balls, 45 to 43! But this 45 is also the highest English figure on the eight tours. Un-fortunately the balls-per-wicket ratio, taking the two sides together, was similarly the highest of the eight: wickets fell on average at about one per hour: hence, as in 1962/3, three Tests out of five were drawn.

England always had enough runs in the bank – this is the only MCC tour to Australia wherein seven men had an average of over 40. True, the captain's was only 17. Yet in contrast to events nine years later no one agitated for his removal. The trouble was that David Brown and Jeff Jones of Glamorgan, well though they bowled at times, could not quite fill the shoes of Statham and Trueman. Smith had to lean heavily on Titmus and Allen, who were both terribly expensive.

Australia on balance were no better off. Graham McKenzie – with 100 Test wickets to his name before the series started and at the tender age of 24 – was a fine bowler with a model action, and he and Neil Hawke made a good opening pair, as they had done in England. But they scarcely got any support worthy of the name. There were three Australians, Simpson, Lawry and Bob Cowper, with batting averages in the eighties, while that of Doug Walters, the find of the series, was 68.

This was the first tour in which I found myself in the company of Geoff Boycott – he had gone to South Africa, also under Mike Smith, the previous winter but I had been following the Australians in the West Indies. Boycott could not play at Perth because of sciatica, and though he got on to the field at Adelaide and made 94 the pain returned, and he had to be left behind for a day or two when the team left for the next stop up-country. It happened that I, too, lingered awhile, and, visiting the patient, came to know a zeal for playing and making runs that was more intense than I have ever encountered. The pain at missing this first chance of an innings at Melbourne of all places was clearly far harder to bear than that of the sciatica, hateful though that can be. Though we have differed since at times regarding his attitudes and decisions I always recall to his credit Geoff's burning ardour for the game in an age wherein even cricket is tainted with 'work to rule'.

Another recollection of that particular Adelaide visit is one of many instances of the violence and contrast of Australian weather. When we arrived – this was in mid-November before South Australia normally gets really hot – the city sweltered breathlessly in the nineties and it was during this period that Gary Player, shooting two fantastical 62s over Royal Adelaide, won the Open Championship. Suddenly play in the Sheffield Shield game before ours was suspended by a dust-storm, after which the wind began to blow so fiercely and so cold that walking abroad was like stepping into the slip-stream of an aeroplane. Instead of air-conditioning we suddenly needed log-fires. That's one side of Australian weather in a nutshell.

A brief but significant sidelight on our way round to Melbourne was some effective leg-spinning by Ken Barrington against Victoria. Eleven overs he bowled in the two innings for a return of four for 33. Here surely might be a useful reinforcement to this slender attack! Not on your life. Twice more he got on, on the entire tour, once in Tasmania, once when the New Year Test was a sure draw and he took a couple of wickets. Barrington used to give it a good tweak, and moreover he loved bowling. But the truth is, silly though it is and however foolish they may sometimes look against it, the modern English cricketer has little use or respect for wrist-spin.

There was another leg-break bowler with MCC, Bob Barber, a youthful prodigy who, however, was nervous of his ability in this direction, and never quite shaped up – though he assuredly did with the bat and also in the field. When we got to Sydney for the New South Wales match Barber really showed how the ball could be hit on Australian pitches by an athletically-built young cricketer with a good eye and aggressive intent. On the first morning of the game he played every stroke in the book until ten minutes before lunch when, needing only 10 for his hundred, he underestimated Brian

Booth's mobility at mid-off and was thrown out at the bowler's end. He and Eric Russell, taking his chance in Boycott's continued absence, made 151 together, and I said I simply could not remember seeing a more attractive opening partnership for an MCC side abroad. Poor Russell was destined to get only one Test in the series, and then had to go in last because of an injury to his hand. But for Barber this innings was the prelude to something even bigger and finer.

MCC gave a foretaste of things to come by making more than 500 against New South Wales, but Doug Walters, a 19-year-old from the country town of Dungog, gave a foretaste too with the first of what turned out to be three hundreds in successive matches. Altogether the game was away out of the ordinary. Jeff Jones was banned from bowling for running too straight down the pitch in defiance of law 46 – the only instance I've seen or know of – thus depleting bowling resources already reduced by an injury to Brown which caused MCC to send in a hurry for Barry Knight. Despite these setbacks Smith, who had caused NSW to follow-on, caught *five* catches, including three brilliant ones near the bat, and so brought about the first defeat of the State at the hands of MCC since 1932/3. (Until very recently – Denness actually won both state games at Sydney – beating New South Wales was just about akin to a touring side beating Yorkshire.)

Though they had been narrowly beaten by Victoria the record of Smith's team on the eve of the Test at Brisbane was better than that of any of the other post-war seven, and their esteem had risen to the extent that in my preview of this First Test I said I thought the odds about the rubber had shifted since the tour started from 7 to 2 to evens.

With the retirement of Davidson it appeared that for the first time in history Australia lacked a great bowler. They were unlucky also in that Simpson, the captain-designate, was hurt, and had to give place to Booth both at Brisbane and later at Sydney. Norman O'Neill was unfit – this most gifted of cricketers was never to play again for Australia. So one way and another, from retirements and sickness, Australia at first had only four survivors from the side of four years ago – Booth, Lawry, Burge and Grout. As it happened, rain which caused the loss of nine playing hours in the first twelve took most of the point from the match which thereafter became an exercise in observation and rehearsal. Australia had substantially the better of it, Walters adding his name to the fairly select list of those who have made a hundred in their first Test: there are ten Australians altogether but only one other, Jimmy Burke, that amusing fellow and blatant, awful chucker, has done it since the war.

After Walters' innings I wrote that with one necessary qualification I thought he would come to be rated as the best bat produced by Australia since Neil Harvey proclaimed himself with his famous hundred at Headingley in 48. The reservation concerned his ability against really fast bowling, as to which I had no evidence. Looking back, it is as well I made the qualification, for Snow and others have sometimes been his master. Yet *has* Australia shown us a better since Harvey, other than Greg Chappell, whose appearance came five years later? Only Lawry and Simpson have made more runs and had records to compare if one is to make a quantitative judgement. At all events my contention is at least arguable. Doug has made eleven hundreds for Australia, some of extreme brilliance, and if he ever played a dull innings I never saw it.

England's scourge of the sixties, Bill Lawry, opened the series with 166, stretched over three days and seven hours of play – a galling experience for England since they all thought that Parks had made a very good leg-side catch off Brown from the seventh ball of the match. That was not a happy start, but Lou Rowan and Col Egar soon won the confidence of both sides, and I would say this was the best-umpired Australian series I saw.

From Brisbane we followed a circuitous route south-west to Adelaide, calling for one-day games at Canberra, Bathurst, Albury and Mount Gambier: 2300 miles in all, mostly by charter flight and staying in the up-to-date motels, quite new ten years ago, which have transformed the Australian out-back. But before the out-back there was the visit to the Federal capital which in the days of Robert Menzies's Prime Ministership was always one of the high points of the tour. We dined marvellously well and listened to the best after-dinner speaker in the business, relaxed, reminiscent, leg-pulling, humorous. The modern professional cricketer very soon has enough and to spare of speeches, but here was the lone exception: they couldn't hear enough of him. It was on the tour previous, when Don Bradman played, that our host, discovering that the game coincided with Fred Trueman's birthday, presented him at the dinner with a silver tankard and some words of high praise to go with it: whereupon the Duke of Norfolk turned on R.G.M. that inscrutable look and said, 'I suppose you know you've just destroyed the disciplinary labours of several months?' There was a sequel to another

Bowlers who changed a series

34. *(right)* Tyson, the destroyer, at fullest stretch of arm, chest, and shoulders. In six weeks, with no mean help from May, Cowdrey and Statham, he won the rubber of 1954/5. **35.** *(below)* Davidson, brilliant opening bowler and all-round successor to Keith Miller, 1953-63. A perfect model.

36. *(below)* Benaud after delivery. Is he the last of the great Australian wrist-spinners? **37.** Rorke: a menace to England in 1958/9. Among others, it was his cultivation of the drag that led to a change in the no-ball law. The back leg will be well over the popping crease before the ball leaves the hand.

38. *(above)* Snow, the best English fast bowler of his decade, whose 31 wickets decided the 1970/1 series. 39. Lillee, with every limb co-ordinated and cocked for violent delivery: a perfect study in rhythm and power. 40. *(below)* Thomson, the Australian find of 1974/5, bowling to Amiss. The rocking motion of his shoulders supported by a strong back generates his great speed. Note Amiss's exemplary position.

earlier game when Ian Peebles and I stood umpire, thus qualifying apparently for the very fine green tie with boomerangs enclosing the legend 'P.M.'s XI' given to those who participated.

A week or two later at the Windsor Hotel, Melbourne, my wife and I were in bed waiting for our breakfast when there came a knock on the door. 'Come in,' I cried, thinking it was the waiter. No response, so I shouted rather loudly. At this the Prime Minister of Australia poked his head round the door, bearing my tie, and much enjoyed my confusion.

One does not look for beauty of the English sort in Australian grounds which are all dual-purpose affairs built for utility, but Manuka Oval, at Canberra, with its tents and gaily-coloured crowd enclosed in a rich frame of silver poplars whispering in the breeze, was well out of the ordinary run, putting one slightly in mind of Arundel – than which one can give no higher praise. The P.M.'s side was a nice blend of the illustrious and the obscure, and in the latter category when Smith's team played at Canberra was a teenager, Paul Sheahan, whose 79 moved me to predict he would soon be playing for Victoria. Now there was a man who, if he had cared – 'concentrated', Sir Donald might say – just a little more could well have been acclaimed the best since Harvey: who fielded furthermore almost as magnificently in the covers as Colin Bland.

The wide pastoral area called the Riverina is as green and pleasant a land as it sounds, 'with milk and honey blest' in the words of the hymn. Thence MCC flew down to the coast at Mount Gambier where they found another thoroughly reputable side containing several in their teens and drawn from the whole of South Australia. Some had flown five hundred miles in order to play. English cricketers often find the parties organized for them by the countrymen more to their taste than the sophisticated hospitality of the cities, and I described this at the time as 'the most enjoyable week of the tour'. The pleasure for Ann and me was enhanced by seeing something of life on a sheep and cattle station, at Nangwarry, presided over by that I. M. McLachlan, who had been twelfth man for Australia during the previous tour. He was reputedly bringing up the hard way his younger jackarooing brother Angus – shacked up, we heard, in a caravan so far into the bush that a loaf of bread had to last him a week – a far cry, he must have thought, from the mellow red-brick courts of Jesus College, Cambridge.

The approach to the Second Test, played as usual at Melbourne over the New Year holiday, illustrated fairly enough the hazards that beset touring sides the world over. Their troubles seldom came singly. Of MCC's cluster of fastish bowlers Brown was laid low with bursitis, or a sort of housemaid's knee of the elbow, David Larter, that tall, pleasant if somewhat remote young man who enjoys the unique distinction of having toured Australia twice with MCC without being chosen for a Test Match, could only bowl half-pace because of a strained side, while Ken Higgs, faithful trier if ever there was one but who looked a little plain on Australian pitches, had picked up a chill, always described on this and subsequent tours more grandiosely as a 'virus'. So the England fast attack consisted perforce of Jones and Knight, the latter until a few weeks previously having been vegetating quietly down in Essex. Thank goodness Boycott was fit again, it was seriously said, as his bowling might well be useful!

It was not surprising that Australia's first innings added up to a solid 358. However, England's reply began with an 'electrifying' 88 in an hour by Boycott and Barber – what a pity that circumstances prevented this glamorous partnership from regularly plaguing England's opponents once this tour was over! From this beginning all those following took profit, so that England, for the first time in Australia since the Bodyline tour thirty-odd years before, topped 500. Edrich and Cowdrey made hundreds and in the 558 there were eight scores of more than 40. I had been chiding Cowdrey in print for forgetting in the placid contemplation of his artistry that the ball needs to be hit. But this innings, lasting only three and a quarter hours, recalled his salad days.

Australia on paper had no difficulty in saving the game, but figures often enough disguise the truth. Two hours were lost to the weather on the fourth evening while next day Australia had four out for 204 – only 4 runs between the scores and four and a half hours remaining – when with Australia's last front-line pair together Parks missed a clear stumping chance offered by Burge off Barber. Had it been taken the Australian tail were doomed to a long struggle. As it was Burge, nearly always a staunch man for his side in a crisis, and young Walters once more made hundreds, and that was that.

Sydney in those days took spin and the toss accordingly mattered there more than anywhere. Smith won it whereupon Barber strode out to play the innings of his life, with substantial help from Boycott. When the latter left, just before tea for 84, the score stood at 234 for one – third, in terms of England opening stands against Australia, only to Hobbs's and Rhodes's 323 at Melbourne in 1911/12, and the 283 of Hobbs and Sutcliffe also at Melbourne the time they batted all day.

Often in bleak moments do I cast back to Bob Barber's 185 in front of 40,000 on that sunny Friday in January 66. He batted without chance for five hours, starting decorously enough and then hitting the ball progressively harder and with a superb disdain to every corner of the field. One recalls the exceptional vigour of his driving and how he brought his wrists into the cut, making room for the stroke. It made blissful watching to English eyes – to one pair in particular, for by a wonderful chance father Barber had flown in from home that very evening.

England this time, thanks finally to another hundred by the dogged, faithful, unexciting Edrich, reached 488, whereupon Smith, after his side had dismissed Australia for 221, caused them to follow-on and duly won the game by an innings with a day to spare. It was a great triumph, for which speed and spin were almost equally responsible. Brown and Jones made the first inroads, after which Titmus and Allen preyed on the Australian dislike of off-spin when the pitch takes some degree of turn. The pitch did not exactly 'go', but it gave increasing encouragement to bowlers who were on top, and whose ascendancy was only likely to be shifted by the sort of onslaught by the middle and tail that one always used to fear from Australian sides, yet now decreasingly so. Bob Cowper, one of Australia's youthful replacements, as at Melbourne batted auspiciously – though, as events proved, we had yet to see the best of him.

Considering Australian critics had hailed Smith's side as the weakest ever to come under the colours of MCC the manner of this win was gratifying, to say the least. Now they were saying they were the most attractive to tour from England since the war. Even our phlegmatic captain seemed to be betraying a gleam of pleasure behind his steel-rimmed specs. He had good reason, with three-quarters of the job done, five first-class matches won, one lost, and four drawn (three favourably). In the manner of their playing MCC had given points to their opponents on almost every occasion. They had made no promises on arrival about 'brighter cricket' – that tiresome phrase – but they had aimed to play better cricket, and by and large events had shown that taking the initiative brought the best results. Everyone knew who was behind this philosophy; it was Doug Insole, the chairman of selectors, and, of course, Billy Griffith, the tour manager.

I tried to capture the background to the tour after the Test victory in a cable home:

> When the last Australian wicket fell last Tuesday afternoon and Smith tried to thrust forward his most successful bowler, David Allen, the latter declined the honour and the team not only insisted on their captain leading them in but applauded him through the gate. It was a pleasant and highly unusual incident: equally so, incidentally, was the gesture of Australia's captain, Brian Booth, who was standing waiting to shake the hand of each member of the England team in congratulation as they reached the dressing-room door.
>
> Four days earlier, just as Barber and Edrich were going out after tea with the score standing at 234 for one, I happened to be passing the nets. There was Smith bowling alone to his No. 11 batsman, Jones. It will be recalled Jones made 16 next day (thus multiplying his previous tour aggregate by eight!) and helped in a stand of 55 for the last wicket.
>
> Smith, though outwardly unconventional and in manner casual to a degree, succeeds as a captain for the conventional reasons. He is thoughtful for his players, unselfish, does not 'fuss' them or panic, shows a grasp of the situation which they deem in general sensible and not least gives an inspiring personal lead in the field.

I went on to note the manager's equal share in promoting the harmony of the side, and to applaud the efforts both of Jack Ikin, and of Miss Daphne Surfleet, who as a rest from strenuous assistance to me, notably in editing the vast *World of Cricket*, was travelling with us as tour secretary. (She is still frequently to be seen at Test Matches under the name of Mrs Richie Benaud.) I ended – luckily! – by saying it would be uncharacteristic if there were no reaction on the field to the English challenge, and that the Ashes weren't regained yet by a long chalk.

Australia's selectors reacted to popular feeling by dropping four of the beaten side, including Graham (or Garth) McKenzie, taker of a hundred Test wickets but only five, as it happened, in the series thus far. Simpson was back as captain, to the exclusion of Booth, McKenzie's place being taken by P. J. Allan of Queensland, who had deputized for him in the First Test. The MCC party greeted the exclusion of McKenzie for Adelaide with satisfaction. However their sentiments were short-lived. Allan dropped out through injury,

McKenzie was drafted back, and a few moments after the start of the second day was being applauded into the pavilion for the best performance of his career:

O	M	R	W
21.7	4	48	6

There had been quite a bit of freshness in the pitch, McKenzie had used it to perfection, and Australia had held every catch, including two beauties by men newly capped and destined to become famous, Ian Chappell and Keith Stackpole.

There had been censure of Australia's slow batting in the series, and the selectors had shown what they thought on the matter by dropping Cowper from their twelve despite scores of 99 and 60 in the preceding two Tests. Simpson now announced that his target was a run a minute, an ordinary rate maybe in days gone by but breakneck almost in the sixties, what with slow overrates and so much accent on defence. Yet Australia, give or take a few minutes, achieved it, the captain leading the way with the highest opening stand ever, in partnership with Lawry, for Australia against England: 244. I never remember seeing better running between wickets than that of these two – and found myself comparing them, in fact, with Hobbs and Sutcliffe. With the field constantly changing over as right- and left-hander alternated, England, in much heat, sweated and chased unavailingly. Playing the same side as at Sydney meant that the third bowler other than the slows was Boycott. It was depressing to see him given the tenth over of the innings. Having headed the England score without the loss of a wicket Australia rubbed in their advantage as it seemed inevitably. After they had fielded out to a score of 516 England's early batsmen failed for a second time, and though Barrington played with the utmost resolution for five hours and a half the end came with a day and a bit to spare. Australia had looked the better at every point. After giving them due credit Smith with unaccustomed vigour described the English effort as 'appalling'.

The verdict was an innings and 9 runs as against the innings and 93 in England's favour at Sydney. Thereby hangs a record, for neither country otherwise has been beaten by an innings in one Test and won by an innings in the next. It seemed to me that, taking the four Tests together, the respective strengths and weaknesses more or less cancelled out. The batting of both sides was stronger than the bowling, as the Fifth Test now confirmed.

What was wanted, as a climax to so much attractive cricket was, naturally, a well-contested finale, but, as at Sydney in 63, this was not forthcoming. Then it was largely the fault of the conditions. Now it was perhaps so in the sense that the pitch was too good and the bowling too ordinary. But there was also the fact that, when the crunch came, the instinct for self-preservation showed uppermost after all. The game began before one of Melbourne's largest crowds (68,476), but after three days Australia had replied to England's 485 for nine with 333 for three, and there could scarcely be any other result than a draw. Rain throughout the fourth day settled the issue beyond the slightest argument, and it was in an inevitably sterile atmosphere on the fifth day that Cowper took his score from 159 overnight to 307, the fourth highest innings in the history of England v Australia. But perhaps the match is worth a closer dissection in its early stages. England clearly needed a brisk start such as Boycott and Barber had given them earlier in the series, but this was far from happening. According to *Wisden*, 'Boycott, though out of touch, took 60 of the first 80 balls bowled, then ridiculously ran out Barber and himself fell twenty minutes later.' Boycott in fact at his worst. Barrington met the needs of the situation by making the fastest and best of his five hundreds against Australia (in two and a half hours), after which many more runs came but against defensive fields and a slow overrate not quite quickly enough.

When Australia batted Lawry, their stumbling-block-extraordinary, took root, and in an interminable left-handed stand with Cowper effectively doused English prospects. When this relentless fellow, having reached his sixth Test hundred against England, at length took a liberty he had made 592 runs in the Tests, average 84, the highest aggregate since Bradman's in 1946/7: not only that, he had scored 979 against Smith's side since they landed at Perth, and had occupied the crease for forty-one and a half hours. There was a gayer side to Lawry as we had seen at Adelaide – but he didn't let it obtrude too often. He just kept that long, sharp nose religiously over the ball, accumulating at his own deliberate gait, and in particular tucking everything away off his pads whenever the English bowlers bowled there, as they all too often did. While Lawry and Cowper were making 212 together they got two runs out of every three on the leg-side – an implicit condemnation of the out-cricket considering that most of the fielders were always on the off. Cowper, need one say, showed the utmost self-discipline and a safe method – and what more can one say? He batted for twelve hours, 7 minutes – the third longest occupation in the history of England v Australia, exceeded only by Len Hutton's 13 hours and 17 minutes for 364 at the Oval in 1938 and Bobby Simpson's 12 hours 42 minutes for 311 at Old Trafford in 1964.

It was sad that the esteem of Smith's side suffered towards the tour's end – disappointing that only two of the five Tests were finished. Yet all the draws were rain-affected, with four days in all lost, and it could even be argued that without the interruptions all *might* have been brought to conclusion. This was one of the wetter Australian summers. Though the profit was well down on the previous tour this halved series was fought with what, looking back, seems a rare good humour.

9

The Ashes, But . . .

We come now to the seventh post-war MCC tour of Australia led by Ray Illingworth, with David Clark of Kent as his manager. Immediately behind us were two halved series in Australia with only two games finished in each, and since Mike Smith's tour yet another shared series in England, again with three draws out of five. Since Bobby Simpson had won in England in 64 by the only Test finished the record of the four rubbers preceding 1970/71 showed three English victories, four Australian – and thirteen draws. Australia, of course, retained the Ashes which Benaud had captured way back in 58/9 and retained in 61. One way and another little had gone right for English cricket in the sixties until Colin Cowdrey won a rubber in the West Indies in 67/8 and Illingworth, in Cowdrey's absence injured, beat the West Indies at home in 69.

Results on the whole were only moderate, but far sadder, of course, was the necessity for the rupture of cricket relations as between England and South Africa with all the bitterness that this provoked. There is no need to tread those prickly, contentious paths again except to mention that it was the Cricket Council's last-minute cancellation, at the Government's urgent plea, of the invitation to South Africa to tour England in 1970 that resulted in the hurriedly-organized series of unofficial Tests against the Rest of the World, on the evidence of which the side for Australia in 1970/71 would be picked.

Notice that I speak of 'unofficial' Test Matches, and since most Australians do not accept that these magnificent games should be included in the record books I should, in parenthesis, re-state the situation which resulted in the Editor of *Wisden* including them, and continuing to do so despite a resolution to the contrary passed by the International Cricket Conference. When the Cricket Council's hand was forced by James Callaghan, the Home Secretary, on 22 May 1970, the ruling body faced not the disruption of games and damage to grounds which would have occurred had the South Africans come over but, instead, an empty void: no Test series, by the profits from which the counties survived, no cricket to counter the soccer World Cup which would thus monopolize English sporting interest all summer, to cricket's lasting disadvantage.

In this critical situation, with the season already in progress, sponsors were rapidly sought and happily discovered in the great brewing firm of Guinness, who *on the understanding that these should be accorded the dignity of unofficial Tests* underwrote a five-match series to the tune of £20,000. There was a ready-made captain at hand in Gary Sobers, who with Freddie Brown as manager and Leslie Ames chose the teams from the many famous overseas players playing county cricket plus several more leading South Africans to augment Barry Richards and Mike Procter, of Hampshire and Gloucestershire respectively. The cricket the two teams provided was some of the finest ever seen in England. It had all the fervour of a Test occasion, and more skill than most such. Into the bargain, the World side of assorted nationality (five in all) showed a fraternal spirit which was a practical illustration of how sportsmen can transcend artificial barriers of race. To those of us who had dreaded our Test arenas being reduced to pitched battlefields the outcome was beyond our best hopes, and of course, with the stern Australian tour in view, it added to the gain that England under Illingworth, though almost inevitably beaten, had been able to flex their muscles.

Considering how much money all their opponents have taken back from England over the years, how inter-dependent, both financially and in other ways, all countries must be, it never occurred to me – nor, I think, to many others close to the game – that Australia and the rest would fail to accept a *fait accompli* in circumstances which were unique and unforeseeable. Yet they have, and so for the first time in history *Wisden* and younger and lesser compilations are out of step, and some newspapers use one set of figures and some another.

It isn't necessary to know much cricket history to appreciate that Test status has been accorded, often posthumously, without any demur to series where the reputations of the players and the quality of play have been more than dubious. Why, in 1929/30 two teams labelled England were playing simultaneously, one in the West Indies, the other in New Zealand. Twenty-five cricketers represented England that winter, yet when Australia came to England a few months later only five of these twenty-five were among the twenty-one thought good enough to play in that great 1930 series. In other words, nearly fifty men played inside a twelvemonth for sides labelled England.

There is no absolute Test standard. It has never been suggested, so far as I know, that Test rank should be taken away from these contests on the ground that England's best were not engaged – as they have often not been, for that matter, at other times in the West Indies, New Zealand and also India.

If anyone wants a precedent for 'Unofficial Tests' counting in the records the answer is that all Tests played by South Africa since 1960 are unofficial, since the ICC rule proclaimed that official Tests could be played only between member-countries of the Commonwealth, from which South Africa seceded in that year. The point would only be an academic one were it not for the obvious desirability of individual records being universally accepted. I wonder if there's any chance of some of those comparatively young, intelligent, forward-looking people who now run the game in Australia and the West Indies (the two countries who dug their toes in on this issue) reading these words and saying to themselves: 'Well, how could we have been so small-minded and dog-in-the-manger about this? Let's swallow our pride and vote to put the record straight at the next ICC.' That would be splendid, and if the ICC remains silent I hope that Norman Preston, the Editor of *Wisden,* sticks to his guns – which technically he is quite justified in doing since by their own rule the ICC can only pronounce as to what are official Test Matches. After which preamble let us return to the choice of the MCC team, which as I say was largely determined by the showing of individuals in the Rest of the World Test series.

The most significant decision to be made, naturally, concerned the captaincy. Illingworth or Cowdrey? Both had strong credentials which are worth recalling. Colin's position as England's reigning captain was unchallenged when in May 1969, playing a John Player League game in front of the TV cameras, he snapped an Achilles tendon when batting. The noise was such he supposed he must have hit the stumps with his bat! This put him out of cricket for the summer, the selectors choosing Ray as England captain in his absence. Now in 1970 Cowdrey was back and in full flow for England as well as Kent, whom in fact he proceeded to lead to the County Championship. He had four Australian tours behind him, three as vice-captain, and was a proved success as a leader overseas.

Illingworth's elevation rather than that of Tom Graveney, who had been vice-captain to Cowdrey, came as a surprise since he had been only an intermittent Test cricketer since being first capped eleven years earlier. But on leaving Yorkshire to lead Leicestershire he had won much respect as a captain while his batting under the added responsibility flowered amazingly. In the Tests of 1969 and 1970 he looked – as the averages proclaimed him to be – the next most dependable bat after Boycott. Add his off-spinning, hitherto his chief qualification, and his credentials for a place in English conditions were unassailable. On the reverse of the coin was his non-success on the overseas pitches of the West Indies in 59/60 and of Australia in 62/3: 23 wickets only on two tours at 60 runs each, in the Tests five in all for 514! It looked as though he needed English conditions to get wickets at reasonable cost.

The selectors for this tour, unlike those in the past, were the home Test selectors – Alec Bedser, Don Kenyon, Alan Smith and Billy Sutcliffe (son of Herbert) – and not, as hitherto, this committee plus some other experienced men named by MCC. They plumped for Illingworth, at the same time nominating Cowdrey – yet again! – as vice-captain. On an assessment of all the qualities necessary I hoped that the decision would have gone the other way, but it was, of course, completely logical and reasonable to give 'Illy' the job, for in England he had done his backers proud.

The two contenders were far from a natural blend of hearts and minds, and those of us who hoped that they might form with David Clark a harmonious partnership united by the common aim of winning back the Ashes were proved over-optimistic. The object was achieved, but it could not be said that the victory owed much to liaison between any two of the three at the top.

This time, as the *Daily Telegraph* and the *Sunday Telegraph* were to be represented by both Michael Melford and myself, I did not fly out until immediately before the First Test, by which time, under the revised itinerary curtailed at its start in order to accommodate a sixth Test at Perth, MCC had had only four first-class games and had shown indifferent form, to say the least. South Australia had made 649 for nine in answer to MCC's 451 for nine, Victoria had beaten them by six wickets, New South Wales had had them following on, while Queensland had made 360 before MCC led on first innings in a very dull match. Several, and notably Boycott, had made plenty of runs, but the out-cricket was such that only in Brisbane had MCC even bowled a side out.

On the face of it the outlook was not rosy – until one recalled how only a year previously Australia had been 'whitewashed' four-nil in South Africa. Eight of that team including Bill Lawry, the captain, were on parade for this First Test at Brisbane. In my preview I rated Australia in their own conditions as favourites to keep the Ashes. A comical misunderstanding lightened the last hours before the battle. In the Queensland match on the last day Geoff Boycott had 'retired hurt' (for 124, his third hundred in four games) in order to give others practice. There was nothing the matter with him, but an English cricket-writer suggested facetiously, for want of anything better to say, that Geoff, whose fondness for batting has always been a by-word, might have sustained a bruise or two in the dressing-room when forcibly prevented from continuing his innings. The remark had joke written all over it, but the captain and manager had quite a time of it denying published reports of 'a scuffle'. What bright spark in London or Sydney, I wonder, cooked that up? The trouble is that on these tours newspapers are greedy for 'news angles', and sometimes go to laughable lengths in their search for a story.

Once the series got under way 'the populars' soon got something a bit more solid to bite on, for Keith Stackpole, who went on to get 207, had made only 18 when the cameras seemed to show him narrowly run out. Lou Rowan gave him in, not unreasonably since there was only a matter of inches and fractions of a second in it, and the batsman is entitled to the benefit of the doubt. So before lunch on the first day we had the old hobby-horse trotted out of the alleged incompetence of Australian umpires. There were ructions ahead, of course, but my view was that Rowan, Tom Brooks and M. G. O'Connell, who shared the umpiring in the series, did a good job all through.

By close of play (Australia 308 for two) I seemed to have seen confirmed all the gloomy forebodings of the English party in the press-box who had been with the team from the start. 28 November 1970 was, however, a highly extraordinary day. With over 400 on the board and only three men out the old pattern of English grief at Brisbane looked all too like being repeated when suddenly the captain took a very fine catch at silly mid-off off Underwood, and within a few minutes Underwood had got two more out including Doug Walters for 112. Snow, who had generally looked the best of the bowlers, now weighed in with a vengeance, and Australia were out for 433. The last seven had fallen for 15. When if ever . . . ? we thought, and the answer proved not to concern Laker at Old Trafford but rather Bedser at Trent Bridge in 1953. The last seven wickets then fell for 12. But there the pitch was difficult, now it was perfect, as England proceeded to show.

By the fourth afternoon they had established a lead of 31, nearly everyone contributing, and thereafter Australia were very much on the back foot, while England for their part seemed at times disinclined to attack all-out, presumably for fear of what Gleeson might do if they had a substantial while to bat in the fourth innings. The cricket was all a bit cagey, with the respective captains reacting according to type. Nevertheless, by bowling out Australia – despite Lawry's patient 84 – for 214 there was no doubt that the moral honours belong to England.

The playing of the Second Test at Perth made a milestone in the history of England v Australia for no fresh venue had been chosen in either country since Brisbane achieved Test status in 1928. The decision came after lengthy agitation by the West Australians, and in the event they have been handsomely justified, for the ground by the Swan River, the accommodation and the general arrangements have all been tip-top. Visitors in successive MCC parties would probably have voted almost to a man for Perth, though not for a six-Test series. They would have preferred a Perth Test either alternating with or succeeding Brisbane, with which city is the great East-West rivalry. When the Perth attendance figures are called over the public-address, showing an advance on the corresponding numbers at Brisbane, the loyal West Australians applaud vigorously!

In many respects the Second Test was not unlike the First. The bat on good pitches, easy-paced, was generally the master of the ball. 'You know,' said Lindsay Hassett, in talk not on the air, 'you can scarcely get a decent Test attack from the two sides.' Yet runs seldom came sufficiently fast to encourage hopes of a result. The clock mostly looked like winning from the point where England, after being sent in by Lawry (to the horror of old Australian cricketers), emerged from the first day with 257 on the board and only the openers out.

Boycott and Luckhurst had established by this time on the tour a convincing partnership wherein here at Perth Yorkshire was distinctly (and unusually) overshadowed by Kent. Lawry's first wicket did not come until after tea, by which time events had condemned his gambit. Luckhurst found little to trouble him in making his first hundred against McKenzie, Thomson, Greg Chappell, Gleeson, Walters and Stackpole. When the younger Chappell was brought into the team for Jenner, the leg-breaker, the selectors were restricting Lawry to three regulars and three change bowlers – a dubious distribution that made his sending-in the more surprising.

But Greg Chappell deserved his promotion all right, as he proceeded to show by starting his Test career with a hundred. He made it when the good citizens of Perth must have been wondering whether, now they'd got their Test Match at last, the whole business was not seriously over-rated. England had needed ten hours to make 397, whereat Snow had both Lawry and Stackpole back in no time, and Redpath and Ian Chappell set about effecting a recovery from 17 for three. Redpath, who obliged with 171, made in just over eight hours, is the most conscientious of cricketers but he is also one of the least spectacular. England naturally made it as hot as they could for the new boy, who, coming in at 107 for five, after forty minutes had only compiled a single. However, gradually Greg blossomed, and in a glorious hour after tea went from 42 to 100. Thus this tall, slim youngster with the upright, classical method made a beginning from which, up to the moment of writing, he has never looked back. England, thinking they needed a third fastish bowler, had supplanted Underwood in favour of Lever, and since a strong, coolish wind blew down the pitch off the Swan River all through the match and Lever was employed for long stretches bowling manfully into it one could see the point. However, after the Redpath-Chappell stand had become established – this despite some fine bowling by Snow – the English attack looked plainly unbalanced and never seemed likely to break through. It was already increasingly clear – to me, at any rate – that a blunder had been made in leaving Greig at home. It was the old problem, with all-rounders scarce, of being obliged to weaken either the batting or the bowling, and it is the bowling which usually suffers.

In these days our Test cricketers still had a wholesome fear of the wrist-spin of Gleeson, who when England went in again 43 runs behind with ten hours stretching ahead might still have had the winning of the game in his hands. Half an hour after tea Gleeson had the wickets of both Boycott and Fletcher in the same over, and with Cowdrey out at the other end in the next Australia's opportunity at this point was clear enough. But now Edrich took root, and with substantial help from d'Oliveira, Illingworth and Knott led England steadily out of harm's way.

This effort of John Edrich led me to couple him with Herbert Sutcliffe and Maurice Leyland, men whose temperament made them better Test than county cricketers. His fifth hundred against Australia was an affair of more than five hours, but, at that, slightly faster than Redpath's retrieving effort for Australia, and only a shade slower than Luckhurst's hundred on the first day. Since 81,494 came to watch, the first-ever Test at Perth was rated a success – despite the heavy loan that the WACA had had to negotiate in order to build the new accommodation that made the match possible.

Thus far personal tour relations had seemed reasonably harmonious, but before MCC left Perth to fly back east David Clark responded to a request of the Australian press for an impression of the series so far. Australian papers seem keener than most English ones on direct quotes from those in authority, and the manager both before this occasion and afterwards was keen to accommodate them in so far as he could. He told them frankly now that he thought both teams had been thinking too defensively, and that 'we need some positive and challenging tactics in the Tests.' Since 15 of the last 22 Anglo-Australian Tests had been drawn David's strictures were perfectly well received in Australia. When pressed whether he would prefer to see the next four Tests drawn or for Australia to win them 3-1 the reply came, after a pause for consideration, that 'I'd rather see four results.' He added that if all four were drawn there might soon be no Ashes to play for. These sentiments went down, as I say, in Australia but not at all favourably with the members of the side. The captain, for instance, could scarcely be expected to agree that he would rather see the rubber lost than drawn.

I well recall the startling reception Mr Clark's words had as they were read by the players in the evening papers on the day following the Test in the aircraft bearing our team and most of the Australians to Adelaide and beyond. For although there is no doubt that the manager from time to time attempted to put an enterprising philosophy across (as Billy Griffith, who had been given wider powers, had done five years earlier) the team had had no inkling that what they rated as an attack on them was going to appear. Granted that the manager was genuinely very surprised by the stir his remarks caused he must have been sorry, looking back, that he had not prepared his charges for what was coming. No doubt a different captain and manager might have had a frank talk and buried the matter over a couple of drinks. This, however, did not happen. As the chairman of the recent Clark Report (into the future of first-class cricket) the manager may have seemed too closely tied to the establishment to be wholly acceptable anyway. At any rate, from this point onwards the regard in which he was held by some of the team – and therefore his authority – declined, with unfortunate consequences.

The next significant occurrence made the situation no better; the complete obliteration of the Melbourne Test by the weather. From every point of view this was a disaster of the first order, bad enough for the members of The Cricket Society, The Forty Club, The *Cricketer* party, and all others which had flown from England on package tours in search of sun and cricket: worst of all for the Australian Board for whom the Melbourne Test at the turn of the year holds the key to the over-all profit.

After rain had prevented play on the first day the authorities of the two countries met to decide whether an extra day should be added at the end. As, however, the toss had taken place, and England had put Australia in, they agreed mutually that the game had technically begun. Therefore the playing time could not be extended. The point, as it happened, could not have been more academic, since there was now no let-up in the weather. It was worse than Sydney in 1955. On the third blank day, with the ground a water-meadow and rain still bucketing down, the Australian Board held a council of war, calling into consultation Sir Cyril Hawker, who as president of MCC was also chairman of the Cricket Council, Gubby Allen, the vice-chairman, and David Clark as manager. The Australians asked the Englishmen to consider, in the circumstances, playing another Test in lieu of the return game against Victoria at Melbourne in between the Fourth at Sydney and the Fifth at Adelaide. Though this would make the programme top-heavy with Tests – in fact four inside six weeks – Sir Cyril and Co. after due deliberation decided that for the general good of cricket they ought to accept.

The important question that needs answering at this point is whether there had been consultation before the Australian proposal was agreed, and as to this David Clark is quite specific. He informed the captain what was in the wind, saying that though it put an extra strain on the players, and was scarcely in the interests of England, who would gain very little financially, it was felt that in the exceptional circumstances and for the broad good of Anglo-Australian cricket they should agree. Ray Illingworth, while naturally not very enthusiastic, after thinking it over said he appreciated the position and would go along with the idea. The manager reported accordingly, and so the deal was done. In his statement to the press David said: 'We are taking a calculated risk in the interests of the image of the game as a whole and of cricket relations between England and Australia'.

It was at a team meeting, hurriedly called, and attended by everyone except Cowdrey, d'Oliveira and Knott, that angry opposition crystallized. Though the Third Test was washed out the series, technically at least, numbered seven matches. That, they said, was too much – and what about some extra cash? I would not identify the majority by any means with an extreme attitude, but several were vociferous in complaining, so that poor Cyril Hawker, whose visit was planned as a goodwill gesture in his year of office, blending business and pleasure, must have imagined he'd stepped into a nest of shop-stewards.

At last the Melbourne skies turned to blue and the first one-day Gillette-style international took place. Having been deprived of the Test Match 46,000 turned up to see Australia win the game quite comfortably – a deceptive indication, as it now seems, of the appeal of this sort of cricket to Australians. They may come to embrace it, but they haven't done so yet. And so via Wagga Wagga for a country game to Sydney and to the game that turned the rubber.

It was played on a pitch that was something near the ideal, with enough response to sustain the spirits of both fast and slow bowlers though of the former only Snow met with much success. England held an advantage from the moment when Boycott on the first morning found his best form: 100 for no wicket at lunch with Boycott 64 was encouraging to say the least, and though he was caught on the leg boundary off a long-hop for 77, and some very good off-spinning by Mallett brought the fall of four wickets for a handful around the tea interval, the tail perked up in the persons of the fast bowlers. These now included Bob Willis, the replacement for Ward who had broken down and been sent home before the First Test.

This was the match which showed Snow – as well as Boycott – at his peak, and though he and Lever had only three first innings wickets between them it was thanks to them that Australia stumbled at the start, after which they were always struggling against spin. Underwood, who had been selected neither for Perth nor Melbourne, was the key figure, the Australians, after Mallett and Gleeson had been their own wicket-takers, confronting him with a mixture of timidity and desperation that restored his confidence with each passing over. He turned only a few, but most of his opponents – eight to be precise – had played at the Oval in 1968, and they cannot have forgotten.

Up to a point Australia, thanks to unaccepted slip chances given by Redpath, Walters and Stackpole, made a strong counter, with 189 for four on the board on the second evening in answer to England's 332. However, the third day was a triumph for England, who polished off the Australian innings for 236 and then answered with 178 for three. Boycott was again in great shape, adding 130 undefeated with d'Oliveira, who in the morning had shown his utility by picking up a couple of wickets. Early in the second innings Boycott threw Edrich's wicket away grossly but redeemed himself in a monumental effort lasting all but seven hours, latterly in company with his captain, who played his biggest and best innings of the tour.

I noted a strange comment to the press by Bill Lawry before the fourth day started. England led by 274 and had seven wickets left – a mighty strong position but not exactly cast-iron – yet. Lawry, however, said there was 'no way' in which Australia could win, and I wondered what that did for home morale. However that might be, England could muster only 76 in the morning two-hour session, during which Boycott made his second hundred (in 15 Tests) against Australia.

By now Illingworth obviously decided that all was completely well, and in forty minutes England added 65 before bringing Australia in and inviting them to make 416 for victory. What a hope! Lawry again took in Ian Chappell, not a regular opener, rather than Stackpole, whom he apparently thought too flirtatious against the new ball. Certainly Snow had had Stackpole cheaply twice at Perth, but what about that 207 at Brisbane only two Tests ago? In fact Snow found a hateful lifter for Chappell's first ball of the innings, and thereafter bowled like a man inspired. I had not seen an Englishman bowl either faster or better than Snow at Sydney since Tyson. I wrote:

> In a fast bowler rhythm and accuracy generally go hand in hand. When everything is absolutely ticking, so to speak, a strong fellow like Snow finds not only an extra yard of pace but seems able to keep an unerring eye on the target. The merit of Snow in this form is not only that that high arm and loose wrist get the utmost life and lift from the pitch but that he is so extraordinarily straight.

To help him he had a dubious dusty spot or two which sowed in the batsmen's minds an uncertainty about the height to which the ball might rise. But what profit was that to the others of his type? Of the 14 English wickets that fell to bowlers in the match McKenzie and Connolly took two for 220: Snow had eight for 63, and by taking seven in the second innings joined a very select company of English fast bowlers – Tom Richardson, Tyson, Statham and Lockwood – who had bagged as many.

There are those who say it takes a bowler to understand a bowler. At all events Illingworth handled his side, and in particular his match-winning bowler, to perfection over these five days. To save the game Australia needed to bat for just over nine hours, which bad light on the penultimate evening reduced by almost an hour. They lasted in fact for just about half the time required, and this in spite of the most steadfast effort by Lawry himself, who in a total of 116 carried his bat for 60. No one could stay long save Stackpole, who did not arrive until No. 6.

When the response of the Australian selectors to loud cries of 'Sack the lot' – or almost the lot – was to retain all the batsmen who had failed and to drop only the opening bowlers one was reminded that their larder was, by Test reckoning, not all that well stocked. Nevertheless, they had the better of the next Test at Melbourne without very much looking like winning it. England's catching throughout had been uncertain, but when Australia won the toss they had actually dropped eight by the time Lawry declared an hour before the close on the second day. Cowdrey, holder of the record number of Test catches (124 at the moment of going to press), spilled three, some said four. Altogether he had a nightmare of a day, for when the young in the crowd saluted Ian Chappell's hundred by invading the field both Colin and the hero of the hour had their caps snatched – a crowning indignity. At Brisbane and Perth time had been lost because of these high-spirited demonstrations. Here many hundreds scaled the iron pickets, and the game was held up ten minutes. What was worse was the patter of innumerable tiny feet on the pitch itself.

Lawry retired hurt following several blows on the hand, whereupon the elder Chappell achieved his first Test hundred against England, and a mighty good one at that, after a horribly sticky start during which he was twice missed. Young Willis had an auspicious bowl while on the other side Rodney Marsh, whose batting had not hitherto looked as though it might be a matter of importance, reached 92. At this point Lawry declared, leaving England three-quarters of an hour's batting. Tactically no doubt this was a good decision, but psychologically I am not so sure. There is a *cachet* attaching to a man who reaches three figures in a Test which is something of an asset to his side ever after. Marsh has now played

in fifteen Tests against England, and never come so near again –
though I should add that three years after this Melbourne innings
he made 132 against New Zealand at Adelaide.

There were two English hundreds in this drawn high-scoring match,
one from Luckhurst, the other from d'Oliveira. The former was
rather quieter than usual, which could have been justified by the
certainty that England had nothing better than a draw to play for.
In fact, however, it became known after he was out that he was
courageously batting for most of his innings with his left hand in
plaster and three fingers of the glove bound together – this the result
of a blow from Australia's 1970/71 Thomson, nicknamed 'Froggie'.
He was an energetic fellow with a strange, whirlwind, running-through
sort of action. He was short of top pace, and was dropped after the
next Test having taken only 12 Test wickets at 54 a time. But he
could make the ball lift at times, and might without flattery have
had better figures.

This was the fourth of 'Dolly's' five hundreds for England, and it
is perhaps the moment to salute this splendid fighting cricketer whose
determination is somewhat belied by his bland, smiling face. In the
history of the game he will be associated inevitably with the sad
rumpus involving England, the country of his adoption, and South
Africa, the land of his birth, the controversy generally known as
'The d'Oliveira Affair'. But his cricket should never be forgotten,
for in my time England have had no better man in a crisis nor one
who in his demeanour on the field was a better advertisement for
the game. As a model for the young perhaps he could have been
improved only in one respect – which is a matter of technique. So
strong is he in the forearms that he has always been able to engineer
exceptional power without the need of a back-lift. Apart from his
batting he often got valuable Test wickets with that deceptively
guileless late out-swing: judging by the number of catches missed
off him it deceived the slip fielders as much as it did the batsmen.
And though he did not run very fast in the field his throw came to
the top of the stumps like a bullet.

There was too much short bowling in this match, chiefly on England's part, and Snow was warned for intimidation after he had
bowled four bouncers in an over to Walters, whose playing of the
short stuff, it must be admitted, as with one or two others of the
Australians, was a regular provocation to the fast bowlers. Snow had
also been warned in the Perth Test, and one got the impression that
he was prepared to go as far as he deemed politic as regards the

short stuff, and that Illingworth was happy for him to do so. The English attitude seemed to be that the matter was simply one for adjudication by the umpires. Some rated this a tenable view, though it went against the general spirit of former days, the Body-line tour excepted. Unfortunately there was a tough young Australian out there in the middle, Ian Chappell by name, whose cricket philosophy was being shaped by the English attitude. The often rough Australian tactics in 74/5 were closely related to these happenings in 70/71. The next development in this particular saga came now with the choice of a new Australian fast bowler for the Adelaide Test, one Dennis Lillee . . .

But before we leave Melbourne another matter arose which briefly aroused controversy, for Illingworth, in a press statement, said that some of his side questioned the legality of the action of Kerry O'Keeffe, Australia's young wrist-spinner. Apparently Snow and Knott when batting together expressed doubts not only to each other but to the square-leg umpire. It was bad that this should have happened and worse that Illingworth should have related it as though it were a normal thing. Thus he identified himself to some extent with the suspicion, which has had no other substance either before or since, so far as I know. One way and another MCC were not exactly endearing themselves. The evidence of this came in the shape of some booing in the later Tests when the captain came in to bat.

In the Adelaide Test England re-established the superiority shown at Sydney, and seemed to be in train to settle the rubber when Illingworth with a lead on first innings of 235 and an hour of the third day to go decided not to enforce the follow-on. I can recall the astonishment of the old Australian Test cricketers at what they considered an extraordinary reprieve. England's dismissal of Australia for 235 (exactly half their own score) was the result of the best piece of out-cricket by either side in the series. The morale of Lawry's side had suffered another heavy blow, and the natural move seemed to be for England to try to knock them down again without giving them a breathing-space.

When I recovered from my surprise I mustered some sort of argument in support of the English tactics. Though the weather by Adelaide standards was cool Snow, Lever and Willis had just bowled 50 overs between them, taking eight of the wickets to the spinners' two. I expect they were tired, especially considering there had been only two days between the end of the Melbourne Test and the start of this one. (Actually the fast bowlers had had four days and a few hours without bowling.) It could be calculated that a strong Australian rally in their second innings, had they followed on, might conceivably have left England three or four hours' batting on the last afternoon with a target to chase. They might then have run into trouble against the spinners. There was a fair case to be made for Illingworth, though to old cricketers and critics on the spot it seemed that he was timidly letting Australia off the hook. One could not avoid the feeling that about the decision there was an element of tacit protest at the imposition of the extra Test. In the end Illingworth's second innings declaration allowed his bowlers eight and three-quarter hours to get Australia out again and so clinch the rubber and the Ashes, but Stackpole and Ian Chappell played so well that they scarcely looked like doing so. A day all but fifty minutes they batted together, giving only one chance in that time and probably fortifying in the process the selectors in their estimation that here were the Australian captain and his deputy of the immediate future. The only casualty in the Australian second innings was a seagull which received a leg-glance from Stackpole full amidships, so reducing the value of the stroke from four to two. Willis, the fielder, rendered first-aid, and a later report gave the patient's condition as satisfactory. Thus it got off better than the swallow which was hit by a ball bowled by Greg Chappell to John Inverarity at Adelaide the preceding season. In this case the ball went on to hit the stumps, but the umpire ruled the ball dead – as well as the bird.

But from these pleasantries I must cast back to the first day of this Test to record the unhappy incident of Boycott's run-out. I happened to be returning from the broadcast point having joined Barry Richards (playing this season for South Australia) as a guest summarizer, and had reached a point square with the stumps at the Cathedral end. As Ian Chappell's throw from mid-wicket hit the stumps I found myself crying 'He's out,' because Boycott's bat was in the air. He scarcely seemed to realize his danger. It was a close thing, and O'Connell, the umpire, who was perfectly placed to see, hesitated a second or two before giving his verdict. When he did so Boycott threw his bat on the ground, and we had the sorry spectacle of Greg Chappell returning it to him without ceremony and, with Boycott glaring at the umpire, more than one fielder indicating with a jerk of the thumb the nearest way to the pavilion gate.

I've no doubt that Boycott was surprised, and if at the earliest moment he had made a full and open expression of regret the Australian public, who knew well enough the depth of his concentration and dedication, would have accepted the apology and thought little the worse of him. As it was all they saw in next day's paper was a picture strongly suggesting if it did not completely prove that the umpire was right, and a statement from Illingworth that Boycott was sorry that 'he showed a degree of displeasure at a decision that he thought was a poor one.' A 'degree', indeed! And second-hand at that. *Some* Yorkshiremen find it terribly hard to say they're sorry, and it can cost them dear. One recalls along with this instance, that of Brian Close whose refusal to apologize after he had been unanimously found guilty of time-wasting in a county match – only a euphemism for cheating, after all – cost him the MCC captaincy in the West Indies. I do not equate the offences: Boycott's was essentially unprecedented, a hasty reaction on the spur of the moment which he now regrets very much. The similarity is that both were perpetrated by distinguished Yorkshire cricketers and both were thoroughly bad for cricket.

Other incidents still worse for cricket were coming up, but the Australian selectors now came to the front of the picture by doing something that none of their predecessors had done for seventy years: they dropped their captain in mid-series: Ian Chappell was to be captain at Sydney, and Lawry was not only out of the captaincy but out of the team. The move was unexpected because in modern times unprecedented, but it was not difficult to follow the reasoning of Sir Donald Bradman and his colleagues, Neil Harvey and Sam Loxton. By Australian standards Lawry's general outlook was unusually defensive – and it had certainly not been blessed with success. He had lost eight Test Matches, more than any modern captain, and there was a case for giving a young man with a more positive approach the chance of squaring the series and so hanging on to the Ashes.

Again, one could imagine it might be embarrassing to his successor if Lawry were still to be a member of the side. But here the decision was more open to criticism for it rather refuted the statement often trotted out, when a comparison is made between English and Australian selection methods, that the Australians always choose their team first and the captain from within its number. On that basis it was hard to exclude Lawry whose back, of all the Australians, England still most wanted to see. However, there it was, out went Lawry in favour of Ken Eastwood, at 35 one of the oldest men to be first capped as a batsman by Australia, and out also went Gleeson, Mallett and Thomson. Their replacements, Jenner, Dell and O'Keeffe, meant that Australia were going into the game with a main quartet who had taken only six Test wickets between them. That, too, had never happened, save in 1946.

As if all this were not drama enough, a limited-over match at Sydney four days before the Test between MCC and Western Australia, as the state one-day champions, had cost England the services of their best bat. On a damp pitch a ball from McKenzie flying off a length had broken Boycott's left arm. So Luckhurst, deprived of practice for those weeks by a broken finger, perforce had to play and go in first with Edrich.

Appalling weather which had prevented the groundsman from producing a dry pitch for this one-day game had so interfered with his preparation that the bowlers were sure to get some help. The English party then were as relieved when they knew that McKenzie was safely flying west home to Perth as they had been on hearing that Lawry had been dropped. McKenzie might be stale, but granted any assistance which was the man they would least want to face from among McKenzie, Lillee and Dell? This argued little against Lillee who had bowled fast and with much promise on the dead Adelaide wicket. Cowdrey, by the way, appeared back among the English twelve, having been dropped after Melbourne, but in the end England played their strongest hand of bowlers. As it happened all six found parts to play.

The weather continued to be so bad that there were doubts whether the ground would be fit, and when this fateful Test began it was before a crowd of only ten thousand. It was all but certain that the toss winner would put his opponents in, and Chappell duly won the right to do so. The pitch started rather better than the worst fears suggested, but the bowlers were always getting something. England made 184, the captain showing up best after half the side were out for 98. The Australian bowling was wayward and inclined to shortness. Trevor Bailey was passing through Sydney, and the scene made his mouth water. As it happened the pitch played better the longer the match lasted. But now for the happenings which scar the memory of the tour – and which sicken the heart to recite again.

When Australia went in that evening Snow bowled Stackpole with an unplayable ball that came back a foot and just brushed the off-stump. Next day Australia were in sore straits at 66 for four before Redpath and Walters engaged in a worthy and successful effort to win back the initiative by some bold batting, especially on the part of Walters, who had the luck to be twice missed. Underwood's contribution in this period – 13 overs for 28 runs and the wickets of them both – was possibly his most valuable effort of the tour. Greg Chappell was playing admirably and the question was whether anyone could stay with him when (at 195 for seven) Jenner was hit on the side of the head ducking into a bouncer from Snow, the ball bouncing off towards cover-point. At first sight the injury looked more serious than it proved, but as Jenner was led bleeding back to the pavilion the crowd's anger mounted. They had seen Snow peppering their side throughout the series, and, certainly, 'Froggie' Thomson doing some peppering on his own account. Now Snow had gone against convention by letting fly at a tail-ender. One did not need to be a psychologist to feel the prevailing mood as Lou Rowan, the umpire at the bowler's end, was seen to give Snow a warning. Snow's reaction was some hot-tempered words and an angry glare while Illingworth approached, not to question his fast bowler but to protest vehemently by word and gesture, claiming, as he afterwards said, that it was the first bouncer in the over. Indignation seethed on all sides as at the end of the over Snow snatched his hat from Rowan and, after a drinks interval, retired to long-leg: not just to the boundary's edge but with one foot literally in the drain beneath the low picket-fence, against which the crowd on what is known as 'the little Hill' were jostling. To go so needlessly close, exchanging comment with spectators as he did so, looked, in the circumstances, like further provocation, and it was too much for one man who grabbed Snow's shirt. As Snow and this fellow (who may well have quenched his thirst not wisely but too well) briefly tangled, a few beer tins thrown from some spectators in the immediate rear fell on to the field. Thereupon Illingworth without further ado, or any word either to the umpires or to the batsmen, motioned his side off the field.

Some left more willingly than others, but when all were in the pavilion the umpires returned thereto, and warned England's captain that if he did not return he would forfeit the match. Illingworth said he had taken his team off to protect them and that they would return when the litter was cleared. This was already accomplished – Ray Robinson, that most diligent of researchers, says in *The Wildest Tests* that the count was forty cans and a few bottles in the gutters to which they had been consigned, many of the cans having contained soft drinks and therefore presumably thrown by boys. The batsmen,

Chappell and Lillee, had remained on the field, and the stoppage, though to anxious eyes it seemed far longer, was timed as seven minutes. In 209 Tests between England and Australia it was the first time such a thing had happened.

Such is a brief resumé of the affair, to which it may be added that of the three previous balls bowled in the over to Jenner two were very short and could well have been interpreted as intimidatory, and that after the second of these, immediately before the one that hit, Illingworth brought a fourth man, Willis, over to the on-side, presumably to catch a mis-hit. After four years and more the impression remains as clear as it was when I wrote from the spot: 'with a modicum of tact and self-discipline all round the situation would never have arisen.'

Greg Chappell seemed less affected by the affair than his opponents, he with some help from Lillee adding 40 more runs before close of play. Jenner, returning next day, made 30 and so Australia after all led by 80. As in England's first innings Chappell made extensive use of the spin of O'Keeffe – quickish stuff rather after the manner of Doug Wright, with the googly turning distinctly more than the leg-break – and of Jenner, after Luckhurst and Edrich had made an exemplary start. Ian Chappell, who had won much applause in the first innings by his aggressive use of spin, gained an improbable trick when he produced Eastwood, who seldom got a bowl with Northcote, his Melbourne club. Eastwood sent down some left-arm wrist spin, as it turned out, and promptly took the important wicket of Fletcher. There was a dash about the new captain that took everyone's fancy, and Chappell added to his laurels with a superb effort running back from slip and taking off in a dive to catch Hampshire, that good and lively cricketer whom I might have introduced into the narrative before this. England's second innings was a good fighting effort all round, to which the captain contributed (in a crucial sixth wicket stand of 69 with d'Oliveira) despite a painful crack on the left knee from the fast-medium left-arm of Dell.

There was a more crippling blow from fate to come, though, when Australia went in a second time needing 223 to win. No sooner had Snow yorked the hapless Eastwood for a duck than he misjudged an awkward swirling hook, aimed by Stackpole off Lever, and, running back into the very spot on the picket-fence that had been the scene of the trouble, caught a finger between two panels and dislocated it horribly. Illingworth's feelings as his ace card ran back to the pavilion with the bone protruding from his little finger can probably be imagined. Luckily he had started with a full string of bowlers. But Snow, with 31 wickets to his name, when it mattered, was worth almost two of any others. The moral effect of his departure can only have uplifted the Australians.

However, it also had the effect of bringing some extra quality out of the rest of the England side. If one could only forget the happenings of the Saturday evening, what a fascinating struggle it was! After Lever in a particularly fine over had had Ian Chappell's wicket Stackpole began to emerge as the man who might see to it that the Ashes remained, after all, in Australia. Illingworth – who everyone thought had under-bowled himself, taking the series as a whole – broke a menacing stand by beating Redpath, while Walters, seldom at ease against the speed, fell headlong into a trap baited by Illingworth and Willis, steering a short one with geometric precision into the hands of d'Oliveira at third man. The alliance of Stackpole and Greg Chappell was an obvious threat, but Illingworth was now very much in the groove, and after half an hour of it Stackpole, sweeping, was bowled off his pads for 67, the highest score in the match. If Knott had stumped Marsh off his captain, Australia's hopes would have sunk out of sight, but the little man missed what was rated his first unaccepted chance since Brisbane, and so the fifth day dawned with five wickets still standing and exactly 100 needed.

Underwood was now brought into the picture, bowling Marsh soon after the start, but it was Illingworth who ended Australian hopes by luring Chappell out to meet a ball that went with the arm, Knott this time making no mistake. It was his twenty-fourth victim, a record but with the extra Test thrown in. Three-quarters of an hour later Illingworth was being borne back to the pavilion on the shoulders of his team, the second man only since Jardine to win a series in Australia. Whatever qualifications had to be made as regards attitudes and behaviour – and it did cricket no service to try to whitewash the blemishes – no one could withhold admiration for Illingworth's keen tactical grasp and for the wholehearted team effort that in the end was proof against the injuries to Boycott before the match and of Snow during it. Neither side could compare with many in the past, but by the end there was no doubt at all which was the better.

10

Defeat Without Dishonour

In the months before MCC were due to fly once again to Australia the signs suggested that whoever was entrusted with the captaincy would have a hard job ahead to retain the Ashes which had been won with not much to spare four years before and retained as a result of the exciting, hard-fought home series of 1972. As usual it was England's batting which on paper looked all too fragile, with the senior men mostly much of a muchness and no younger ones announcing themselves in a way that appealed to the TCCB selectors. The latter oddly-assorted body were accused of being allergic to youth, to which Alec Bedser, the long-serving chairman, answered that any young batsman would be welcomed so long as he was thought good enough. How do you tell, ran the counter-argument, unless new men are given a chance? Why, in 1972 even M. J. K. Smith, the MCC captain in Australia seven years before, who had subsequently retired and then returned to Warwickshire, had been brought back for three Tests along with Peter Parfitt, who in the last six years had been chosen only once for England, and who was destined to retire for good at the end of the season.

However, in the summer of 1974 England's batsmen, to the surprise of all, first slaughtered the Indian spinners, and then against Pakistan played well enough at least to halve the short series, if not to win it. It was easy for optimists to forget that in the West Indies the previous winter England had been heavily outplayed in three Tests out of the five, even if a narrow victory in the last enabled them, against all the odds, to get away with a drawn rubber.

After Ray Illingworth in the latter half of the summer of 1973 had led England to defeat at the hands of the West Indies – an innings and 226 runs was the shattering margin at Lord's after West Indies had declared at 652 for eight – the selectors had decided that the time for a change had come, and instead of turning to one of the regular England players, or going back to a tried elder in Colin

Cowdrey, suddenly plumped for Michael Denness. Faced with as tough an assignment as has confronted any English touring captain, since he had to prove himself against the strongest opposition as a batsman as well as a leader, Denness improved upon a diffident start in the West Indies, and in the decisive Test there handled his side extremely well.

The England captaincy, unless it be in the hands of a great cricketer with an almost prescriptive right to it who is moreover being success-ful – Hutton, May, and – for a brief period until injury in 1969 – Cowdrey, are post-war examples – has never been a sinecure. Criti-cism surrounds the holder as surely as the sparks fly upward. Denness was given short shrift in much of the media. Some favoured Boy-cott, some Close (though he was 42 and highly suspect round the joints), while others would have stuck to Illingworth, even though in his last six Tests he had taken only six wickets at 75 a time. However, Denness's authority on the field had strengthened in the West Indies with experience, he had shown an admirable fielding example, and he had made just about enough runs to be worth his place as a batsman. Accordingly he was retained for the series against India, who were duly whitewashed three-nil with the captain getting two hundreds. Short of making a great mess of the short Pakistan series Denness after this was all but sure to take the side to Australia. He didn't, and was duly appointed.

Granted their original choice for the West Indies I believe the selectors made the right and proper decision for the captaincy in Australia, but in choosing the side they fell surely into the cardinal error of picking more fast – or rather fastish – bowlers than could possibly be kept exercised: five, plus Tony Greig if he should be called upon to bowl in that style (as in fact he was). There was no rectifying the balance of the party after that, and it was lucky indeed that Greig, the only all-rounder, kept fit all through. Another man who could do three things well would have been a godsend. I don't think the selectors were guilty of any other culpable choices or omissions, but there is no blinking the fact that they did not enjoy enough esteem for the job, and in particular suffered a lack of experience of touring needs in Australia (or, for that matter, any-where else). Brian Taylor, the retired captain of Essex, was a wicket-keeper, Ossie Wheatley, one-time captain of Glamorgan, was a bowler pure and simple, Jack Bond, former captain of Lancashire and now of Notts, was a county batsman who had never threatened to go higher. Bedser alone knew Australia, and of the others only Taylor, many years before in South Africa, had gone on a major tour. All good men and true, they were nevertheless as a body an inadequate appointment, for which the TCCB had no one to blame but themselves.

There was much speculation whether John Snow, who had been omitted at Illingworth's instigation after the first Test against the West Indies in 1973, would be recalled. It was his 31 wickets in six Tests, after all, which had had the chief part in bringing back the Ashes in 1971, and on his day and in the mood he could still perhaps produce a more dangerous spell than anyone. But there was a good deal on the other side of the ledger. Since the fracas at Sydney he had been dropped by Sussex for not trying, he had been dropped by the England selectors for the following Test Match when he had barged Sunil Gavaskar on to the ground at Lord's, and on a private tour of D. H. Robins's team in South Africa, managed by Leslie Ames and led by Close, he had been dropped for disobedience. Temperamental cricketers who are acceptable – on a balance of advantage, if you like – in their prime are apt to be soon discarded when they become expendable. Snow was now 33. Maybe another manager would have taken the chance of finding a way to his heart and accepted the risk, but with Bedser the things that count most are team-spirit and the maximum effort at all times – the virtues he himself had illustrated so well. When Alec accepted the managership in Australia Snow's chances flew out of the window.

England's other problem-cricketer of distinction was, of course, Geoffrey Boycott, who had made no secret of his own ambitions towards the England captaincy. When Illingworth asked not to be considered for the leadership of MCC in India and Pakistan in 1972/3 and Tony Lewis was appointed captain Boycott declared himself unavailable. He went to the Caribbean under Denness, to whom Greig was vice-captain, but after failing in six innings against the Indians at home, including two in the First Test, requested not to be picked for the next because he was dissatisfied with his form. (He had made a hundred in each innings of the Test Trial at Worcester only a fortnight previously.) Against the Rest of the World in 1970 he had likewise asked not to be picked for the same reason.

As England's most experienced and successful Test batsman Boycott was naturally chosen now for Australia, but almost at the last minute he again pulled out, saying he needed a further rest from Test cricket. In the cricket world Yorkshire's egocentric perfectionist came in for much criticism from old-fashioned folk like me who feel that cricketers owe the debt of service to the game that has made their fame and fortune. Weighing up the effect of his absence one could reflect that since there was no rapport between him and Denness the team would no doubt be happier without him. Again, he was injury-prone against fast bowlers, and very few of his runs for England had been made against extreme speed which this side would be up against if Dennis Lillee were to make a come-back. (Jeff Thomson at this stage was no more than a vague rumour.) Allow all this, and the team was still substantially the weaker for the late substitution of Brian Luckhurst in Boycott's place.

All this makes a longish preamble, but the story is incomplete without this background. Anyway, let us now to Brisbane where I found a contented and reasonably confident camp with all singing the praises of the manager, and the only fly in the ointment the batting form of the captain, who had been unlucky enough to contract a virus of some kind as soon as he arrived, and so had missed most of the first invaluable weeks.

The first day's play of this First Test was notable, in the light of what was to happen thereafter, in that England took three of the six wickets that fell from bouncers mishooked, and next day thus captured two more. Most of the Australian batsmen were still short of form and runs, and were dealing so poorly with the short stuff that the temptation was irresistible. Still, up to a point at least, the mode of dismissal of half the Australian side gave their own bowlers the green light so far as bouncers were concerned, and from the first ball there was no doubt that Lillee and Thomson had got the message.

Lillee's pace was perhaps a yard ahead of that of Willis, fastest and best of the England bowlers, while Thomson's was a yard and more greater than Lillee's. Thomson's speed indeed was a revelation, and when he replaced Lillee at the downwind end, with Clem Jones's ridge to bowl at, England were soon in grave trouble. As was to happen all through the series, Thomson bowled better when the first of the shine was off than when the ball was new. I cannot be sure whether Lindsay Hassett was talking about the first innings or the second when at the end of the tour he, Chris Martin-Jenkins and I attempted a survey of the tour over the Australian air, but which-ever it was he said he thought an over by Thomson at Brisbane was the *best* he had ever seen from a fast bowler.

That will give an idea of what England were up against – for no one will have played and seen much more cricket over the last forty

years than Lindsay. The purists talked of Thomson's action as slinging, and maybe the left shoulder does fall away a shade early in the
delivery stride. Yet there was no lack of rhythm, and the muzzle
velocity he generated from a relatively short run was amazing. From
the back, as he ran to the crease, I could see more than a hint of
Keith Miller.

Greig saved England's bacon in the first innings, even more completely than Ian Chappell saved Australia's, for he came in at 57
for four to join John Edrich with Lillee and Thomson rampant, each
in turn playing on the uncertainty of the bounce at the city end. I
can't think of an innings calculated to do more for English morale
than Greig's hundred since Ted Dexter took Hall and Griffith apart
on that memorable day at Lord's. He took risks certainly, getting runs
over the slips and gully sometimes accidentally as well as by malice
aforethought. But generally with his great height he got over the
short stuff well, and gave it the full weight of his bat – which is
getting on for three pounds. It was the innings of a strong man and
a fearless one, the stroke-diagram of which shows how only 5 runs
came behind the wicket on the leg-side and only 12 on the leg-side
in front. There were three strokes for four past mid-off, and the
remaining 81 were made in the arc between first slip and extra-
cover.

When he was finally out, having made 110 out of 191 in five hours,
Greig got a tremendous ovation, but when I read a certain respected
Australian newspaper next day I reached the sixteenth paragraph
before it was apparent that anyone called Greig was playing in the
match. The Aussies are not slow to criticize the English press, and
often not without reason, so I shall take leave now and then to have a
tilt at theirs. Alas for objectivity! This reminds me that after the
fourth day of the Sixth Test when Australia with seven wickets left
were 103 runs behind we woke up to the banner headline WE'VE
SAVED IT! For once one rather relished the verbal castigation of the
batsmen next morning after Australia had been beaten by an innings.

Despite all that Greig achieved on the second and third days
Australia duly won on the fifth with an hour and a quarter to spare,
England departing for Perth much sobered by the happenings of the
game, by the unexpected speed of Thomson, by the realization that
Lillee was still a power, and not least by the knowledge that their
two foremost batsmen, Dennis Amiss and Edrich, were nursing
broken hands that would keep them out of the Second Test.

For those of us who were looking on with as much detachment

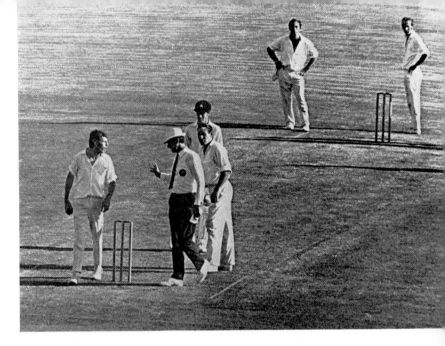

Sorry scenes from the '71 Tour

41. *(above)* At Sydney: Snow and Illingworth in angry altercation with Umpire Rowan after he has warned the bowler for intimidation. **42.** *(below)* At Adelaide: Ian Chappell and Mallett show Boycott the way home after he had thrown down his bat on being given run out.

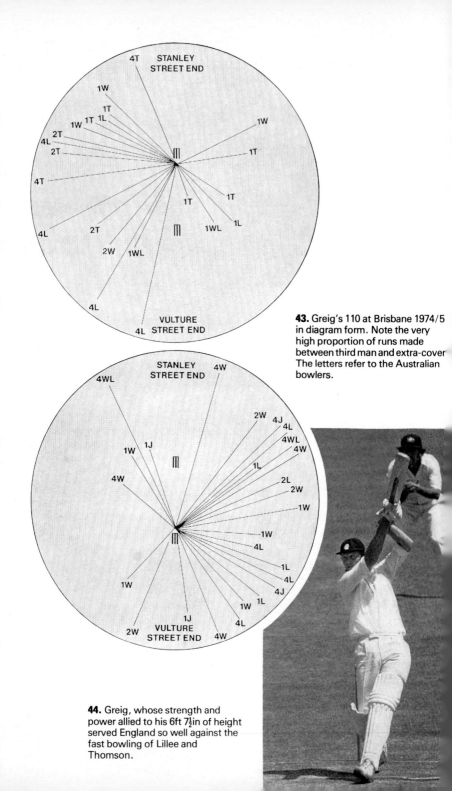

Top diagram labels:
STANLEY STREET END
4T
1W
1T
1W 1T 1L
2T
4L
2T
4T
4L
2T
1WL
2W 1WL
4L
VULTURE STREET END
4L
1W
1T
1T
1T
1L
1WL
1L

43. Greig's 110 at Brisbane 1974/5 in diagram form. Note the very high proportion of runs made between third man and extra-cover The letters refer to the Australian bowlers.

Bottom diagram labels:
STANLEY STREET END
4W
4WL
1W 1J
4W
1W
1W
2W
1J
2W
VULTURE STREET END
4W
2W 4J
4L
4WL
4W
1L
2L 2W
1W
1W
4L
1L
4L
4J
1L
4L

44. Greig, whose strength and power allied to his 6ft 7½in of height served England so well against the fast bowling of Lillee and Thomson.

as we could muster there was also the threat that the series might be ruined by the intent to intimidate. The short stuff was not one-sided, and Peter Lever had been warned on the second day when bowling to Australia's No. 8. However, it was the Australian pair who posed the chief threat, and the senior of these had actually been frank and foolish enough to declare his intentions both in a book published on the eve of the tour and, just in case anyone had not heard or read what he said, on TV the evening before the Test ended. 'I aim to hit him somewhere between the stomach and the rib-cage,' he remarked in a matter-of-fact tone, adding that he did not want to do a man serious injury, just 'to hurt him a bit', and no doubt generally soften him up.

The interviewer did his best to temper Lillee's statement by suggesting that what he was hoping for was mistimed strokes when he bowled short, but Lillee repeated that although 'that comes into it' what he was aiming for was hits. In his book *Back to the Mark* he had been just as specific: 'I bowl bouncers for one reason and that is to hit the batsman and thus intimidate him.' I wish I could say what must have got into Lillee, since I had come to know and like him in England two years earlier.

I am quite sure that the Australian Cricket Board were displeased by all this, just as they were by attitudes and talk at times on the field. They had recently lifted the ban on players writing and talking on the air about matches in which they were engaged because it was argued that this meant greater publicity for cricket, the only stipulation being that they might write nothing calculated to bring the game into disrepute *in the opinion of the Chairman of the Board*. I felt that the Board should have dissociated themselves publicly from Lillee's philosophy, as I do not doubt they did to him in private. It did not make for an auspicious start to a series. However, although articles by the Chappell brothers in addition to Lillee were regularly syndicated there was no more inflammatory stuff, and one could only conclude that the Chairman in question, T. C. J. (Tim) Caldwell, had laid down the law with those concerned, just as Bedser did when anyone on his side stepped out of line on the field.

The Woolloongabba ground, trim and well-equipped nowadays in contrast to the old primitive amenities and run-down state, had maintained its reputation as an English graveyard – this was the fifth defeat in the eight post-war Tests. I've seen England win four times apiece at Melbourne and Sydney, once at Adelaide, but never here.

Before MCC left Brisbane for Perth the tour committee comprising, in addition to the captain and manager, Alan Smith (the assistant-manager), Edrich (vice-captain) and Greig decided that with two batsmen out of action already, and the prospect of others succumbing in the five Tests to come, they needed another batsman. Of their six specialists David Lloyd had also been unavailable at Brisbane with a finger break – which reduced the fit batsmen at this point to three, Denness, Fletcher, and Luckhurst.

But imagine the surprise when the name the tour selectors came up with after all the water that had flown under the bridge was that of Colin Cowdrey. They wanted him, they said, because he had the best technique of anyone against fast bowling. So at the ripe age of 42 the veteran of 113 Tests promptly packed his bags down at Limpsfield and three days later was airborne for Perth, in company, as it happened, with my wife. A delay of 19 hours at Bombay meant that he arrived just four days before the Second Test in which it was already clear that he would be needed.

The Australians, who scarcely ever bring anyone back, thought the recall of Cowdrey incomprehensible, and had to be reminded of several notable come-backs: for instance of David Sheppard (113) at Old Trafford, of Cyril Washbrook (98) at Headingley, of Denis Compton (94) at the Oval – a remarkable hat-trick achieved by Gubby Allen and company in 1956. There was a lot of comment about Santa Claus and *Dad's Army,* but the crowds on each ground when Colin came in to bat showed their admiration in the clearest possible way. Keith Miller could not understand how, after all he had done, he should want to subject himself to the world's fastest, but the victim's reaction to his first Test innings was 'I did enjoy it so' – an interesting difference in attitudes.

England's only feasible hope was a holding action at Perth where they found a perfect pitch, mild in pace, on which Chappell, the day being overcast, invited them to bat. Lloyd (49 and 35) made a reasonably auspicious beginning against Australia, while Father Christmas, going in No. 3 in the first innings and first in the second (Luckhurst had become yet another finger casualty), notched 22 and 41. There were fourteen double-figure scores in England's two innings, but only Knott (No. 7) and Fred Titmus (No. 8) reached fifty, and Australia had won by nine wickets by the fourth evening.

Their batting prospered on the perfect surface even if England's did not – 481 in a day and a half with all but one contributing, and Doug Walters stealing the show on a sunny Sunday evening by taking a hundred between tea and the close. He got there – repeating, incidentally, the Test hundred he made in an afternoon at Port-of-Spain – by hitting the last ball of the day high over the ropes at long-leg for six.

Who better than Walters when the mood is on him? Doug never quite touched this form again in the series, though one was always fearing he might. Greg Chappell, who had announced himself in Test cricket with a hundred here four years earlier, played beautifully as usual, while Ross Edwards on his home ground made a quiet, compact, stylish hundred in five hours and a quarter.

Again it was Thomson and Lillee who had shown themselves too good, helped by close catching nearly as brilliant and infallible as at Brisbane. Fourteen of England's twenty wickets fell to catches by the keeper, slips or gully – almost a repeat of the First Test. It was not that anyone was 'running away'. No one did that, among the first eight in the order anyway. But, aiming square rather than to mid-off, one man after another was drawn into error by the pace and the lift. Almost everything above ground Australia caught. Ian Chappell, Redpath, Walters and Mallett were all very good, and Greg Chappell just a bit better even than any of them. He took in fact seven catches in the match, something never hitherto done in Tests though his grandfather Vic Richardson came close.

England approached the Third Test at Melbourne in better heart, with Amiss and Edrich now restored, but the luck continued to run ill for them since on winning the toss for the third time Chappell again put them in on a typically fresh first day pitch. Denness had decided to do likewise if he had had the opportunity. Moreover Hendrick, sharing the new ball with Willis when Australia went in against England's 242, pulled up with a torn ham-string in his third over and could not bowl another ball in the match – or, as it turned out, in the series.

However, despite their misfortunes, England had their full share in the glory of a marvellously even tight-fought game watched by quarter of a million people. On Boxing Day – the first day – the crowd was given as 77,165, which is the most I have ever seen for certain at a cricket match. I put it this way since no one seemed to know how many got in at Calcutta at the New Year of 1973, the figure being given as a round 75,000 each day.

Here both sides were on top in turn, only to let the chance slip, Australia once doing so in uncharacteristic circumstances. On the second afternoon the openers, Redpath and Wally Edwards, were making runs more easily than at any time in the game (apart from Amiss's performance subsequently), and had reached 63 together when the light grew dull, and the umpires according to the law gave them the option of continuing. Redpath decided to go in, saying afterwards that he thought that to bat on would have been hard on young Edwards who was struggling to keep his place in the team. It subsequently rained, but Australia might have had the best part of an hour's more batting. As it was young Edwards was promptly out next day, and all ten Australian wickets went down for 178 runs.

On the fourth day it was England who surrendered what at one stage was a formidable position. This was the one occasion when Australia saw the vintage Amiss. There was no better batting on either side in the series than the 70 he made before lunch, chiefly with Lloyd in their opening stand of 115. For once Lillee and Thomson were hit and hit hard, and naturally their control faltered. This is specially likely to happen when as now bowlers are required to change direction for the combination of a right- and left-hander. I thought Denness might have sent in Edrich rather than Cowdrey on Lloyd's departure, or alternatively either come in himself or promoted Greig to keep up the pressure. As it was, Amiss could not recover the magic touch in the afternoon, and in a fateful two hours England descended to 182 for eight.

Thomson, whose first seven overs had given him 0 for 46, now took 3 for 9, all as usual caught by the keeper or at slip. Again it was Greig who staged the rescue, and with the minimum of help until Willis came in – looking wide-eyed, as usual, like someone who has lost his way – at No. 10. Appearances this time were deceptive, for Willis played his stopping role admirably while Greig gave another sterling performance, forcing whenever he could but clearly conscious that all depended on his staying in.

Since his 60 took only two hours and a half, with the field spread to allow singles but deny the fours, it may be accepted that his stroke-play was of a high order. It was, with the *bonne bouche* a towering six over long-off at the Southern end which had the older hands wondering when they had seen the like. Sir Robert Menzies recalled such a hit by Warwick Armstrong while Leslie Ames mentioned Walter Hammond but didn't think even he had effected such a carry at Melbourne. Ted Dexter I've seen hit straight sixes here, but nothing comparable on the off-side. Greig made 29 out of the last 30 from the bat, and so it was that Australia with an over and one full day remaining needed 246 to win.

The last day was a memorable struggle on a pitch that lasted well without withholding the prospect of reward to good bowling. With Hendrick a casualty and Titmus limping badly from a cruel blow on the inside of the right knee sustained during his brief innings, England were patently handicapped. However, everyone pulled his weight, the fielding touched its best, and one by one the Australians succumbed. There was one major slice of luck when Greg Chappell was LBW to what was almost a shooter. At tea it was 145 for five, and odds on England. Walters, Marsh and (as usual) Walker improved matters, however, so that with an hour and its minimum of 15 overs to go the board showed 191 for six: 55 to get and Marsh and Walker well established.

A strange thing then happened which was never fully explained, Ian Chappell afterwards saying he had given no special orders. In seven overs by Titmus and Underwood, bowling to normal containing fields, Australia added only seven runs. The sudden retirement into their shells of these two competent players was said to be a protest against Titmus bowling to six leg-side fielders and Underwood operating for a while without a slip. But what did they want – England to serve up the Ashes on a plate with, as Neville Cardus once observed, parsley round them? There were plenty of vacant spots in Melbourne's broad acres, well as these two bowled.

Perhaps Marsh and Walker were merely ensuring they would still be together when the new ball was produced. At any rate the sight of Willis wielding it spurred them to renewed action. Three overs from Willis cost 22, but at the other end Greig accounted for Marsh. With three overs left Australia at 230 for seven needed 16 runs. Greig, now bowling off-breaks, in the thirteenth over conceded only two. Denness swopped Underwood for Willis, and amid the utmost tension he bowled an exemplary maiden to Lillee. So it was 14 to get in the last over. Lillee had a bang, was caught fourth ball in the covers, and lo! Australia ended just eight short of the target with two wickets left.

If they had scored normally between five and five-thirty the game would have been theirs. Yet if England had rooted Walker out quickly they would probably have won. On the whole the result was fair enough – the closest-fought draw in my experience of Tests between England and Australia.

All England's batsmen being now fit and Denness having so few runs, the captain for the Fourth Test stepped down in favour of Edrich. In answer to pointed questions at the start of the tour he had said he would do so at any time if it seemed better for the side. There was absolutely no pressure either by the managers or from within the side for Denness to rest himself – rather the contrary. Yet in the climate of the moment it seemed the best solution, even though Australia's first innings – they won the toss as they had every time hitherto, and this time chose to bat – had not gone very far before the loss to the out-cricket was painfully apparent.

England's mobility in the field was usually under strain, and this Sydney performance was the weakest of the six. If they were to pick from the party the best fielding side, ignoring other considerations, it would have contained all five of those (leaving the reserve wicket-keeper out of the reckoning) who for one reason or another were not included here. Edrich had an unenviable job, and could only be criticized in his refusal when the Australian tail were scoring freely to bring on either of his two admirable spinners. It is a curious modern fallacy that it's 'dangerous' to give Nos. 8 to 11 a taste of slow bowling. Walker in particular never looked half the bat when he had to wait for the ball to come to him.

From the Australian angle the best thing about their batting was the success of Rick McCosker, the tall, dark New South Welshman they had brought in as opening partner for Redpath. He looked a thoroughly good player off his legs, where England conveniently concentrated their attack, less sure outside the off-stump. He gave two chances in that area before the third was taken just when it seemed he might add his name to those ten Australians who in the course of history have made 100 against England in their first Test. Two of them were in this side, incidentally – Greg Chappell, who played beautifully for 84 before he was out to a lovely slip catch, low to his left, by Greig, and Doug Walters, the local hero, who was LBW to Arnold for 1 at the start of the second day. Arnold's five for 86 was due reward for his best effort for England abroad.

Whether or not Walters's misfortune put The Hill in a bad humour I can't say, but what with the beer and the overcrowding and the heat the denizens thereof had one of their noisiest, most refractory days. The members of the Sydney Cricket Ground Trust, whose guest for the day I happened to be, were given ample evidence to support a general feeling that The Hill, as it is, is a dangerous ana-chronism urgently in need of more civilized facilities. It was all right maybe in times when spectators were better behaved and before the days of iced containers ('Eskies'), and when in any case those in the popular sections could not afford the vast quantities of beer which

146

are now consumed. How some of this fluid is ultimately disposed of on a crowded day when there is no access to lavatories I leave to the imagination.

It was The Hill's fevered cries of 'Lill-ee, Lill-ee!', as Australia's premier bowler began to accelerate on his run-up to the stumps, that seemed to add a yard to his daunting speed and to shorten his average length distinctly. Maybe also he remembered that when batting Greig had had the effrontery to hit him on the left elbow, thereby provoking some highly unparliamentary remarks and an apparent loss of temper on Lillee's part. Mallett likewise when batting had seemed highly aggrieved by a blow on the hand that hampered his bowling next day. It might be a question whether England were tactically wise to provoke the Australian bowlers by short stuff in view of their own very inferior fire-power. However, Richie Benaud, who might sometimes be thought chary of criticizing his fellows, wrote in the Sydney *Daily Mirror* that he had 'absolutely no sympathy with the lower half of the Australian order when they complain about an excess of short-pitched bowling against them.' Another great Australian cricketer, Bill O'Reilly, wrote of this Sunday's cricket in the *Sydney Morning Herald* 'the situation looks dangerously close now to getting right out of hand.' He concluded that 'the whole future of these engagements depends upon some very quick, sane thinking on the part of the authorities concerned and, more importantly, the captains.'

I fear the great man's words will have fallen on stony ground so far as Ian Chappell is concerned, for he made it clear more than once that he regarded the control of his side on the field as the concern solely of the umpires. Poor wretched men! I wonder what Ian thought might have happened if either Tom Brooks or Robin Bailhache had applied the final sanction under Law 46, and had banned either Lillee or Thomson on that emotion-charged Sunday afternoon. How many beer cans might have bespattered the field, and angry spectators invaded the playing area? As it was the umpires contented themselves with friendly warnings afterwards described as 'unofficial'. In the circumstances it was hard to blame them. I gathered from Alec Bedser that after close of play the teams repaired to one another's dressing-rooms, as usual on this tour, for a glass of beer. It was the manager who reintroduced this regular old custom, by the way, and it indeed said a lot that this chance could be taken to salve sore feelings. The best thing I heard about Lillee during the series was how the evening after some heated exchange on the field he took Tony Greig's arm, saying 'come on you old—, come and have a beer.' That's something, as I say, but the TV cameras weren't in the dressing-room. No young Australian sportsman saw the sequel, but perhaps a million or more had witnessed the abrasive, ill-tempered behaviour in the middle. The modern player is inclined to think that these public outbursts are all part of the show. What they do not seem to realize is the great harm they do the game by such deplorable example.

After the last Test I did a longish nation-wide broadcast review of the series under the chairmanship of Norman May and in company with Lindsay Hassett. When the subject of behaviour on the field, and in particular the use of foul language, came up Lindsay said with great deliberation 'during my time I never heard a single player of either side swear at another.' In other words, the habit is confined to the last twenty years. My impression is that it has grown much worse during the last five, and I grieve to say I think that some English counties led the fashion in the first place.

Enough, perhaps, of this particular day. I left the ground with a nasty taste in my mouth and the conviction that a deliberate attempt had been made to intimidate the first five men in the England order. Strangely enough, the only serious casualty had been to a fielder, who was hit on the temple at short-leg by a stroke that Edrich said would have gone for four. Next day the victim, McCosker, tried to field but desisted, and he was not needed to bat a second time.

England in their first innings, facing 405, were at one time on the third morning (a slightly cooler day in all respects) half-out for 123, but were rescued by Knott in his best and most aggressive form. Titmus and Underwood gave notable assistance, the new ball being hit hard and often. In the first hour after lunch England actually made 92.

Still, they ended 110 behind, whereupon Redpath and Greg Chappell in the longest stand of the series (220) made sure Australia had enough runs to declare on, in good time. Redpath in his second hundred against England was much as usual, correct, the ideal second string, while Greg showed all the strokes and especially the favourite on-drive wide of mid-on. Four and a quarter hours must be reckoned very good time for 144 in these days, considering the rate at which overs are bowled. Ian Chappell's declaration soon after three o'clock on the fourth afternoon left England no impossible job on the face of it, little though previous form suggested that they might make 400 to win, in whatever number of hours. As it was, a thunderstorm – one of only two sizeable interruptions during the series – kept Australia off the field for an hour and a half, thereby improving England's prospects of a draw which, in turn, would have left the Ashes still in dispute at Adelaide.

It was half past eleven on the fifth morning before England's first wicket fell, and the pitch was playing blamelessly enough. A rearguard was very much on, but Edrich retired hurt first ball, hit in the ribs ducking to a short one that skidded low, and the middle batting thereafter was either disappointingly limp or in the case of Greig foolhardy, as though he felt the situation was beyond saving – which later events denied. On Greig's dismissal – a wild swing at Mallett gave Marsh his only stumping of the series – Edrich returned to the fray, the X-ray having revealed no broken bones, and at last found in Willis a man intending to drop anchor. For an hour and a half these two stuck it out in relative safety, Willis repeating his valuable innings with Greig at Melbourne. Unfortunately when Lillee grasped the new ball Willis's enthusiasm waned somewhat. He was yorked in the third over of the last hour, whereupon Lillee's first ball to Arnold, a prodigious bouncer, flew past his nose and out of Marsh's reach for four byes. One was almost too disillusioned with the spirit of the game to note this opening salvo to England's No. 11. Arnold lasted seven overs, and there were only five to go (for it was all but six o'clock) when Mallett had him at short-leg and the fight for the Ashes was over. Edrich, who with 50 and 33 not out had a good match with the bat, scarcely looked like getting out, and the last two stands illustrated how the day might well have been saved.

I can cover England's next and fourth defeat more briefly. The game was particularly disappointing from the English angle since after rain had washed out the first day – no one recalled when this had happened before in Adelaide – the pitch was still wet at one end on the second morning, and Denness, winning the toss, naturally put Australia in. In these days of total covering to get Australia in on a damp pitch was almost too good to be true: what had happened was that a high wind had lifted the pins holding down the tarpaulins. Up to a point all went well for England, since directly after lunch Australia were 84 for five. Underwood – four for six at one time – had taken all five at the end that gave help, and but for some excellent defensive batting from Redpath against the lifting, turning ball and a promising effort by McCosker the situation must have been worse.

As it was, Walters and Jenner took the traditional Australian way out of a tight situation and chanced their arms. The pitch now was all but harmless, the sun having done its work, and Underwood's support was quite inadequate – Greig none for 63 off ten overs. At the same time all praise to Walters, who played brilliantly, and also to Jenner who on his home ground surpassed himself by making 74 in little more than two hours. Underwood had them both in the end, having taken all seven wickets so far, but against a dispirited attack the tail completed the recovery.

Denness came in for strong criticism for giving Titmus only the last over before lunch at the opposite end to Underwood. From the press-box at square-leg it could not be seen that the dampness did not extend to what would have been Titmus's length: hence the captain sticking to Arnold, who bowled without luck, and Greig who had one of his off-est days. (I find myself alternately lauding and scolding England's outstanding cricketer.)

England's innings on Australia Day was a disaster mitigated only by a really good innings of 51 against the speed by Denness until, having batted less than an hour and a half, he fell to the besetting flick. So also did Fletcher after another much better innings. For the fourth time in four Tests then Australia got themselves into the driving seat and there they stayed. Once again they declared their second innings, leaving England eight and a half hours to get 405: oceans of time.

The package tour parties from England had but a few minutes to enjoy the luxury of speculating whether at last England would make the most of conditions now perfect and pull out a stirring perform-ance. The chance was surely the greater – and Chappell's declaration accordingly the more demanding – since Jeff Thomson had wrenched his right shoulder playing lawn-tennis of all things at the lavish jamboree which 'Windy' Hill-Smith always gives to the cricket world on the Adelaide rest-day at his Yalumba winery. To be exact, he had strained the musculatendinous cuff.

Yet after a few minutes England were 10 for three with Amiss again out for 0 to a perfect ball from Lillee impelling a stroke. Lloyd was picked up in the slips off Walker, and Cowdrey was out to a catch just as brilliant as his first innings dismissal. Then Walker at backward short-leg had jumped feet in the air to catch him high right-handed: now Mallett in the gully threw himself left and took inches from the ground what had seemed a safe cut played as in-tended. It was easy, watching this series, in frequent dejection at

England's batting frailties, to overlook the excellence of the Australian close catching. Granted that the batsmen generally gave them every cause to keep the sharpest look-out, the standards of such men as the Chappells, Mallett, Redpath and Walters were marvellously high. It was true enough that the fast bowlers won the series, but what extraordinary support they had! I at least have never seen so many outstanding catches in a Test series. Denness this time was caught at fly-slip posted for the purpose thirty yards behind the regular ring, just as Snow had had Ian Chappell at Sydney four years earlier. The most calamitous day of the series ended with England 94 for five. Though the weather had reverted to what one expects of Adelaide in January, with the temperature high in the nineties, and though Australia were a bowler short, no last day recovery was feasible from such a situation. Knott batted easily and fluently enough to show what might have been, granted a respectable start. He improved on his Sydney performance in fact to make his first Test hundred against Australia, a chanceless innings of four and a half hours. Fletcher too maintained the improvement that was due to culminate so richly at Melbourne and in New Zealand.

The usual medical bulletin preceded England's choice for the last Test. Hendrick was still unfit for a five-day match, Willis had broken down once more, while Lloyd's neck had played up again, and the last two would have to be sent home. But there, for once, misfortune ended, since though Chappell won the toss for the fifth time he surprisingly chose to bat on what turned out a normally fresh first day Melbourne pitch. Lever, back in Willis's place, used his chance superbly, every catch stuck, he came back full of spirit despite a shade temperature of 100, and sure enough by tea-time Australia had been bowled out for 152, the lowest total of the series. Lever six for 38! He kept the ball up to the bat, showed admirable control, and occasional lift and late movement did the rest. Four out of the first five batsmen made 2 runs between them, the captain alone coming to terms with the attack. There was a further factor which, though not responsible for a wicket, added to the batsmen's apprehensions. Water from the covers had been allowed to spill on a spot about the circumference of a bucket short of a length at Lever's end. It was only hit once, the ball taking a divot before connecting painfully with Greg Chappell's jaw.

When Amiss and Cowdrey opened in very dull light the former was at once LBW to Lillee, so collecting his third successive duck, all at Lillee's hands. After half an hour the umpires ruled the light unfit, and when the innings was resumed next morning (43,000 present on Sunday as against 32,000 on Saturday) Cowdrey was at once caught behind off a very awkward lifter from Walker. I recalled the pessimistic comment of one of England's leading batsmen overnight: 'we'll be lucky to get 250.' Now it was 18 for two with Denness joining Edrich and the bowling fresh. Who in their dreams could have supposed that the captain would return six hours later with the board showing 273 for three, the Australians following him with only Edrich's wicket in mid-afternoon to show for their labours? Cowdrey's ball was the first and last of the day to misbehave, Denness made strokes soundly and confidently from the first, and soon Lillee was walking off the field with his right boot in his hand, having strained his foot.

The Australian attack was thus reduced to something like its 1970/71 shape and quality: Walker, Dymock (the left-arm quick-medium Queenslander), Walters, Mallett and Ian Chappell. They performed with accurate perseverance, and the fielding – especially of Edwards and Redpath in the covers – was marvellously good. The batting, however, held the eye, first Edrich and Denness in concert, then when Edrich was caught at first slip, the captain almost unaided, until Fletcher towards the end blossomed forth somewhat as his partner tired.

Next day the pair of them were at it again with Denness the chief aggressor until shortly after lunch he drove hard and low back to Walker's right and was excellently caught and bowled for 188. He played most of the strokes at one time or another in his eight hours at the crease but it is those between point and extra-cover that one chiefly recalls, the body leaning, left knee bent, into the hits off the front leg and poised on the toes, right foot back, when the shorter ball could be watched on to the bat and cracked hard and true at the selected angle in the off-side arc. A slice and a half of luck Mike enjoyed. He whipped Walters off his toes hard but straight to McCosker at square-leg when 36, while at 121 soon after the new ball came Ian Chappell might have got a hand to an edge off Dymock. Otherwise the number of unintended hits over such a long span was extraordinarily small.

What better man than Greig to come in at 359 for four with bowlers and fielders enduring their ninth hour in the sun? Greig played with the utmost power and no little disdain throughout the afternoon while Fletcher after reaching his hundred relaxed and also punched the ball hard. Between lunch and tea England made 145 runs, 83 of them to Greig, and as they came in at 496 for four opinion was divided as to when if at all Denness should declare. Now? After an hour? Or not at all? I was in a minority in supposing that he should get all the runs he could by the close, leaving Australia twelve hours' batting to save the game with a deficit approaching 500 that they could not hope to reach. As it was the manner of the after-tea batting made it evident that Australia were going to be got in pretty soon. Fletcher and Greig were promptly caught respectively at mid-on and mid-off, driving, whereupon as one ambitious stroke after another was attempted Walker cashed in gleefully to gain handsome recompense for all his toil. From three for 136 his analysis in the course of 20 balls became eight for 143, England were all out for 529, and by five o'clock they were in the field again. It was the seventh highest score ever made by England in Australia, and another 30 runs would have made it the highest for all but fifty years. Denness's 188 beat by 15 runs the next best score by an England captain in Australia, A. E. Stoddart's great innings on this ground just eighty years before. It was also the highest Test score made by an English batsman in Australia since the war – a fact which escaped general notice at the time.

These were gay garlands of a sort to uplift a bruised and battered touring party, but only victory could underline the point they needed to make – take Lillee and Thomson away and who then were the better side? Australia had lost no wicket by the close of the third day, and by tea on the fourth afternoon England, deprived by illness of Lever, had only prised out McCosker for a very worthy 76. Ian Chappell and Redpath had gone by the close, Redpath after an utterly composed, patient stay of six hours. But the deficit now was only 103. Hence the *Sun* heading, WE'VE SAVED IT.

They hadn't, of course. Next day Lever, weakened but game, returned to share with Arnold a ball still red. Between them they had three of Greg Chappell's fellows out within an hour while he batted with ease and calm. Arnold produced a snorter for Walters, pitching about leg-stump and flicking out the off-bail. Looking with some interest for descriptions of this ball I read:

The ball from Arnold which came in on Walters and shattered his wicket was a good one – but, what the heck, Dougie's a great batsman and he was playing in a time of crisis. *Something much better was needed, and expected.*

The last sentence in black type. One could only conclude that in a time of crisis no great batsman has any business getting out, whatever the merit of the ball . . .

At lunch Australia with four wickets, including Chappell's, still standing were only 13 behind. Afterwards Greig, bowling slow, caught and bowled Walker (thereby depriving him of top place in the averages, a distinction that was looking well within his compass) while Lever bowled Greg with a break-back immediately he reached his hundred. So the end was unexpectedly sudden, and England after all did not need to bat again.

Thus England in a significant way at the last opportunity took heartening revenge for four defeats just as Freddie Brown's side had done in 1951 and, in reverse, Australia in 1929. So my last reporting assignment before retirement from the *Daily Telegraph* turned out a happy one, and I ended the final description on this nostalgic note:

My last sight of Melbourne Cricket Ground was an impromptu little gathering on the outfield in front of the banner reading 'MCC Fans Thank Colin – six Tours.' The central figure, wearing a large straw sun-hat, was signing endless autographs, posing for photographs and exchanging friendly talk with young and old in the way that has made him as popular a cricketer as has ever visited Australia.

There being no compulsive urge to return (as we ultimately did, spending a happy week in Bombay and Baroda) Ann and I lingered awhile in Melbourne and Sydney. I was surprised in both places at the number of people, including taxi-drivers and casual acquaintances, who professed delight not so much at England having won the last Test as at Mike Denness having done so much towards the victory. The view seemed unanimous that both the Australian and English press had given him a raw deal. This fortified a long-held view of mine that there is a sense of sportsmanship among followers of games which is sometimes far from reflected in newspapers. I was aiming, of course, to express the contrary philosophy when I began my review of the tour in the *Daily Telegraph* by saying that 'the sixteenth tour of MCC in Australia will only be regarded as a failure by those sad, misguided followers of sport – a small proportion, surely – who equate defeat with dishonour.' Anyone sympathetic to the win-at-all-costs mentality will have discovered long since that this was the wrong book for him.

11

A Sundry or Two

So I come to the end of the road with a feeling of strenuous times well spent, of the good things heavily outnumbering the bad. I look back on a kaleidoscopic background of crowded, clamorous grounds; of official welcomes and strictly unofficial parties of every sort; of endless moves from city to city made as painless as possible by ANA (Ansett Airlines of Australia); of a profusion of fine golf courses, and a variety of populous beaches; of good Anglican churches, fuller than most at home; of the friendly dignity of clubs and Government Houses; of the over-swelling traffic and of countless salty exchanges with taxi-drivers; of a vast country of almost limitless resources awaiting the further pioneering skills of Australian man.

All the eight tours have had their special merits and points of attraction, and there have inevitably been respects in which things might have been ordered a good deal better. England have had the worst of the cricket to the extent of nine Tests won and double the number lost. Perhaps in their own country Australian cricketers would always have the edge over a period, but not necessarily to such a degree as this.

Occasionally England's chances have been jeopardized by inadequacy in the partnership between captain and manager. The selecting has brought forth a few queer picks and some expensive omissions. Remember all those meetings in 1950 with the party emerging in dribs and drabs. It's strange to think that Jim Laker had to wait until he was 36 to be chosen for Australia. It appeared at the time (to me at least) that Ted Dexter should have been chosen originally in 1958 and Tony Greig in 1970: the Australians wouldn't have left such talent at home for fear of bringing it on too quickly. The overloading with fast bowlers was a self-inflicted handicap in 1974/5. But presumably there may be corresponding Australian cases, though with a smaller field of choice the margin of error with them is proportionately less.

I believe the strongest Australian side in the all but thirty years to have been that of 1946/7, with 1962/3 next in quality and 1950/51 somewhere in the running. The feats of Lillee and Thomson bring 1974/5 into contention for a place though no serious critic who has seen both in action could rate them, as some tried to do, with 1946/7. At the end of the last series the *Melbourne Herald* published some articles comparing the Test teams of various eras, leaving the last word with Sir Donald Bradman. As captain of the team in 1946/7 and a selector of the next six he is, of course, in a unique position to arbitrate as between 1946/7 and 1974/5, and he did so in the detached, logical manner one would expect, using the simple, sensible method of writing down the two batting orders side by side and making a man-for-man comparison. Don made the 'score' 9-1 to his side of the late 'forties with one pair balancing out. (Incidentally he also compared England 1948 with England 1975, giving 1948 the verdict $8\frac{1}{2}$-$2\frac{1}{2}$.)

What about the respective merits of Lillee and Thomson on the one hand, Lindwall and Miller on the other? Hear what the Don says:

In this past series Lillee and Thomson were probably, as a pair, the fastest and most lethal opening pair in Australia's history. They possessed remarkable physique, strength and stamina, and ability and (may I add within the confines of diplomacy) a willingness to exploit the short-pitched ball to an extent *which would have unnerved any side*. (My italics.)

But did that make them better than Lindwall and Miller?

For deep understanding of the subtleties of the bowling art, the use of swing, cut, change of pace, etc., Lindwall and Miller would be far more knowledgeable, though I appreciate the finer points play a lesser part in speed than they do in spin. On balance there would be mighty little between the two pairs.

If Australia 1946/7 were the strongest what England side would have the best chance against them? One would have to go for 1954/5, with 1962/3 *proxime accessunt*. What might really be needed would be the England bowling of 1954/5 with the 1962/3 batting, the strongest selection from the two captained by Len Hutton. Some might prefer the only other side to have won a rubber in Australia in the period, that of 1970/71 – but this would be to ignore the crucial point that Australia 1970/71 were surely the weakest side of the eight.

As to individuals, how can one pick and choose amid such a

'Ashes to ashes, dust to dust—if Thomson don't get ya, Lillee must . . .'

Sunday Telegraph, Sydney

45. Epitaph for England 1974/5.

46. Six to Walters, off Willis's last ball of the day, brings up his hundred, made between tea and the close: Perth 1974/5.

The best sides from each country, 1946-75

47. MCC 1954/5 with Commodore Whinfield on the *Orsova*. From left to right.
Back row: McConnon, Tyson, Cowdrey, Graveney, Bedser, Appleyard. *Middle row:*
Simpson, Wilson, Edrich, Evans, May (behind Evans), Commodore Whinfield,
Mr C. G. Howard *(Manager)*, Hutton, Bailey, Duckworth *(Scorer)*. *Front row:* Dalton
(Masseur), Loader, Statham, Andrews, Wardle. (Compton arrived later by air.)

48. Brisbane 1946/7: Australia's first post-war Test side which (apart from Tribe and
Dooland) was identical with the men who quickly established their supremacy.
At the back: Johnson, Miller, Morris, Toshack, Lindwall, Tallon, McCool. Seated:
Dooland, Hassett, Bradman, Barnes, Tribe.

galaxy? England have used 79 men in these eight series, Australia 76 – and of these at least a full thirty can be described according to my personal rating anyway as great cricketers. If one were asked to find a handful to best epitomize the cricketing virtues of their respective countries I could not suggest any names more appropriate than Bradman, Miller, Harvey and Benaud for Australia, Hutton, Bedser, May and Evans for England. But so many have played the part of heroes at one time or another. How many of those whose deeds are enumerated factually in the Appendix that follows have I not applauded back to the pavilion in spirit, and with a lump in the throat? Not actually, of course, since we do not clap or express other outward signs of emotion in the press-box!

Those who have stayed with me to the end may not be surprised if in the light of the evidence of the last two tours I finish on a warning note. Cricket in Australia in many respects is as healthy as it has ever been – perhaps healthier. According to Alan Barnes, secretary of the Australian Cricket Board, there could be as many as half a million practising cricketers – and they normally retire from the game earlier than in England. There have never been so many. Likewise in an age when gates at the popular spectator sports have tended to fall those for cricket are scarcely lower – for Test Matches anyway – than in the peak periods just before and just after the war. The number watching Denness's team over the tour was estimated at around 900,000.

But in these disorderly days the very popularity of the event poses problems, these being much accentuated, as the last two Sydney Tests have illustrated vividly enough, when there are fast bowlers around. Manners both on the cricket field and beyond the boundary will only be a broad reflection of the times in which we live, and the subtleties of cricket are such that its character is dangerously dependent on the old conventions and unwritten laws being observed. If sides are determined to stretch the letter of the law to the uttermost limit, and if the battle is waged with the mouth as well as with bats and balls, with the crowd picking up, as it always does, the atmosphere prevailing in the middle, the conflict is likely to be unedifying, to say the least. One of the biggest differences between the Tests of today and of yesterday and the day before is the modern inter-action between players and crowd. This development reached its most dangerous pitch in Australia in 1974/5. The most explosive place was Sydney where it seemed that an element in the crowd were determined on retribution for the Snow and Illingworth versus Rowan confrontation of four years earlier. Lillee was their willing instrument of revenge, the hostility in the air being something akin, I imagine, to that of the Bodyline series with the vital difference that the popular sections of the crowd were now in favour of the bowlers' assault rather than against it.

On that Sydney Sunday afternoon Australia were the aggressors in word and deed, but I would be far from saying that English behaviour of late has been all it might have been. Taking the last two MCC tours together I dare say the provocation and the misdemeanours may have just about cancelled one another out. The worst aspect of this most publicized face of cricket is the dreadful example it sets to the young who – at least by certain cricketers at some stages – have been shown exactly how not to comport themselves on the cricket field.

With which thoroughly square, reactionary, old-fashioned sentiment let me close in hopes of an improvement in these respects when MCC visit again in 1978/9 – and in final gratitude for the vast pleasure in the continuing saga of England v Australia enjoyed by so many for so long.

Results of all series in Australia 1946-75

	Tests	Won	Lost	Drawn
1946/7	5	0	3	2
1950/1	5	1	4	0
1954/5	5	3	1	1
1958/9	5	0	4	1
1962/3	5	1	1	3
1965/6	5	1	1	3
1970/1	6	2	0	4
1974/5	6	1	4	1
Totals	42	9	18	15

MCC Teams in Australia 1946-75

	1946–7		1950–1		1954–5		1958–9	
CAPTAIN	Hammond	43	Brown	39	Hutton	38	May	28
BATSMEN	Hutton	30	Hutton	34	Graveney	27	Cowdrey	25
	Compton	28	Simpson	30	May	24	May	28
	Edrich	30	Parkhouse	24	Compton	36	Graveney	31
	Washbrook	31	Washbrook	35	Cowdrey	21	Richardson	27
	Hammond	43	Sheppard	21	Hutton	38	Watson	38
	Ikin	28	Compton	32	Edrich	38	Milton	30
	Hardstaff	35	Dewes	23	Simpson	34	(Dexter)	23
	Fishlock	39	Close	19	*Wilson*	21	*Subba Row*	26
ALL-ROUNDERS	Yardley	31	Brown	39	Bailey	30	Bailey	34
	Langridge	40	Bailey	26				
FAST AND MEDIUM	Bedser	28	Bedser	32	Statham	24	Statham	28
	Voce	37	Warr	23	Tyson	24	Trueman	27
	Pollard	34	(Statham)	20	Bedser	36	Tyson	28
					Loader	24	Loader	28
SPINNERS	Smith	38	(Tattersall)	28	Appleyard	30	Laker	36
	Wright	32	Wright	36	Wardle	31	Lock	29
			Hollies	38	*McConnon*	31	(Mortimore)	25
			Berry	24				
WICKET-KEEPERS	Evans	26	Evans	30	Evans	34	Evans	38
	Gibb	33	McIntyre	32	Andrew	24	Swetman	24
MANAGERS	R. Howard		{ Green / Nash		C. G. Howard		Brown / Eager (asst.)	
No. in party	17		19		18		18	
Average Age	33		29		29		29	

Author's Note: Names in italics are of players who did not play in Test Matches.
Names in brackets either arrived late or departed early through injury.

1962–3		1965–6		1970–1		1974–5	
Dexter	27	Smith	32	Illingworth	38	Denness	33
Barrington	31	Barrington	34	Boycott	29	Denness	33
Dexter	27	Cowdrey	32	Edrich	33	Edrich	37
Cowdrey	29	Edrich (J. H.)	28	Luckhurst	31	Amiss	31
Sheppard	33	Boycott	24	D'Oliveira	38	Fletcher	30
Graveney	35	Barber	30	Fletcher	26	Lloyd	27
Parfitt	25	Smith	32	Hampshire	29	Luckhurst	35
Pullar	27	Russell	29	Cowdrey	37	(Cowdrey)	39
		Parfitt	28				
Titmus	29	Titmus	32	Illingworth	38	Greig	27
Knight	24	Knight	27				
Trueman	31	Jones	23	Willis	21	Arnold	30
Statham	32	Brown	23	Lever	30	Hendrick	25
Coldwell	29	Higgs	28	Shuttleworth	25	Lever	34
Larter	22	*Larter*	25	Snow	28	Old	25
				(*Ward*)	23	Willis	25
Illingworth	30	Allen	29	Underwood	25	Titmus	41
Allen	26			Wilson	33	Underwood	29
Smith	25	Parks	33	Knott	24	Knott	28
Murray	27	*Murray*	30	*Taylor*	29	*Taylor*	33
Norfolk		Griffith		Clark		Bedser	
Bedser (asst.)		Ikin (asst.)		Thomas		Smith (asst.)	
17		17		16		17	
28		29		31		31	

Test scores and averages 1946-75

1946/7 First Test, Brisbane

November 29, 30, December 2, 3, 4   Toss: Australia
Result: AUSTRALIA WON BY AN INNINGS AND 332 RUNS

AUSTRALIA

S. G. Barnes, c Bedser b Wright	31
A. R. Morris, c Hammond b Bedser	2
*D. G. Bradman b Edrich	187
A. L. Hassett, c Yardley b Bedser	128
K. R. Miller, lbw b Wright	79
C. L. McCool, lbw b Wright	95
I. W. Johnson, lbw b Wright	47
†D. Tallon, lbw b Edrich	14
R. R. Lindwall, c Voce b Wright	31
G. E. Tribe, c Gibb b Edrich	1
E. R. H. Toshack, not out	1
Extras, (b 5, lb 11, w 2, nb 11)	29
Total	645

FALL OF WICKETS. *First Innings:* 1–9, 2–46, 3–322, 4–428, 5–465, 6–596, 7–599, 8–629, 9–643, 10–645.

ENGLAND

L. Hutton, b Miller	7	c Barnes b Miller	0
C. Washbrook, c Barnes b Miller	6	c Barnes b Miller	13
W. J. Edrich, c McCool b Miller	16	lbw b Toshack	7
D. C. S. Compton, lbw b Miller	17	c Barnes b Toshack	15
*W. R. Hammond, lbw b Toshack	32	b Toshack	23
J. T. Ikin, c Tallon b Miller	0	b Tribe	32
N. W. D. Yardley, c Tallon b Toshack	29	c Hassett b Toshack	0
†P. A. Gibb, b Miller	13	lbw b Toshack	11
W. Voce, not out	1	c Hassett b Tribe	18
A. V. Bedser, lbw b Miller	0	c and b Toshack	18
D. V. P. Wright, c Tallon b Toshack	4	not out	10
Extras, (b 8, lb 3, w 2, nb 3)	16	(b 15, lb 7, w 1, nb 2)	25
Total	141		172

FALL OF WICKETS. *First Innings:* 1–10, 2–25, 3–49, 4–56, 5–56, 6–121, 7–134, 8–136, 9–136, 10–141. *Second Innings:* 1–0, 2–13, 3–33, 4–62, 5–65, 6–65, 7–112, 8–114, 9–143, 10–172.

BOWLING

ENGLAND. *First Innings:* Voce 28, 9, 92, 0; Bedser 41, 5, 159, 2; Wright 43·6, 4, 167, 5; Edrich 25, 2, 107, 3; Yardley 13, 1, 47, 0; Ikin 2, 0, 24, 0; Compton 6, 0, 20, 0.

AUSTRALIA. *First Innings:* Lindwall 12, 4, 23, 0; Miller 22, 4, 60, 7; Toshack 16·5, 11, 17, 3; Tribe 9, 2, 19, 0; McCool 1, 0, 5, 0; Barnes 1, 0, 1, 0. *Second Innings:* Miller 11, 3, 17, 2; Toshack 20·7, 2, 82, 6; Tribe 12, 2, 48, 2.

Umpires: G. Borwick, J. D. Scott

1946/7 Second Test, Sydney

December 13, 14, 16, 17, 18, 19   Toss: England
Result: AUSTRALIA WON BY AN INNINGS AND 33 RUNS

ENGLAND

L. Hutton, c Tallon b Johnson	39	hit wkt b Miller	37
C. Washbrook, b Freer	1	c McCool b Johnson	41
W. J. Edrich, lbw b McCool	71	b McCool	119
D. C. S. Compton, c Tallon b McCool	5	c Bradman b Freer	54
*W. R. Hammond, c Tallon b McCool	1	c Toshack b McCool	37
J. T. Ikin, c Hassett b Johnson	60	b Freer	17
N. W. D. Yardley, c Tallon b Johnson	25	b McCool	35
T. P. B. Smith, lbw b Johnson	4	c Hassett b Johnson	2
†T. G. Evans, b Johnson	5	st Tallon b McCool	9
A. V. Bedser, b Johnson	14	not out	3
D. V. P. Wright, not out	15	c Tallon b McCool	0
Extras, (b 4, lb 11)	15	(b 8, lb 6, w 1, nb 2)	17
Total	255		371

FALL OF WICKETS. *First Innings:* 1–10, 2–88, 3–97, 4–99, 5–148 6–187, 7–197, 8–205, 9–234, 10–255. *Second Innings:* 1–49, 2–118 3–220, 4–280, 5–309, 6–327, 7–346, 8–366, 9–369, 10–371.

AUSTRALIA

S. G. Barnes, c Ikin b Bedser	234
A. R. Morris, b Edrich	5
I. W. Johnson, c Washbrook b Edrich	7
A. L. Hassett, c Compton b Edrich	34
K. R. Miller, c Evans b Smith	40
*D. G. Bradman, lbw b Yardley	234

C. L. McCool, c Hammond b Smith	12
†D. Tallon, c and b Wright	30
F. W. Freer, not out	28
G. E. Tribe, not out	25
E. R. H. Toshack, did not bat	
Extras, (lb 7, w 1, nb 2)	10
Total (8 wkts dec)	659

FALL OF WICKETS. *First Innings:* 1–24, 2–37, 3–96, 4–159, 5–564, 6–564, 7–595, 8–617.

BOWLING

ENGLAND. *First Innings:* Miller 9, 2, 24, 0; Freer 7, 1, 25, 1; Toshack 7, 2, 6, 0; Tribe 20, 3, 70, 0; Johnson 30·1, 12, 42, 6; McCool 23, 2, 73, 3. *Second Innings:* Miller 11, 3, 37, 1; Freer 13, 2, 49, 2; Toshack 6, 1, 16, 0; Tribe 12, 0, 40, 0; Johnson 29, 7, 92, 2; McCool 32·4, 4, 109, 5; Barnes 3, 0, 11, 0.
AUSTRALIA. *First Innings:* Bedser 46, 7, 153, 1; Edrich 26, 3, 79, 3; Wright 46, 8, 169, 1; Smith 37, 1, 172, 2; Ikin 3, 0, 15, 0; Compton 6, 0, 38, 0; Yardley 9, 0, 23, 1.

Umpires: G. Borwick, J. D. Scott

1946/7 Third Test, Melbourne

January 1, 2, 3, 4, 6, 7   Toss: Australia
Result: MATCH DRAWN

AUSTRALIA

S. G. Barnes, lbw b Bedser	45	c Evans b Yardley	32
A. R. Morris, lbw b Bedser	21	b Bedser	155
*D. G. Bradman, b Yardley	79	c and b Yardley	49
A. L. Hassett, c Hammond b Wright	12	b Wright	9
K. R. Miller, c Evans b Wright	33	c Hammond b Yardley	34
I. W. Johnson, lbw b Yardley	0	(7) run out	0
C. L. McCool, not out	104	(6) c Evans b Bedser	43
†D. Tallon, c Evans b Edrich	35	c and b Wright	92
R. R. Lindwall, b Bedser	9	3 Washbrook b Bedser	100
B. Dooland, c Hammond b Edrich	19	c Compton b Wright	1
E. R. H. Toshack, c Hutton b Edrich	6	not out	2
Extras, (nb2)	2	(b 14, lb 2, nb 3)	19
Total	365		536

FALL O F WICKETS. *First Innings:* 1–32, 2–108, 3–143, 4–188, 5–188, 6–192, 7–255, 8–272, 9–355, 10–365. *Second Innings:* 1–68, 2–159, 3–177, 4–242, 5–333, 6–335, 7–341, 8–495, 9–511, 10–536.

ENGLAND

L. Hutton, c McCool b Lindwall	2	c Bradman b Toshack	40
C. Washbrook, c Tallon b Dooland	62	b Dooland	112
W. J. Edrich, lbw b Lindwall	89	lbw b McCool	13
D. C. S. Compton, lbw b Toshack	11	run out	14
*W. R. Hammond, c and b Dooland	9	b Lindwall	26
J. T. Ikin, c Miller b Dooland	48	c Hassett b Miller	5
N. W. D. Yardley, b McCool	61	not out	53
†T. G. Evans, b McCool	17	(9)not out	0
W. Voce, lbw b Dooland	0		
A.V. Bedser, not out	27	(8)lbw b Miller	25
D. V. P. Wright, b Johnson	10		
Extras, (b 1, lb 12, nb 2)	15	(b 15, lb 6, w 1)	22
Total	351	(7 wkts)	310

FALL OF WICKETS. *First Innings:* 1–8, 2–155, 3–167, 4–176, 5–179, 6–292, 7–298, 8–298, 9–324, 10–351. *Second Innings:* 1–138, 2–163, 3–186, 4–197, 5–221, 6–249, 7–294.

BOWLING

ENGLAND. *First Innings:* Voce 10, 2, 40, 0; Bedser 31, 4, 99, 3; Wright 26, 2, 124, 2; Yardley 20, 4, 50, 2; Edrich 10·3, 2, 50, 3. *Second Innings:* Voce 6, 1, 29, 0; Bedser 34·3, 4, 176, 3; Wright 32, 3, 131, 3; Yardley 20, 0, 67, 3; Edrich 18, 1, 86, 0; Hutton 3, 0, 28, 0.

AUSTRALIA. *First Innings:* Lindwall 20, 1, 64, 2; Miller 10, 0, 34, 0; Toshack 26, 5, 88, 1; McCool 19, 3, 53, 2; Dooland 27, 5, 69, 4; Johnson 6·5, 1, 28, 1. *Second Innings:* Lindwall 16, 2, 59, 1; Miller 11, 0, 41, 2; Toshack 16, 5, 39, 1; McCool 24, 9, 41, 1; Dooland 21, 1, 84, 1; Johnson 12, 4, 24, 0.

Umpires: G. Borwick, J. D. Scott

1946/7 Fourth Test, Adelaide

January 31, February 1, 3, 4, 5, 6   Toss: England
Result: MATCH DRAWN

ENGLAND

L. Hutton, lbw b McCool	94	b Johnson	76
C. Washbrook, c Tallon b Dooland	65	c Tallon b Lindwall	39
W. J. Edrich, c and b Dooland	17	c Bradman b Toshack	46
*W. R. Hammond, b Toshack	18	c Lindwall b Toshack	22

D. C. S. Compton, c and b

Lindwall	147	not out	103
J. Hardstaff, b Miller	67	b Toshack	9
J. T. Ikin, c Toshack b Dooland	21	lbw b Toshack	1
N. W. D. Yardley, not out	18	c Tallon b Lindwall	18
A. V. Bedser, b Lindwall	2	c Tallon b Miller	3
†T. G. Evans, b Lindwall	0	not out	10
D. V. P. Wright, b Lindwall	0		
Extras, (b 4, lb 5, w 2)	11	(b 5, lb 3, w 2, nb 3)	13
Total	460	(8 wkts dec)	340

FALL OF WICKETS. *First Innings:* 1–137, 2–173, 3–196, 4–202, 5–320, 6–381, 7–455, 8–460, 9–460, 10–460. *Second Innings:* 1–100, 2–137, 3–178, 4–188, 5–207, 6–215, 7–250, 8–255.

AUSTRALIA

M. R. Harvey, b Bedser	12	b Yardley	31
A. R. Morris, c Evans b Bedser	122	not out	124
*D. G. Bradman, b Bedser	0	not out	56
A. L. Hassett, c Hammond			
b Wright	78		
K. R. Miller, not out	141		
I. W. Johnson, lbw b Wright	52		
C. L. McCool, c Bedser b Yardley	2		
†D. Tallon, b Wright	3		
R. R. Lindwall, c Evans b Yardley	20		
B. Dooland, c Bedser b Yardley	29		
E. R. H. Toshack, run out	0		
Extras, (b 16, lb 6, w 2, nb 4)	28	(lb 2, nb 2)	4
Total	487	(1 wkt)	215

FALL OF WICKETS. *First Innings:* 1–18, 2–18, 3–207, 4–222, 5–372, 6–389, 7–396, 8–423, 9–486, 10–487. *Second Innings:* 1–116.

BOWLING
AUSTRALIA. *First Innings:* Lindwall 23, 5, 52, 4; Miller 16, 0, 45, 1; Toshack 30, 13, 59, 1; McCool 29, 1, 91, 1; Johnson 22, 3, 69, 0; Dooland 33, 1, 133, 3. *Second Innings:* Lindwall 17·1, 4, 60, 2; Miller 11, 0, 34, 1; Toshack 36, 6, 76, 4; McCool 19, 3, 41, 0; Johnson 25, 8, 51, 1; Dooland 17, 2, 65, 0.
ENGLAND. *First Innings:* Bedser 30, 6, 97, 3; Edrich 20, 3, 88, 0; Wright 32·4, 1, 152, 3; Yardley 31, 7, 101, 3; Ikin 2, 0, 9, 0; Compton 3, 0, 12, 0. *Second Innings:* Bedser 15, 1, 68, 0; Edrich 7, 2, 25, 0; Wright 9, 0, 49, 0; Yardley 13, 0, 69, 1.

Umpires: G. Borwick, J. D. Scott

1946/7 Fifth Test, Sydney

February 28, March 1, 3, 4, 5   Toss: England
Result: AUSTRALIA WON BY FIVE WICKETS

ENGLAND

L. Hutton, retired ill	122	absent ill	—
C. Washbrook, b Lindwall	0	b McCool	24
W. J. Edrich, c Tallon b Lindwall	60	st Tallon b McCool	24
L. B. Fishlock, b McCool	14	(1)lbw b Lindwall	0
D. C. S. Compton, hit wkt b Lindwall	17	(4)Miller b Toshack	76
*N. W. D. Yardley, c Miller b Lindwall	2	b McCool	11
J. T. Ikin, b Lindwall	0	(5)st Tallon b McCool	0
†T. G. Evans, b Lindwall	29	(7)b Miller	20
T. P. B. Smith, b Lindwall	2	(8)c Tallon b Lindwall	24
A. V. Bedser, not out	10	(9)st Tallon b McCool	4
D. V. P. Wright, c Tallon b Miller	7	(10)not out	1
Extras, (b 7, lb 8, w 1, nb 1)	17	(b 1, lb 1)	2
Total	280		186

FALL OF WICKETS. *First Innings:* 1–1, 2–151, 3–188, 4–215, 5–225, 6–225, 7–244, 8–269, 9–280. *Second Innings:* 1–0, 2–42, 3–65, 4–65, 5–85, 6–120, 7–157, 8–184, 9–186.

AUSTRALIA

S. G. Barnes, c Evans b Bedser	71	c Evans b Bedser	30
*A. R. Morris, lbw b Bedser	57	run out	17
D. G. Bradman, b Wright	12	c Compton b Bedser	63
A. L. Hassett, c Ikin b Wright	24	c Ikin b Wright	47
K. R. Miller, c Ikin b Wright	23	not out	34
R. A. Hamence, not out	30	c Edrich b Wright	1
C. L. McCool, c Yardley b Wright	3	not out	13
†D. Tallon, c Compton b Wright	0		
R. R. Lindwall, c Smith b Wright	0		
G. E. Tribe, c Fishlock b Wright	9		
E. R. H. Toshack, run out	5		
Extras, (b 7, lb 6, nb 6)	19	(b 4, lb 1, nb 4)	9
Total	253	(5 wkts)	214

FALL OF WICKETS. *First Innings:* 1–126, 2–146, 3–146, 4–187, 5–218, 6–230, 7–230, 8–233, 9–245, 10–253. *Second Innings:* 1–45, 2–51, 3–149, 4–173, 5–180.

BOWLING

AUSTRALIA. *First Innings:* Lindwall 22, 3, 63, 7; Miller 15·3, 2, 3· 1; Tribe 28, 2, 95, 0; Toshack 16, 4, 40, 0; McCool 13, 0, 34, 1. *Second Innings:* Lindwall 12, 1, 46, 2; Miller 6, 1, 11, 1; Tribe 14, 0, 58, 0; Toshack 4, 1, 14, 1; McCool 21·4, 5, 44, 5; Barnes 3, 0, 11, 0.

ENGLAND. *First Innings:* Bedser 27, 7, 49, 2; Edrich 7, 0, 34, 0; Smith 8, 0, 38, 0; Wright 29, 4, 105, 7; Yardley 5, 2, 8, 0; *Second Innings:* Bedser 22, 4, 75, 2; Edrich 2, 0, 14, 0; Smith 2, 0, 8, 0; Wright 22, 1, 93, 2; Yardley 3, 1, 7, 0; Compton 1·2, 0, 8, 0.

Umpires: G. Borwick, J. D. Scott

Averages : 1946/7

AUSTRALIA

BATTING	M.	*Inns.*	N.O.	*Runs*	H.S.	*Av.*
D. G. Bradman	5	8	1	680	234	97·14
K. R. Miller	5	7	2	384	141*	76·80
S. G. Barnes	4	6	0	443	234	73·83
A. R. Morris	5	8	1	503	155	71·85
C. L. McCool	5	7	2	272	104*	54·40
A. L. Hassett	5	7	0	332	128	47·42
R. R. Lindwall	4	5	0	160	100	32·00
D. Tallon	5	6	0	174	92	29·00
I. W. Johnson	4	5	0	106	52	21·20
G. E. Tribe	3	3	1	35	25*	17·50
B. Dooland	2	3	0	49	29	16·33
E. R. H. Toshack	5	5	2	14	6	4·66

PLAYED IN ONE TEST: F. W. Freer 28*, M. R. Harvey 12 and 31, R. A. Hamence 30* and 1.

BOWLING	*Overs*	Mds.	*Runs*	Wkts.	*Av.*
R. R. Lindwall	122·1	20	367	18	20·38
K. R. Miller	122·3	15	334	16	20·87
E. R. H. Toshack	178·4	50	437	17	25·70
C. L. McCool	182	27	491	18	27·27
I. W. Johnson	124·6	35	306	10	30·60
B. Dooland	98	9	351	8	43·87

ALSO BOWLED: F. W. Freer 20–3–74–3, G. E. Tribe 95–9–330–2, S. G. Barnes 7–0–23–0.

ENGLAND

BATTING	M.	Inns.	N.O.	Runs	H.S.	Av.
L. Hutton	5	9	1	417	122*	52·12
D. C. S. Compton	5	10	1	459	147	51·00
W. J. Edrich	5	10	0	462	119	46·20
C. Washbrook	5	10	0	363	112	36·30
N. W. D. Yardley	5	10	2	252	61	31·50
W. R. Hammond	4	8	0	168	37	21·00
J. T. Ikin	5	10	0	184	60	18·40
A. V. Bedser	5	10	3	106	27*	15·14
T. G. Evans	4	8	2	90	29	15·00
W. Voce	2	3	1	19	18	9·50
D. V. P. Wright	5	8	3	47	15*	9·40
T. P. B. Smith	2	4	0	32	24	8·00

PLAYED IN ONE TEST: P. A. Gibb 13 and 11, J. Hardstaff 67 and 9.
L. B. Fishlock 14 and 0.

BOWLING	Overs	Mds.	Runs	Wkts.	Av.
N. W. D. Yardley	114	15	372	10	37·20
D. V. P. Wright	240·2	23	990	23	43·04
W. J. Edrich	115·3	13	483	9	53·66
A. V. Bedser	246·3	38	876	16	54·75

ALSO BOWLED: T. P. B. Smith 47–1–218–2, L. Hutton 3–0–28–0,
J. T. Ikin 7–0–48–0, D. C. S. Compton 16·2–0–78–0, W. Voce 44–12–
161–0.

1950/1 First Test, Brisbane

December 1, 2, 4, 5   Toss: Australia
Result: AUSTRALIA WON BY 70 RUNS

AUSTRALIA

J. A. R. Moroney, c Hutton b Bailey	0	lbw b Bailey	0
A. R. Morris, lbw b Bedser	25	c Bailey b Bedser	0
R. N. Harvey, c Evans b Bedser	74	(6)c Simpson b Bedser	12
K. R. Miller, c McIntyre b Wright	15	(7)c Simpson b Bailey	8
*A. L. Hassett, b Bedser	8	lbw b Bailey	3
S. J. E. Loxton, c Evans b Brown	24	(4)c Bailey b Bedser	0
R. R. Lindwall, c Bedser b Bailey	41	(8)not out	0
†D. Tallon, c Simpson b Brown	5		
I. W. Johnson, c Simpson b Bailey	23	(3)lbw b Bailey	8
W. A. Johnston, c Hutton b Bedser	1		
J. B. Iverson, not out	1		
Extras, (b 5, lb 3, nb 3)	11	(nb 1)	1
Total	228	(7 wkts dec)	32

FALL OF WICKETS. *First Innings:* 1–0, 2–69, 3–116, 4–118, 5–129, 6–156, 7–172, 8–219, 9–226, 10–228. *Second Innings:* 1–0, 2–0, 3–0, 4–12, 5–19, 6–31, 7–32.

ENGLAND

R. T. Simpson, b Johnston	12	b Lindwall	0
C. Washbrook, c Hassett b Johnston	19	c Loxton b Lindwall	6
†T. G. Evans, c Iverson b Johnston	16	(6)c Loxton b Johnston	5
D. C. S. Compton, c Lindwall b Johnston	3	(9)c Loxton b Johnston	0
J. G. Dewes, c Loxton b Miller	1	(3)b Miller	9
L. Hutton, not out	8	(8)not out	62
A. J. W. McIntyre, b Johnston	1	run out	7
*F. R. Brown, c Tallon b Miller	4	(10)c Loxton b Iverson	17
T. E. Bailey, not out	1	(4)c Johnston b Iverson	7
A. V. Bedser		(5)c Harvey b Iverson	0
D. V. P. Wright		c Lindwall b Iverson	2
Extras, (lb 2, nb 1)	3	(b 6, nb 1)	7
Total (7 wkts dec)	68		122

FALL OF WICKETS. *First Innings:* 1–28, 2–49, 3–52, 4–52, 5–56, 6–57, 7–67. *Second Innings:* 1–0, 2–16, 3–22, 4–23, 5–23, 6–30, 7–46, 8–46, 9–77, 10–122.

BOWLING

ENGLAND. *First Innings:* Bailey 12, 4, 28, 3; Bedser 16·5, 4, 45, 4; Wright 16, 0, 81, 1; Brown 11, 0, 63, 2. *Second Innings:* Bailey 7, 2, 22, 4; Bedser 6·5, 2, 9, 3.
AUSTRALIA. *First Innings:* Lindwall 1, 0, 1, 0; Johnston 11, 2, 35, 5; Miller 10, 1, 29, 2. *Second Innings:* Lindwall 7, 3, 21, 2; Johnston 11, 2, 30, 2; Miller 7, 3, 21, 1; Iverson 13, 3, 43, 4.

Umpires: A. N. Barlow, H. Elphinston

1950/1 Second Test, Melbourne

December 22, 23, 26, 27   Toss: Australia
Result: AUSTRALIA WON BY 28 RUNS

AUSTRALIA

K. A. Archer, c Bedser b Bailey	26	c Bailey b Bedser	46
A. R. Morris, c Hutton b Bedser	2	lbw b Wright	18
R. N. Harvey, c Evans b Bedser	42	run out	31
K. R. Miller, lbw b Brown	18	b Bailey	14
*A. L. Hassett, b Bailey	52	c Bailey b Brown	19

S. J. E. Loxton, c Evans b Close	32	c Evans b Brown	2
R. R. Lindwall, lbw b Bailey	8	c Evans b Brown	7
†D. Tallon, not out	7	lbw b Brown	0
I. W. Johnston, c Parkhouse b Bedser	0	c Close b Bedser	23
W. A. Johnston, c Hutton b Bedser	0	b Bailey	6
J. B. Iverson, b Bailey	1	not out	0
Extras, (b 4, lb 2)	6	(b 10, lb 5)	15
Total	194		181

FALL OF WICKETS. *First Innings:* 1–6, 2–67, 3–89, 4–93, 5–177, 6–177, 7–192, 8–193, 9–193, 10–194. *Second Innings:* 1–43, 2–99, 3–100, 4–126, 5–131, 6–151, 7–151, 8–156, 9–181, 10–181.

ENGLAND

R. T. Simpson, c Johnson b Miller	4	b Lindwall	23
C. Washbrook, lbw b Lindwall	21	b Iverson	8
J. G. Dewes, c Miller b Johnston	8	(5)c Harvey b Iverson	5
L. Hutton, c Tallon b Iverson	12	c Lindwall b Johnston	40
W. G. A. Parkhouse, c Hassett b Miller	9	(6)lbw b Johnston	28
D. B. Close, c Loxton b Iverson	0	(7)lbw b Johnston	1
*F. R. Brown, c Johnson b Iverson	62	(8)b Lindwall	8
T. E. Bailey, b Lindwall	12	(3)b Johnson	0
†T. G. Evans, c Johnson b Iverson	49	b Lindwall	2
A. V. Bedser, not out	4	not out	14
D. V. P. Wright, lbw b Johnston	2	lbw b Johnston	2
Extras, (b 8, lb 6)	14	(b 17, lb 2)	19
Total	197		150

FALL OF WICKETS. *First Innings:* 1–11, 2–33, 3–37, 4–54, 5–54, 6–61, 7–126, 8–153, 9–194, 10–197. *Second Innings:* 1–21, 2–22, 3–52, 4–82, 5–92, 6–95, 7–122, 8–124, 9–134, 10–150.

BOWLING

ENGLAND. *First Innings:* Bailey 17·1, 5, 40, 4; Bedser 19, 3, 37, 4; Wright 8, 0, 63, 0; Brown 9, 0, 28, 1; Close 6, 1, 20 1. *Second Innings:* Bailey 15, 3, 47, 2; Bedser 16·3, 2, 43, 2; Wright 9, 0, 42, 1; Brown 12, 2, 26, 4; Close 1, 0, 8, 0.

AUSTRALIA. *First Innings:* Lindwall 13, 2, 46, 2; Miller 13, 0 39, 2; Johnston 9, 1, 28, 2; Iverson 18, 3, 37, 4; Johnson 5, 1, 19, 0; Loxton 4, 1, 14, 0. *Second Innings:* Lindwall 12, 1, 29, 3; Miller 5, 2, 16, 0; Johnston 13·7, 1, 26, 4; Iverson 20, 4, 36, 2; Johnson 13, 3, 24, 1.

Umpires: G. C. Cooper, R. Wright

1950/1 Third Test, Sydney

January 5, 6, 8, 9   Toss: England
Result: AUSTRALIA WON BY AN INNINGS AND 13 RUNS

ENGLAND

L. Hutton, lbw b Miller	62	c Tallon b Iverson	9
C. Washbrook, c Miller b Johnson	18	b Iverson	34
R. T. Simpson, c Loxton b Miller	49	c Tallon b Iverson	0
D. C. S. Compton, b Miller	0	c Johnson b Johnston	23
W. G. A. Parkhouse, c Morris b Johnson	25	run out	15
*F. R. Brown, b Lindwall	79	b Iverson	18
T. E. Bailey, c Tallon b Johnson	15	(8)not out	0
†T. G. Evans, not out	23	(7)b Johnson	14
A. V. Bedser, b Lindwall	3	b Iverson	4
J. J. Warr, b Miller	4	b Iverson	0
D. V. P. Wright, run out	0	absent hurt	—
Extras, (lb 10, nb 2)	12	(b 1, lb 5)	6
Total	290		123

FALL OF WICKETS. *First Innings:* 1–34, 2–128, 3–128, 4–137, 5–187, 6–258, 7–267, 8–281, 9–286, 10–290. *Second Innings:* 1–32, 2–40, 3–45, 4–74, 5–91, 6–119, 7–119, 8–123, 9–123.

AUSTRALIA

K. A. Archer, c Evans b Bedser	48
A. R. Morris, b Bedser	0
*A. L. Hassett, c Bedser b Brown	70
R. N. Harvey, b Bedser	39
K. R. Miller, not out	145
S. J. E. Loxton, c Bedser b Brown	17
†D. Tallon, lbw b Bedser	18
I. W. Johnson, b Brown	77
R. R. Lindwall, lbw b Brown	1
W. A. Johnston, run out	0
J. B. Iverson, run out	1
Extras, (b 3, lb 7)	10
Total	426

FALL OF WICKETS. *First Innings:* 1–1, 2–122, 3–122, 4–190, 5–223, 6–252, 7–402, 8–406, 9–418, 10–426.

BOWLING

AUSTRALIA. *First Innings:* Lindwall 16, 0, 60, 2; Miller 15·7, 4, 37, 4; Johnson 31, 8, 94, 3; Johnston 21, 5, 50, 0; Iverson 10, 1, 25, 0; Loxton 5, 0, 12, 0. *Second Innings:* Lindwall 4, 1, 12 0; Miller 6, 2, 15, 0; Johnson 10, 2, 32, 1; Johnston 13, 6, 31, 1; Iverson 19·4, 8, 27, 6.
ENGLAND. *First Innings:* Bedser 43, 4, 107, 4; Warr 36, 4, 142, 0; Brown 44, 4, 153, 4; Compton 6, 1, 14, 0.

Umpires: A. N. Barlow, H. Elphinston

1950/1 Fourth Test, Adelaide

February 2, 3, 5, 6, 7, 8   Toss: Australia
Result: AUSTRALIA WON BY 274 RUNS

AUSTRALIA

K. A. Archer, c Compton b Bedser	0	c Bedser b Tattersall	32
A. R. Morris, b Tattersall	206	run out	16
*A. L. Hassett, c Evans b Wright	43	lbw b Wright	31
R. N. Harvey, b Bedser	43	b Brown	68
K. R. Miller, c Brown b Wright	44	b Wright	99
J. W. Burke, b Tattersall	12	not out	101
I. W. Johnson, c Evans b Bedser	16	c Evans b Warr	3
R. R. Lindwall, lbw b Wright	1	run out	31
†D. Tallon, b Tattersall	1	c Hutton b Compton	5
W. A. Johnston, c Hutton b Wright	0	not out	9
J. B. Iverson, not out	0		
Extras, (b 2, lb 1, w 1, nb 1)	5	(b 7, lb 1)	8
Total	371	(8 wkts dec)	403

FALL OF WICKETS. *First Innings:* 1–0, 2–95, 3–205, 4–281, 5–310, 6–357, 7–363, 8–366, 9–367, 10–371. *Second Innings:* 1–26, 2–79, 3–95, 4–194, 5–281, 6–297, 7–367, 8–378.

ENGLAND

L. Hutton, not out	156	c sub (S. J. E. Loxton) b Johnston	45
C. Washbrook, c Iverson b Lindwall	2	lbw b Johnston	31
R. T. Simpson, b Johnston	29	c Burke b Johnston	61
D. C. S. Compton, c Tallon b Lindwall	5	c sub (S. J. E. Loxton) b Johnston	0
D. S. Sheppard, b Iverson	9	lbw b Miller	41
*F. R. Brown, b Miller	16	absent hurt	—
†T. G. Evans, c Burke b Johnston	13	(6)c Johnson b Miller	21
A. V. Bedser, lbw b Iverson	7	(7)c Morris b Miller	0
R. Tattersall, c Harvey b Iverson	0	(8)c Morris b Johnson	6

J. J. Warr, b Johnston	0	(9)b Johnson	0
D. V. P. Wright, lbw b Lindwall	14	(10)not out	0
Extras, (b 15, lb 5, nb 1)	21	(b 15, lb 3, w 2, nb 3)	23
Total	272		228

FALL OF WICKETS. *First Innings:* 1–7, 2–80, 3–96, 4–132, 5–161, 6–195, 7–206, 8–214, 9–219, 10–272. *Second Innings:* 1–74, 2–90, 3–90, 4–181, 5–221, 6–221, 7–228, 8–228, 9–228.

BOWLING
ENGLAND. *First Innings:* Bedser 26, 4, 74, 3; Warr 16, 2, 63, 0; Wright 25, 1, 99, 4; Tattersall 25·5, 5, 95, 3; Brown 3, 0, 24, 0; Compton 1, 0, 11, 0. *Second Innings:* Bedser 25, 6, 62, 0; Warr 21, 0, 76, 1; Wright 21, 2, 109, 2; Tattersall 27, 2, 116, 1; Brown 3, 1, 14, 1; Compton 4·6, 1, 18, 1. AUSTRALIA. *First Innings:* Lindwall 13·3, 0, 51, 3; Miller 13, 2, 36, 1; Johnson 15, 2, 38, 0; Iverson 26, 4, 68, 3; Johnston 25, 4, 58, 3. *Second Innings:* Lindwall 10, 2, 35, 0; Miller 13, 4, 27, 3; Johnson 25·6, 6, 63, 2; Johnston 27, 4, 73, 4; Burke 3, 1, 7, 0.

Umpires: A. N. Barlow, A. F. Cocks

1950/1 Fifth Test, Melbourne

February 23, 24, 26, 27, 28   Toss: Australia
Result: ENGLAND WON BY EIGHT WICKETS

AUSTRALIA

J. W. Burke, c Tattersall b Bedser	11	c Hutton b Bedser	1
A. R. Morris, lbw b Brown	50	lbw b Bedser	4
*A. L. Hassett, c Hutton b Brown	92	b Wright	48
R. N. Harvey, c Evans b Brown	1	lbw b Wright	52
K. R. Miller, c and b Brown	7	c and b Brown	0
G. B. Hole, b Bedser	18	b Bailey	63
I. W. Johnson, lbw b Bedser	1	c Brown b Wright	0
R. R. Lindwall, c Compton b Bedser	21	b Bedser	14
†D. Tallon, c Hutton b Bedser	1	not out	2
W. A. Johnston, not out	12	b Bedser	1
J. B. Iverson, c Washbrook b Brown	0	c Compton b Bedser	0
Extras, (b 2, lb 1)	3	(b 2, lb 8, w 1, nb 1)	12
Total	217		197

FALL OF WICKETS. *First Innings:* 1–23, 2–111, 3–115, 4–123, 5–156, 6–166, 7–184, 8–187, 9–216, 10–217. *Second Innings:* 1–5, 2–6, 3–87, 4–89, 5–142, 6–142, 7–192, 8–196, 9–197, 10–197.

ENGLAND

L. Hutton, b Hole	79	not out	60
C. Washbrook, c Tallon b Miller	27	c Lindwall b Johnston	7
R. T. Simpson, not out	156	run out	15
D. C. S. Compton, c Miller b Lindwall	11	not out	11
D. S. Sheppard, c Tallon b Miller	1		
*F. R. Brown, b Lindwall	6		
†T. G. Evans, b Miller	1		
A. V. Bedser, b Lindwall	11		
T. E. Bailey, c Johnson b Iverson	5		
D. V. P. Wright, lbw b Iverson	3		
R. Tattersall, b Miller	10		
Extras, (b 9, lb 1)	10	(lb 2)	2
Total	320	(2 wkts)	95

FALL OF WICKETS. *First Innings:* 1–40, 2–171, 3–204, 4–205, 5–212, 6–213, 7–228, 8–236, 9–246, 10–320. *Second Innings:* 1–32, 2–62.

BOWLING

ENGLAND. *First Innings:* Bedser 22, 5, 46, 5; Bailey 9, 1, 29, 0; Brown 18, 4, 49, 5; Wright 9, 1, 50, 0; Tattersall 11, 3, 40 0. *Second Innings:* Bedser 20·3, 4, 59, 5; Bailey 15, 3, 32, 1; Brown 9, 1, 32, 1; Wright 15, 2, 56, 3; Tattersall 5, 2, 6, 0.

AUSTRALIA. *First Innings:* Lindwall 21, 1, 77, 3; Miller 21·7, 5, 76, 4; Johnston 12, 1, 55, 0; Iverson 20, 4, 52, 2; Johnson 11, 1, 40, 0; Hole 5, 0, 10, 1. *Second Innings:* Lindwall 2, 0, 12, 0; Miller 2, 0, 5, 0; Johnston 11, 3, 36, 1; Iverson 12, 2, 32 0; Johnson 1, 0, 1, 0; Hole 1, 0, 3, 0; Hassett 0·6, 0, 4, 0.

Umpires: A. N. Barlow, H. Elphinston

Averages: 1950/1

AUSTRALIA

BATTING	M.	*Inns.*	N.O.	*Runs*	H.S.	*Av.*
K. R. Miller	5	9	1	350	145*	43·75
J. W. Burke	2	4	1	125	101*	41·66
A. L. Hassett	5	9	0	366	92	40·66
R. N. Harvey	5	9	0	362	74	40·22
A. R. Morris	5	9	0	321	206	35·66
K. A. Archer	3	5	0	152	48	30·40
I. W. Johnson	5	9	0	151	77	16·77
R. R. Lindwall	5	9	1	124	41	15·50
S. J. E. Loxton	3	5	0	75	32	15·00
D. Tallon	5	8	2	39	18	6·50

BATTING	M.	Inns.	N.O.	Runs	H.S.	Av.
W. A. Johns	5	8	2	29	12*	4·83
J. B. Iverson	5	7	3	3	1*	0·75

PLAYED IN ONE TEST: J. A. R. Moroney 0 and 0, G. B. Hole 18 and 63.

BOWLING	Over	Mds.	Runs	Wkts.	Av.
J. B. Iverson	138·4	29	320	21	15·23
K. R. Miller	106·6	23	301	17	17·70
W. A. Johnston	153·7	29	422	22	19·18
R. R. Lindwall	99·3	10	344	15	22·93
I. W. Johnson	111·6	23	311	7	44·42

ALSO BOWLED: S. J. E. Loxton 9–1–26–0, J. W. Burke 3–1–7–0, G. B. Hole 6–0–13–1, A. L. Hassett 0·6–0–4–0.

ENGLAND

BATTING	M.	Inns.	N.O.	Runs	H.S.	Av.
L. Hutton	5	10	4	533	156*	88·83
R. T. Simpson	5	10	1	349	156*	38·77
F. R. Brown	5	8	0	210	79	26·25
W. G. A. Parkhouse	2	4	0	77	28	19·25
T. G. Evans	5	9	1	144	49	18·00
C. Washbrook	5	10	0	173	34	17·30
D. S. Sheppard	2	3	0	51	41	17·00
T. E. Bailey	4	7	2	40	15	8·00
D. C. S. Compton	4	8	1	53	23	7·57
A. V. Bedser	5	8	2	43	14*	7·16
J. G. Dewes	2	4	0	23	9	5·75
R. Tattersall	2	3	0	16	10	5·33
D. V. P. Wright	5	7	1	23	14	3·83
J. J. Warr	2	4	0	4	4	1·00

PLAYED IN ONE TEST: D. B. Close 0 and 1, A. J. W. McIntyre 1 and 7.

BOWLING	Overs	Mds.	Runs	Wkts.	Av.
T. E. Bailey	75·1	18	198	14	14·14
A. V. Bedser	195	34	482	30	16·06
F. R. Brown	109	12	389	18	21·61
D. V. P. Wright	103	6	500	11	45·45

ALSO BOWLED: R. Tattersall 68·5–12–257–4, J. J. Warr 73–6–281–1, D. B. Close 7 1 28 1, D. C. S. Compton 11·6–2–43–1.

1954/5 First Test, Brisbane

November 26, 27, 29, 30, December 1   Toss: England
Result: AUSTRALIA WON BY AN INNINGS AND 154 RUNS

AUSTRALIA

L. E. Favell, c Cowdrey b Statham	23
A. R. Morris, c Cowdrey b Bailey	153
K. R. Miller, b Bailey	49
R. N. Harvey, c Bailey b Bedser	162
G. B. Hole, run out	57
R. Benaud, c May b Tyson	34
R. G. Archer, c Bedser b Statham	0
R. R. Lindwall, not out	64
†G. R. A. Langley, b Bailey	16
*I. W. Johnson, not out	24
W. A. Johnston, did not bat	
Extras, (b 11, lb 7, nb 1)	19
Total (8 wkts dec)	601

FALL OF WICKETS. *First Innings:* 1–51, 2–123, 3–325, 4–456, 5–463, 6–464, 7–545, 8–572.

ENGLAND

*L. Hutton, c Langley b Lindwall	4	lbw b Miller	13
R. T. Simpson, b Miller	2	run out	9
W. J. Edrich, c Langley b Archer	15	b Johnston	88
P. B. H. May, b Lindwall	1	lbw b Lindwall	44
M. C. Cowdrey, c Hole b Johnston	40	b Benaud	10
T. E. Bailey, b Johnston	88	c Langley b Lindwall	23
F. H. Tyson, b Johnson	7	not out	37
A. V. Bedser, b Johnson	5	c Archer b Johnson	5
†K. V. Andrew, b Lindwall	6	b Johnson	5
J. B. Statham, b Johnson	11	(11)c Harvey b Benaud	14
D. C. S. Compton, not out	2	(10)c Langley b Benaud	0
Extras, (b 3, lb 6)	9	(b 7, lb 2)	9
Total	190		257

FALL OF WICKETS. *First Innings:* 1–4, 2–10, 3–11, 4–25, 5–107, 6–132, 7–141, 8–156, 9–181, 10–190. *Second Innings:* 1–22, 2–23, 3–147, 4–163, 5–181, 6–220, 7–231, 8–242, 9–243, 10–257.

BOWLING

ENGLAND. *First Innings:* Bedser 37, 4, 131, 1; Statham 34, 2, 123, 2; Tyson 29, 1, 160, 1; Bailey 26, 1, 140, 3; Edrich 3, 0, 28, 0.

AUSTRALIA. *First Innings:* Lindwall 14, 4, 27, 3; Miller 11, 5, 19, 1; Archer 4, 1, 14, 1; Johnson 19, 5, 46, 3; Benaud 12, 5, 28, 0; Johnston 16·1, 5, 47, 2. *Second Innings:* Lindwall 17, 3, 50, 2; Miller 12, 2, 30, 1; Archer 15, 4, 28, 0; Johnson 17, 5, 38, 2; Benaud 8·1, 1, 43, 3; Johnston 21, 8, 59, 1.

Umpires: M. J. McInnes, C. Hoy

1954/5 Second Test, Sydney

December 17, 18, 20, 21, 22   Toss: Australia
Result: ENGLAND WON BY 38 RUNS

ENGLAND

*L. Hutton, c Davidson b Johnston	30	c Benaud b Johnston	28
T. E. Bailey, b Lindwall	0	c Langley b Archer	6
P. B. H. May, c Johnston b Archer	5	b Lindwall	104
T. W. Graveney, c Favell b Johnston	21	c Langley b Johnston	0
M. C. Cowdrey, c Langley b Davidson	23	c Archer b Benaud	54
W. J. Edrich, c Benaud b Archer	10	b Archer	29
F. H. Tyson, b Lindwall	0	b Lindwall	9
†T. G. Evans, c Langley b Archer	3	c Lindwall b Archer	4
J. H. Wardle, c Burke b Johnston	35	lbw b Lindwall	8
R. Appleyard, c Hole b Davidson	8	not out	19
J. B. Statham, not out	14	c Langley b Johnston	25
Extras, (lb 5)	5	(lb 6, nb 4)	10
Total	154		296

FALL OF WICKETS. *First Innings:* 1–14, 2–19, 3–58, 4–63, 5–84, 6–85, 7–88, 8–99, 9–111, 10–154. *Second Innings:* 1–18, 2–55, 3–55, 4–171, 5–222, 6–232, 7–239, 8–249, 9–250, 10–296.

AUSTRALIA

L. E. Favell, c Graveney b Bailey	26	c Edrich b Tyson	16
*A. R. Morris, c Hutton b Bailey	12	lbw b Statham	10
J. W. Burke, c Graveney b Bailey	44	b Tyson	14
R. N. Harvey, c Cowdrey b Tyson	12	not out	92
G. B. Hole, b Tyson	12	b Tyson	0
R. Benaud, lbw b Statham	20	c Tyson b Appleyard	12
R. G. Archer, c Hutton b Tyson	49	b Tyson	6
A. K. Davidson, b Statham	20	c Evans b Statham	5
R. R. Lindwall, c Evans b Tyson	19	b Tyson	8
†G. R. A. Langley, b Bailey	5	b Statham	0
W. A. Johnston, not out	0	c Evans b Tyson	11
Extras, (b 5, lb 2, nb 2)	9	(lb 7, nb 3)	10
Total	228		184

178

FALL OF WICKETS. *First Innings:* 1-18, 2-65, 3-100, 4-104, 5-122, 6-141, 7-193, 8-213, 9-224, 10-228. *Second Innings:* 1-27, 2-34, 3-77, 4-77, 5-102, 6-122, 7-127, 8-136, 9-145, 10-184.

BOWLING
AUSTRALIA. *First Innings:* Lindwall 17, 3, 47, 2; Archer 12, 7, 12, 3; Davidson 12, 3, 34, 2; Johnston 13·3, 1, 56, 3. *Second Innings:* Lindwall 31, 10, 69, 3; Archer 22, 9, 53, 3; Davidson 13, 2, 52, 0; Johnston 19·3, 2, 70, 3; Benaud 19, 3, 42, 1.
ENGLAND. *First Innings:* Statham 18, 1, 83, 2; Bailey 17·4, 3, 59, 4; Tyson 13, 2, 45, 4; Appleyard 7, 1, 32, 0. *Second Innings:* Statham 19, 6, 45, 3; Bailey 6, 0, 21, 0; Tyson 18·4, 1, 85, 6; Appleyard 6, 1, 12, 1; Wardle 4, 2, 11, 0.

Umpires: M. J. McInnes, R. Wright

1954/5 Third Test, Melbourne

December 31, January 1, 3, 4, 5   Toss: England
Result: ENGLAND WON BY 128 RUNS

ENGLAND

*L. Hutton, c Hole b Miller	12	lbw b Archer	42
W. J. Edrich, c Lindwall b Miller	4	b Johnston	13
P. B. H. May, c Benaud b Lindwall	0	b Johnston	91
M. C. Cowdrey, b Johnson	102	b Benaud	7
D. C. S. Compton, c Harvey b Miller	4	c Maddocks b Archer	23
T. E. Bailey, c Maddocks b Johnston	30	not out	24
†T. G. Evans, lbw b Archer	20	c Maddocks b Miller	22
J. H. Wardle, b Archer	0	b Johnson	38
F. H. Tyson, b Archer	6	c Harvey b Johnston	6
J. B. Statham, b Archer	3	c Favell b Johnston	0
R. Appleyard, not out	1	b Johnston	6
Extras, (b 9)	9	(b 2, lb 4, w 1)	7
Total	191		279

FALL OF WICKETS. *First Innings:* 1-14, 2-21, 3-29, 4-41, 5-115, 6-169, 7-181, 8-181, 9-190, 10-191. *Second Innings:* 1-40, 2-96, 3-128, 4-173, 5-185, 6-211, 7-257, 8-273, 9-273, 10-279.

AUSTRALIA

L. E. Favell, lbw b Statham	25	b Appleyard	30
A. R. Morris, lbw b Tyson	3	c Cowdrey b Tyson	4
K. R. Miller, c Evans b Statham	7	(5)c Edrich b Tyson	6
R. N. Harvey, b Appleyard	31	c Evans b Tyson	11
G. B. Hole, b Tyson	11	(6)c Evans b Statham	5
R. Benaud, c sub (J. V. Wilson) b Appleyard	15	(3)b Tyson	22
R. G. Archer, b Wardle	23	b Statham	15
†L. V. Maddocks, c Evans b Statham	47	b Tyson	0
R. R. Lindwall, b Statham	13	lbw b Tyson	0
*I. W. Johnson, not out	33	not out	4
W. A. Johnston, b Statham	11	c Evans b Tyson	0
Extras, (b 7, lb 3, nb 2)	12	(b 1, lb 13)	14
Total	231		111

FALL OF WICKETS. *First Innings:* 1–15, 2–38, 3–43, 4–65, 5–92, 6–115, 7–134, 8–151, 9–205, 10–231. *Second Innings:* 1–23, 2–57, 3–77, 4–86, 5–87, 6–97, 7–98, 8–98, 9–110, 10–111.

BOWLING

AUSTRALIA. *First Innings:* Lindwall 13, 0, 59, 1; Miller 11, 8, 14, 3; Archer 13·6, 4, 33, 4; Benaud 7, 0, 30, 0; Johnston 12, 6, 26, 1; Johnson 11, 3, 20, 1. *Second Innings:* Lindwall 18, 3, 52, 0; Miller 18, 6, 35, 1; Archer 24, 7, 50, 2; Benaud 8, 2, 25, 1; Johnston 24·5, 2, 85, 5; Johnson 8, 2, 25, 1.

ENGLAND. *First Innings:* Tyson 21, 2, 68, 2; Statham 16·3, 0, 60, 5; Bailey 9, 1, 33, 0; Appleyard 11, 3, 38, 2; Wardle 6, 0, 20, 1. *Second Innings:* Tyson 12·3, 1, 27, 7; Statham 11, 1, 38, 2; Bailey 3, 0, 14, 0; Appleyard 4, 1, 17, 1; Wardle 1, 0, 1, 0.

Umpires: M. J. McInnes, C. Hoy

1954/5 Fourth Test, Adelaide

January 28, 29, 31, February 1, 2   Toss: Australia
Result: ENGLAND WON BY FIVE WICKETS

AUSTRALIA

C. C. McDonald, c May b Appleyard	48	b Statham	29
A. R. Morris, c Evans b Tyson	25	c and b Appleyard	16
J. W. Burke, c May b Tyson	18	b Appleyard	5
R. N. Harvey, c Edrich b Bailey	25	b Appleyard	7
K. R. Miller, c Bailey b Appleyard	44	b Statham	14
R. Benaud, c May b Appleyard	15	(7)lbw b Tyson	1

†L. V. Maddocks, run out	69	(6)lbw b Statham	2
R. G. Archer, c May b Tyson	21	c Evans b Tyson	3
A. K. Davidson, c Evans b Bailey	5	lbw b Wardle	23
*I. W. Johnson, c Statham b Bailey	41	(11)not out	3
W. A. Johnston, not out	0	(10)c Appleyard b Tyson	3
Extras, (b 3, lb 7, nb 2)	12	(b 4, lb 1)	5
Total	323		111

FALL OF WICKETS. *First Innings:* 1–59, 2–86, 3–115, 4–129, 5–175, 6–182, 7–212, 8–229, 9–321, 10–323. *Second Innings:* 1–24, 2–40, 3–54, 4–69, 5–76, 6–77, 7–79, 8–83, 9–101, 10–111.

ENGLAND

*L. Hutton, c Davidson b Johnston	80	c Davidson b Miller	5
W. J. Edrich, b Johnson	21	b Miller	0
P. B. H. May, c Archer b Benaud	1	c Miller b Johnston	26
M. C. Cowdrey, c Maddocks b Davidson	79	c Archer b Miller	4
D. C. S. Compton, lbw b Miller	44	not out	34
T. E. Bailey, c Davidson b Johnston	38	lbw b Johnston	15
†T. G. Evans, c Maddocks b Benaud	37	not out	6
J. H. Wardle, c and b Johnson	23		
F. H. Tyson, c Burke b Benaud	1		
R. Appleyard, not out	10		
J. B. Statham, c Maddocks b Benaud	0		
Extras, (b 1, lb 2, nb 4)	7	(b 3, lb 4)	7
Total	341	(5 wkts)	97

FALL OF WICKETS. *First Innings:* 1–60, 2–63, 3–162, 4–232, 5–232, 6–283, 7–321, 8–323, 9–336, 10–341. *Second Innings:* 1–3, 2–10, 3–18, 4–49, 5–90.

BOWLING

ENGLAND. *First Innings:* Tyson 26·1, 4, 85, 3; Statham 19, 4, 70, 0; Bailey 12, 3, 39, 3; Appleyard 23, 7, 58, 3; Wardle 19, 5, 59, 0. *Second Innings:* Tyson 15, 2, 47, 3; Statham 12, 1, 38, 3; Appleyard 12, 7, 13, 3; Wardle 4·2, 1, 8, 1.

AUSTRALIA. *First Innings:* Miller 11, 3, 34, 1; Archer 3, 0, 12, 0; Johnson 36, 17, 46, 2; Davidson 25, 8, 55, 1; Johnston 27, 11, 60, 2; Benaud 36·6, 6, 120, 4; Burke 2, 0, 7, 0. *Second Innings:* Miller 10·4, 2, 40, 3; Archer 4, 0, 13, 0; Davidson 2, 0, 7, 0; Johnston 8, 2, 20, 2; Benaud 6, 2, 10, 0.

Umpires: M. J. McInnes, R. Wright

1954/5 Fifth Test, Sydney

February 25, 26, 28, March 1, 2, 3   Toss: Australia
Result: MATCH DRAWN

ENGLAND

*L. Hutton, c Burge b Lindwall	6
T. W. Graveney, c and b Johnson	111
P. B. H. May, c Davidson b Benaud	79
M. C. Cowdrey, c Maddocks b Johnson	0
D. C. S. Compton, c and b Johnson	84
T. E. Bailey, b Lindwall	72
†T. G. Evans, c McDonald b Lindwall	10
J. H. Wardle, not out	5
F. H. Tyson ⎫	
R. Appleyard ⎬ did not bat	
J. B. Statham ⎭	
Extras, (b 1, lb 3)	4
Total (7 wkts dec)	371

FALL OF WICKETS. *First Innings:* 1–6, 2–188, 3–188, 4–196, 5–330, 6–359, 7–371.

AUSTRALIA

W. Watson, b Wardle	18	c Graveney b Statham	3
C. C. McDonald, c May b Appleyard	72	c Evans b Graveney	37
L. E. Favell, b Tyson	1	c Graveney b Wardle	9
R. N. Harvey, c and b Tyson	13	c and b Wardle	1
K. R. Miller, run out	19	b Wardle	28
P. J. Burge, c Appleyard b Wardle	17	not out	18
R. Benaud, b Wardle	7	b Hutton	22
†L. V. Maddocks, c Appleyard b Wardle	32		
A. K. Davidson, c Evans b Wardle	18		
*I. W. Johnson, run out	11		
R. R. Lindwall, not out	2		
Extras, (b 10, lb 1)	11		
Total	221	(6 wkts)	118

FALL OF WICKETS. *First Innings:* 1–52, 2–53, 3–85, 4–129, 5–138, 6–147, 7–157, 8–202, 9–217, 10–221. *Second Innings:* 1–14, 2–27, 3–29, 4–67, 5–87, 6–118.

BOWLING

AUSTRALIA. *First Innings:* Lindwall 20·6, 5, 77, 3; Miller 15, 1, 71, 0; Davidson 19, 3, 72, 0; Johnson 20, 5, 68, 3; Benaud 20, 4, 79, 1.
ENGLAND. *First Innings:* Tyson 11, 1, 46, 2; Statham 9, 1, 31, 0; Appleyard 16, 2, 54, 1; Wardle 24·4, 6, 79, 5. *Second Innings:* Tyson 5, 2, 20, 0; Statham 5, 0, 11, 1; Wardle 12, 1, 51, 3; Graveney 6, 0, 34, 1; Hutton 0·6, 0, 2, 1.

Umpires: M. J. McInnes, R. Wright

Averages : 1954/5

AUSTRALIA

BATTING	M.	Inns.	N.O.	Runs	H.S.	Av.
I. W. Johnson	4	6	4	116	41	58·00
C. C. McDonald	2	4	0	186	72	46·50
R. N. Harvey	5	9	1	354	162	44·25
A. R. Morris	4	7	0	223	153	31·85
L. V. Maddocks	3	5	0	150	69	30·00
R. R. Lindwall	4	6	2	106	64*	26·50
K. R. Miller	4	7	0	167	49	23·85
J. W. Burke	2	4	0	81	44	20·35
L. E. Favell	4	7	0	130	30	18·57
G. B. Hole	3	5	0	85	57	17·00
R. G. Archer	4	7	0	117	49	16·71
R. Benaud	5	9	0	148	34	16·44
A. K. Davidson	3	5	0	71	23	14·20
G. R. A. Langley	2	3	0	21	16	7·00
W. A. Johnston	4	6	2	25	11	6·25

PLAYED IN ONE TEST: W. Watson 18 and 3, P. J. Burge 17 and 18*.

BOWLING	Overs	Mds.	Runs	Wkts.	Av.
R. G. Archer	97·6	32	215	13	16·53
I. W. Johnson	111	37	243	12	20·25
W. A. Johnston	141·4	37	423	19	22·26
K. R. Miller	88·4	27	243	10	24·30
R. R. Lindwall	130·6	28	381	14	27·21
R. Benaud	116·7	23	377	10	37·70

ALSO BOWLED: A. K. Davidson 71–16–220–3, J. W. Burke 2–0–7–0.

ENGLAND

BATTING	M.	Inns.	N.O.	Runs	H.S.	Av.
T. W. Graveney	2	3	0	132	111	44·00
P. B. H. May	5	9	0	351	104	39·00
D. C. S. Compton	4	7	2	191	84	38·20
T. E. Bailey	5	9	1	296	88	37·00

BATTING	M.	*Inns.*	N.O.	*Runs*	H.S.	*Av.*
M. C. Cowdrey	5	9	0	319	102	35·44
L. Hutton	5	9	0	220	80	24·44
W. J. Edrich	4	8	0	180	83	22·50
R. Appleyard	4	5	3	44	19*	22·00
J. H. Wardle	4	6	1	109	38	21·80
T. G. Evans	4	7	1	102	37	17·00
J. B. Statham	5	7	1	67	25	11·16
F. H. Tyson	5	7	1	66	37*	11·00

PLAYED IN ONE TEST: R. T. Simpson 2 and 9, K. V. Andrew 6 and 5, A. V. Bedser 5 and 5.

BOWLING	*Overs*	*Mds.*	*Runs*	*Wkts.*	*Av.*
R. Appleyard	79	22	224	11	20·36
F. H. Tyson	151	16	583	28	20·82
J. H. Wardle	70·6	15	229	10	22·90
J. B. Statham	143·3	16	499	18	27·72
T. E. Bailey	73·4	8	306	10	30·60

ALSO BOWLED: A. V. Bedser 37–4–131–1, W. J. Edrich 3–0–28–0, T. W. Graveney 6–0–34–1, L. Hutton 0·6–0–2–1.

1958/9 First Test, Brisbane

December 5, 6, 8, 9, 10   Toss: England
Result: AUSTRALIA WON BY EIGHT WICKETS

ENGLAND

P. E. Richardson, c Mackay b Davidson	11	c and b Benaud	8
C. A. Milton, b Meckiff	5	c Grout b Davidson	17
T. W. Graveney, c Grout b Davidson	19	(4)run out	36
*P. B. H. May, c Grout b Meckiff	26	(5)lbw b Benaud	4
M. C. Cowdrey, c Kline b Meckiff	13	(6)c Kline b Meckiff	28
T. E. Bailey, st Grout b Benaud	27	(3)b Mackay	68
†T. G. Evans, c Burge b Davidson	4	lbw b Davidson	4
G. A. R. Lock, c Davidson b Benaud	5	b Meckiff	1
J. C. Laker, c Burke b Benaud	13	b Benaud	15
J. B. Statham, c Grout b Mackay	2	c McDonald b Benaud	3
P. J. Loader, not out	6	not out	0
Extras, (lb 1, w 1, nb 1)	3	(b 10, lb 4)	14
Total	134		198

FALL OF WICKETS. *First Innings:* 1–16, 2–16, 3–62, 4–75, 5–79, 6–83, 7–92, 8–112, 9–116, 10–134. *Second Innings:* 1–28, 2–34, 3–96, 4–102, 5–153, 6–161, 7–169, 8–190, 9–198, 10–198.

AUSTRALIA

C. C. McDonald, c Graveney b Bailey	42	c Statham b Laker	15
J. W. Burke, c Evans, b Loader	20	not out	28
R. N. Harvey, lbw b Loader	14	c Milton b Lock	23
N. C. O'Neill, c Graveney b Bailey	34	not out	71
P. J. Burge, c Cowdrey b Bailey	2		
K. D. Mackay, c Evans b Laker	16		
*R. Benaud, lbw b Loader	16		
A. K. Davidson, lbw b Laker	25		
†A. T. W. Grout, b Statham	2		
I. Meckiff, b Loader	5		
L. F. Kline, not out	4		
Extras, (b 4, lb 1, nb 1)	6	(b 2, lb 3, nb 5)	10
Total	186	(2 wkts)	147

FALL OF WICKETS. *First Innings:* 1–55, 2–65, 3–88, 4–94, 5–122, 6–136, 7–162, 8–165, 9–178, 10–186. *Second Innings:* 1–20, 2–58.

BOWLING

AUSTRALIA. *First Innings:* Davidson 16, 4, 36, 3; Meckiff 17, 5, 33, 3; Mackay 8, 1, 16, 1; Benaud 18·4, 9, 46, 3. *Second Innings:* Davidson 28, 12, 30, 2; Meckiff 19, 7, 30, 2; Mackay 9, 6, 7, 1; Benaud 39·2, 10, 66, 4; Kline 14, 4, 34, 0; Burke 10, 5, 17, 0.

ENGLAND. *First Innings:* Statham 20, 2, 57, 1; Loader 19, 4, 56, 4; Bailey 13, 2, 35, 3; Laker 10·1, 3, 15, 2; Lock 10, 4, 17, 0. *Second Innings:* Statham 6, 1, 13, 0; Loader 9, 1, 27, 0; Bailey 5, 1, 21, 0; Laker 17, 3, 39, 1; Lock 14·7, 5, 37, 1.

Umpires: M. J. McInnes, C. Hoy

1958/9 Second Test, Melbourne

December 31, January 1, 2, 3, 5   Toss: England
Result: AUSTRALIA WON BY EIGHT WICKETS

ENGLAND

P. E. Richardson, c Grout b Davidson	3	c Harvey b Meckiff	2
T. E. Bailey, c Benaud b Meckiff	48	c Burke b Meckiff	14
W. Watson, b Davidson	0	b Davidson	7
T. W. Graveney, lbw b Davidson	0	c Davidson b Meckiff	3
*P. B. H. May, b Meckiff	113	c Davidson b Meckiff	17
M. C. Cowdrey, c Grout b Davidson	44	c Grout b Meckiff	12
†T. G. Evans, c Davidson b Meckiff	4	run out	11

G. A. R. Lock, st Grout b Benaud	5	c and b Davidson	6
J. C. Laker, not out	22	c Harvey b Davidson	3
J. B. Statham, b Davidson	13	not out	8
P. J. Loader, b Davidson	1	b Meckiff	0
Extras, (b 1, lb 2, w 3)	6	(b 1, lb 1, nb 2)	4
Total	259		87

FALL OF WICKETS. *First Innings:* 1–7, 2–7, 3–7, 4–92, 5–210, 6–218, 7–218, 8–233, 9–253, 10–259. *Second Innings:* 1–3, 2–14, 3–21, 4–27, 5–44, 6–57, 7–71, 8–75, 9–80, 10–87.

AUSTRALIA

C. C. McDonald, c Graveney b Statham	47	lbw b Statham	5
J. W. Burke, b Statham	3	not out	18
R. N. Harvey, b Loader	167	(4)not out	7
N. C. O'Neill, c Evans b Statham	37		
K. D. Mackay, c Evans b Statham	18		
R. B. Simpson, lbw b Loader	0		
*R. Benaud, lbw b Statham	0		
A. K. Davidson, b Statham	24		
†A. T. W. Grout, c May b Loader	8	(3)st Evans b Laker	12
I. Meckiff, b Statham	0		
L. F. Kline, not out	1		
Extras, (lb 3)	3		
Total	308	(2 wkts)	42

FALL OF WICKETS. *First Innings:* 1–11, 2–137, 3–255, 4–257, 5–261, 6–262, 7–295, 8–300, 9–300, 10–308. *Second Innings:* 1–6, 1–26.

BOWLING
AUSTRALIA. *First Innings:* Davidson 25·5, 7, 64, 6; Meckiff 24, 4, 69, 3; Mackay 9, 2, 16, 0; Benaud 29, 7, 61, 1; Kline 11, 2, 43, 0. *Second Innings:* Davidson 15, 2, 41, 3; Meckiff 15·2, 3, 38, 6; Benaud 1, 0, 4, 0.
ENGLAND. *First Innings:* Statham 28, 6, 57, 7; Loader 27·2, 4, 97, 3; Bailey 16, 0, 50, 0; Laker 12, 1, 47, 0; Lock 17, 2, 54, 0. *Second Innings:* Statham 5, 1, 11, 1; Loader 5, 1, 13, 0; Laker 4, 1, 7, 1; Lock 3·1, 1, 11, 0.

Umpires: M. J. McInnes, R. Wright

1958/9 Third Test, Sydney

January 9, 10, 12, 13, 14, 15   Toss: England
Result: MATCH DRAWN

ENGLAND

T. E. Bailey, lbw b Meckiff	8	c sub (R. B. Simpson) b Benaud		25
C. A. Milton, c Meckiff b Davidson	8	c Davidson b Benaud		8
T. W. Graveney, c Harvey b Benaud	33	lbw b Davidson		22
*P. B. H. May, c Mackay b Slater	42	b Burke		92
M. C. Cowdrey, c Harvey b Benaud	34	not out		100
E. R. Dexter, lbw b Slater	1	c Grout b Benaud		11
†R. Swetman, c Mackay b Benaud	41	lbw b Burke		5
G. A. R. Lock, lbw b Mackay	21	(9)not out		11
F. S. Trueman, c Burke b Benaud	18	(8)st Grout b Benaud		0
J. C. Laker, c Harvey b Benaud	2			
J. B. Statham, not out	0			
Extras, (b 4, lb 5, w 2)	11	(b 11, lb 1, w 1)		13
Total	219	(7 wkts dec)		287

FALL OF WICKETS. *First Innings:* 1–19, 2–23, 3–91, 4–97, 5–98, 6–155, 7–194, 8–200, 9–202, 10–219. *Second Innings:* 1–30, 2–37, 3–64, 4–246, 5–262, 6–269, 7–270.

AUSTRALIA

C. C. McDonald, c Graveney b Lock	40	b Laker	16
J. W. Burke, c Lock b Laker	12	b Laker	7
R. N. Harvey, b Laker	7	not out	18
N. C. O'Neill, c Swetman b Laker	77	not out	7
L. E. Favell, c Cowdrey b Lock	54		
K. D. Mackay, b Trueman	57		
*R. Benaud, b Laker	6		
A. K.Davidson, lbw b Lock	71		
†A. T. W. Grout, c Statham b Laker	14		
K. N. Slater, not out	1		
I. Meckiff, b Lock	2		
Extras, (b 5, lb 10, nb 1)	16	(b 6)	6
Total	357	(2 wkts)	54

FALL OF WICKETS. *First Innings:* 1–26, 2–52, 3–87, 4–197, 5–199, 6–208, 7–323, 8–353, 9–355, 10–357. *Second Innings:* 1–22, 2–33.

BOWLING

AUSTRALIA. *First Innings:* Davidson 12, 3, 21, 1; Meckiff 15, 2, 45, 1; Benaud 33·4, 10, 83, 5; Slater 14, 4, 40, 2; Mackay 8, 3, 19, 1. *Second Innings:* Davidson 33, 11, 65, 1; Meckiff 3, 1, 7, 0; Benaud 33, 7, 94, 4; Slater 18, 5, 61, 0; Mackay 11, 2, 21, 0; Burke 11, 3, 26, 2.
ENGLAND. *First Innings:* Statham 16, 2, 48, 0; Trueman 18, 3, 37, 1; Lock 43·2, 9, 130, 4; Laker 46, 9, 107, 5; Bailey 5, 0, 19, 0. *Second Innings:* Statham 2, 0, 6, 0; Trueman 4, 1, 9, 0; Lock 11, 4, 23, 0; Laker 8, 3, 10, 2.

Umpires: M. J. McInnes, C. Hoy

1958/9 Fourth Test, Adelaide

January 30, 31, February 2, 3, 4, 5   Toss: England
Result: AUSTRALIA WON BY TEN WICKETS

AUSTRALIA

C. C. McDonald, b Trueman	170		
J. W. Burke, c Cowdrey b Bailey	66	not out	16
R. N. Harvey, run out	41		
N. C. O'Neill, b Statham	56		
L. E. Favell, b Statham	4	not out	15
K. D. Mackay, c Evans b Statham	4		
*R. Benaud, b Trueman	46		
A. K. Davidson, c Bailey b Tyson	43		
†A. T. W. Grout, lbw b Trueman	9		
R. R. Lindwall, b Trueman	19		
G. F. Rorke, not out	2		
Extras, (b 2, lb 8, w 4, nb 2)	16	(b 4, lb 1)	5
Total	476	(0 wkts)	36

FALL OF WICKETS. *First Innings:* 1–171, 2–276, 3–286, 4–294, 5–369, 6–388, 7–407, 8–445, 9–473, 10–476.

ENGLAND

P. E. Richardson, lbw b Lindwall	4	lbw b Benaud	43
T. E. Bailey, b Davidson	4	(6)c Grout b Lindwall	6
*P. B. H. May, b Benaud	37	lbw b Rorke	59
M. C. Cowdrey, b Rorke	84	b Lindwall	8
T. W. Graveney, c Benaud b Rorke	41	not out	53
W. Watson, b Rorke	25	(2)c Favell b Benaud	40
F. S. Trueman, c Grout b Benaud	0	c Grout b Davidson	0
G. A. R. Lock, c Grout b Benaud	2	b Rorke	9
F. H. Tyson, c and b Benaud	0	c Grout b Benaud	33
†T. G. Evans, c Burke b Benaud	4	(11)c Benaud b Davidson	0

J. B. Statham, not out	36	(10)c O'Neill b Benaud	2
Extras, (lb 2, nb 1)	3	(b 5, lb 5, w 3, nb 4)	17
Total	240		270

FALL OF WICKETS. *First Innings:* 1–7, 2–11, 3–74, 4–170, 5–173, 6–180, 7–184, 8–184, 9 188, 10 240. *Second Innings:* 1–89, 2–110, 3–125, 4–177, 5–198, 6–199, 7–222, 8–268, 9–270, 10–270.

BOWLING
ENGLAND. *First Innings:* Statham 23, 0, 83, 3; Trueman 30·1, 6, 90, 4; Tyson 28, 1, 100, 1; Bailey 22, 2, 91, 1; Lock 25, 0, 96, 0. *Second Innings:* Statham 4, 0, 11, 0; Trueman 3, 1, 3, 0; Lock 2, 0, 8, 0; Cowdrey 1·3, 0, 9, 0.
AUSTRALIA. *First Innings:* Davidson 12, 0, 49, 1; Lindwall 15, 0, 66, 1; Rorke 18·1, 7, 23, 3; Benaud 27, 6, 91, 5; O'Neill 2, 1, 8, 0. *Second Innings:* Davidson 8·3, 3, 17, 2; Lindwall 26, 6, 70, 2; Rorke 34, 7, 78, 2; Benaud 29, 10, 82, 4; Burke 4, 2, 6, 0.

Umpires: M. J. McInnes, R. Wright

1958/9 Fifth Test, Melbourne

February 13, 14, 16, 17, 18   Toss: Australia
Result: AUSTRALIA WON BY NINE WICKETS

ENGLAND

P. E. Richardson, c and b Benaud	68	lbw b Benaud	23
T. E. Bailey, c Davidson b Lindwall	0	b Lindwall	0
*P. B. H. May, c Benaud b Meckiff	11	c Harvey b Lindwall	4
M. C. Cowdrey, c Lindwall b Davidson	22	run out	46
T. W. Graveney, c McDonald b Benaud	19	c Harvey b Davidson	54
E. R. Dexter, c Lindwall b Meckiff	0	c Grout b Davidson	6
†R. Swetman, c Grout b Davidson	1	lbw b Lindwall	9
J. B. Mortimore, not out	44	b Rorke	11
F. S. Trueman, c and b Benaud	21	b Rorke	36
F. H. Tyson, c Grout b Benaud	9	c Grout b Rorke	6
J. C. Laker, c Harvey b Davidson	2	not out	5
Extras, (b 4, w 4)	8	(b 9, lb 3, w 2)	14
Total	205		214

FALL OF WICKETS. *First Innings:* 1–0, 2–13, 3–61, 4–109, 5–112, 6–124, 7–128, 8–191, 9–203, 10–205. *Second Innings:* 1–0, 2–12, 3–78, 4–105, 5–131, 6–142, 7–158, 8–172, 9–182, 10–214.

AUSTRALIA

C. C. McDonald, c Cowdrey b Laker	133	not out	51
J. W. Burke, c Trueman b Tyson	16	lbw b Tyson	13
R. N. Harvey, c Swetman b Trueman	13	not out	1
N. C. O'Neill, c Cowdrey b Trueman	0		
K. D. Mackay, c Graveney b Laker	23		
A. K. Davidson, b Mortimore	17		
*R. Benaud, c Swetman b Laker	64		
†A. T. W. Grout, c Trueman b Laker	74		
R. R. Lindwall, c Cowdrey b Trueman	0		
I. Meckiff, c and b Trueman	2		
G. F. Rorke, not out	0		
Extras, (b 5, lb 4)	9	(lb 4)	4
Total	351	(1 wkt)	69

FALL OF WICKETS. *First Innings:* 1–41, 2–83, 3–83, 4–154, 5–207, 6–209, 7–324, 8–327, 9–329, 10–351. *Second Innings:* 1–66.

BOWLING

AUSTRALIA. *First Innings:* Davidson 12·5, 2, 38, 3; Lindwall 14, 2, 36, 1; Meckiff 15, 2, 57, 2; Rorke 6, 1, 23, 0; Benaud 17, 5, 43, 4. *Second Innings:* Davidson 21, 1, 95, 2; Lindwall 11, 2, 37, 3; Meckiff 4, 0, 13, 0; Rorke 12·4, 2, 41, 3; Benaud 6, 1, 14, 1.

ENGLAND. *First Innings:* Trueman 25, 0, 92, 4; Tyson 20, 1, 73, 1; Bailey 14, 2, 43, 0; Laker 30·5, 4, 93, 4; Mortimore 11, 1, 41, 1. *Second Innings:* Trueman 6·7, 0, 45, 0; Tyson 6, 0, 20, 1.

Umpires: R. Wright, L. Townsend

Averages: 1958/9

AUSTRALIA

BATTING	M.	*Inns.*	N.O.	*Runs*	H.S.	*Av.*
C. C. McDonald	5	9	1	519	170	64·87
N. C. O'Neill	5	7	2	282	77	56·40
R. N. Harvey	5	9	3	291	167	48·50
L. E. Favell	2	3	1	73	54	36·50
A. K. Davidson	5	5	0	180	71	36·00
J. W. Burke	5	10	3	199	66	28·42
R. Benaud	5	5	0	132	64	26·40
K. D. Mackay	5	5	0	118	57	23·60

APPENDIX

BATTING	M.	*Inns.*	N.O.	*Runs*	H.S.	*Av.*
A. T. W. Grout	5	6	0	119	74	19·83
R. R. Lindwall	2	2	0	19	19	9·50
I. Meckiff	4	4	0	9	5	2·25

PLAYED IN TWO TESTS: L. Kline 4* and 1*, G. F. Rorke 2* and 0*.
PLAYED IN ONE TEST: P. J. Burge 2, R. B. Simpson 0, K. N. Slater 1*.

BOWLING	*Overs*	*Mds.*	*Runs*	*Wkts.*	*Av.*
I. Meckiff	112·2	24	292	17	17·17
R. Benaud	233·2	65	584	31	18·83
A. K. Davidson	183·5	45	456	24	19·00
G. F. Rorke	70·5	17	165	8	20·62
K. D. Mackay	45	14	79	3	26·33
R. R. Lindwall	66	10	209	7	29·85

ALSO BOWLED: L. Kline 25–6–77–0, J. W. Burke 25–10–49–2, K. N. Slater 32–9–101–2, N. C. O'Neill 2–1–8–0.

ENGLAND

BATTING	M.	*Inns.*	N.O.	*Runs*	H.S.	*Av.*
M. C. Cowdrey	5	10	1	391	100*	43·44
P. B. H. May	5	10	0	405	113	40·50
T. W. Graveney	5	10	1	280	54	31·11
P. E. Richardson	4	8	0	162	68	20·25
T. E. Bailey	5	10	0	200	68	20·00
W. Watson	2	4	0	72	40	18·00
J. B. Statham	4	7	3	64	36*	16·00
R. Swetman	2	4	0	56	41	14·00
F. S. Trueman	3	6	0	75	36	12·50
J. C. Laker	4	7	2	62	22*	12·40
F. H. Tyson	2	4	0	48	33	12·00
C. A. Milton	2	4	0	38	17	9·50
G. A. R. Lock	4	8	1	60	21	8·57
T. G. Evans	3	6	0	27	11	4·50
E. R. Dexter	2	4	0	18	11	4·50
P. J. Loader	2	4	2	7	6*	3·50

PLAYED IN ONE TEST: J. B. Mortimore 44* and 11.

BOWLING	*Overs*	*Mds.*	*Runs*	*Wkts.*	*Av.*
J. C. Laker	127·6	24	318	15	21·20
J. B. Statham	104	12	286	12	23·83
P. J. Loader	60·2	10	193	7	27·57
F. S. Trueman	87	11	276	9	30·66
F. H. Tyson	54	2	193	3	64·33
T. E. Bailey	75	7	259	4	64·75
G. A. R. Lock	126·2	25	376	5	75·20

ALSO BOWLED: M. C. Cowdrey 1·3–0–9–0, J. B. Mortimore 11–1–41–1.

191

1962/3 First Test, Brisbane

November 30, December 1, 3, 4, 5   Toss: Australia
Result: MATCH DRAWN

AUSTRALIA

W. M. Lawry, c Smith b Trueman	5	c Sheppard b Titmus	98
R. B. Simpson, c Trueman b Dexter	50	c Smith b Dexter	71
N. C. O'Neill, c Statham b Trueman	19	lbw b Statham	56
R. N. Harvey, b Statham	39	c Statham b Dexter	57
P. J. Burge, c Dexter b Trueman	6	not out	47
B. C. Booth, c Dexter b Titmus	112	not out	19
A. K. Davidson, c Trueman b Barrington	23		
K. D. Mackay, not out	86		
*R. Benaud, c Smith b Knight	51		
G. D. McKenzie, c and b Knight	4		
†B. N. Jarman, c Barrington b Knight	2		
Extras, (b 5, lb 1, nb 1)	7	(b 4, lb 10)	14
Total	404	(4 wkts dec)	362

FALL OF WICKETS. *First Innings:* 1–5, 2–46, 3–92, 4–101, 5–140, 6–194, 7–297, 8–388, 9–392, 10–404. *Second Innings:* 1–136, 2–216, 3–241, 4–325.

ENGLAND

G. Pullar, c and b Benaud	33	c and b Davidson	56
Rev. D. S. Sheppard, c McKenzie b Benaud	31	c Benaud b Davidson	53
*E. R. Dexter, b Benaud	70	b McKenzie	99
M. C. Cowdrey, c Lawry b Simpson	21	c and b Benaud	9
K. F. Barrington, c Burge b Benaud	78	c McKenzie b Davidson	23
†A. C. Smith, c Jarman b McKenzie	21		
P. H. Parfitt, c Davidson b Benaud	80	(6)c Jarman b McKenzie	4
F. J. Titmus, c Simpson b Benaud	21	(7)not out	3
B. R. Knight, c Davidson b McKenzie	0		
F. S. Trueman, c Jarman b McKenzie	19	(8) not out	4
J. B. Statham, not out	8		
Extras, (b 4, lb 2, w 1)	7	(b 15, lb 10, nb 2)	27
Total	389	(6 wkts)	278

FALL OF WICKETS. *First Innings:* 1–62, 2–65, 3–145, 4–169, 5–220, 6–297, 7–361, 8–362, 9–362, 10–389. *Second Innings:* 1–114, 2–135, 3–119, 4–257, 5–257, 6–261.

BOWLING

ENGLAND. *First Innings:* Statham 16, 1, 75, 1; Trueman 18, 0, 76, 3; Knight 17·5, 2, 65, 3; Titmus 33, 8, 91, 1; Dexter 10, 0, 46, 1; Barrington 12, 3, 44, 1. *Second Innings:* Statham 16, 1, 67, 1; Trueman 15, 0, 59, 0; Knight 14, 1, 63, 0; Titmus 26, 3, 81, 1; Dexter 16, 0, 78, 2.
AUSTRALIA. *First Innings:* Davidson 21, 4, 77, 0; McKenzie 25·3, 2, 78, 3; Mackay 28, 7, 55, 0; Benaud 42, 12, 115, 6; Simpson 18, 6, 52, 1; O'Neill 1, 0, 5, 0. *Second Innings:* Davidson 20, 6, 43, 3; McKenzie 20, 4, 61, 2; Mackay 7, 0, 28, 0; Benaud 27, 7, 71, 1; Simpson 7, 0, 48, 0; O'Neill 2, 2, 0, 0.

Umpires: C. J. Egar, E. F. Wykes

1962/3 Second Test, Melbourne

December 29, 31, January 1, 2, 3   Toss: Australia
Result: ENGLAND WON BY SEVEN WICKETS

AUSTRALIA

W. M. Lawry, b Trueman	52	b Dexter	57
R. B. Simpson, c Smith b Coldwell	38	b Trueman	14
N. C. O'Neill, c Graveney b Statham	19	c Cowdrey b Trueman	0
R. N. Harvey, b Coldwell	0	run out	10
P. J. Burge, lbw b Titmus	23	b Statham	14
B. C. Booth, c Barrington b Titmus	27	c Trueman b Statham	103
A. K. Davidson, c Smith b Trueman	40	c Smith b Titmus	17
K. D. Mackay, lbw b Titmus	49	lbw b Trueman	9
*R. Benaud, c Barrington b Titmus	36	c Cowdrey b Trueman	4
G. D. McKenzie, b Trueman	16	b Trueman	0
†B. N. Jarman, not out	10	not out	11
Extras, (b 2, lb 4)	6	(b 4, lb 5)	9
Total	316		248

FALL OF WICKETS. *First Innings:* 1–62, 2–111, 3–112, 4–112, 5–155, 6–164, 7–237, 8–289, 9–294, 10–316. *Second Innings:* 1–30, 2–30, 3–46, 4–69, 5–161, 6–193, 7–212, 8–228, 9–228, 10–248.

ENGLAND

Rev. D. S. Sheppard, lbw b Davidson	0	run out	113
G. Pullar, b Davidson	11	c Jarman b McKenzie	5
*E. R. Dexter, c Simpson b Benaud	93	run out	52
M. C. Cowdrey, c Burge b McKenzie	113	not out	58
K. F. Barrington, lbw b McKenzie	35	not out	0
T. W. Graveney, run out	41		
F. J. Titmus, c Jarman b Davidson	15		
†A. C. Smith, not out	6		
F. S. Trueman, c O'Neill b Davidson	6		
J. B. Statham, b Davidson	1		
L. J. Coldwell, c Benaud b Davidson	1		
Extras, (b 4, lb 4, nb 1)	9	(b 5, lb 3, nb 1)	9
Total	331	(3 wkts)	237

FALL OF WICKETS. *First Innings:* 1–0, 2–19, 3–194, 4–254, 5–255, 6–292, 7–315, 8–324, 9–327, 10–331. *Second Innings:* 1–5, 2–129, 3–233.

BOWLING

ENGLAND. *First Innings:* Trueman 23, 1, 83, 3; Statham 22, 2, 83, 1; Coldwell 17, 2, 58, 2; Barrington 6, 0, 23, 0; Dexter 6, 1, 10, 0; Titmus 15, 2, 43, 4; Graveney 3, 1, 10, 0. *Second Innings:* Trueman 20, 1, 62, 5; Statham 23, 1, 52, 2; Coldwell 25, 2, 60, 0; Barrington 5, 0, 22, 0; Dexter 9, 2, 18, 1; Titmus 14, 4, 25, 1.
AUSTRALIA. *First Innings:* Davidson 23·1, 4, 75, 6; McKenzie 29, 3, 95, 2; Mackay 6, 2, 17, 0; Benaud 18, 3, 82, 1; Simpson 7, 1, 34, 0; O'Neill 5, 1, 19, 0. *Second Innings:* Davidson 19, 2, 53, 0; McKenzie 20, 3, 58, 1; Mackay 9, 0, 34, 0; Benaud 14, 1, 69, 0; Simpson 2, 0, 10, 0; Booth 0·2, 0, 4, 0.

Umpires: C. J. Egar, W. Smyth

1962/3 Third Test, Sydney

January 11, 12, 14, 15   Toss: England
Result: AUSTRALIA WON BY EIGHT WICKETS

ENGLAND

G. Pullar, c Benaud b Simpson	53	b Davidson	0
Rev. D. S. Sheppard, c McKenzie b Davidson	3	c Simpson b Davidson	12
*E. R. Dexter, c Lawry b Benaud	32	c Simpson b Davidson	11

M. C. Cowdrey, c Jarman b Simpson	85	c Simpson b Benaud	8
K. F. Barrington, lbw b Davidson	35	b McKenzie	21
P. H. Parfitt, c Lawry b Simpson	0	c O'Neill b McKenzie	28
F. J. Titmus, b Davidson	32	c Booth b O'Neill	6
†J. T. Murray, lbw b Davidson	0	not out	3
F. S. Trueman, b Simpson	32	c Jarman b McKenzie	9
J. B. Statham, c Benaud b Simpson	0	b Davidson	2
L. J. Coldwell, not out	2	c Shepherd b Davidson	0
Extras, (lb 3, w 2)	5	(b 2, lb 2)	4
Total	279		104

FALL OF WICKETS. *First Innings:* 1–4, 2–65, 3–132, 4–201, 5–203, 6–221, 7–221, 8–272, 9–272, 10–279. *Second Innings:* 1–0, 2–20, 3–25, 4–37, 5–53, 6–71, 7–90, 8–100, 9–104, 10–104.

AUSTRALIA

W. M. Lawry, c Murray b Coldwell	8	b Trueman	8
R. B. Simpson, b Titmus	91	not out	34
R. N. Harvey, c Barrington b Titmus	64	lbw b Trueman	15
B. C. Booth, c Trueman b Titmus	16	not out	5
N. C. O'Neill, b Titmus	3		
B. K. Shepherd, not out	71		
†B. N. Jarman, run out	0		
A. K. Davidson, c Trueman b Titmus	15		
*R. Benaud, c and b Titmus	15		
G. D. McKenzie, lbw b Titmus	4		
C. E. J. Guest, b Statham	11		
Extras, (b 10, lb 11)	21	(b 5)	5
Total	319	(2 wkts)	67

FALL OF WICKETS. *First Innings:* 1–14, 2–174, 3–177, 4–187, 5–212, 6–216, 7–242, 8–274, 9–280, 10–319. *Second Innings:* 1–28, 2–54.

BOWLING
AUSTRALIA. *First Innings:* Davidson 24·5, 7, 54, 4; McKenzie 15, 3, 52, 0; Guest 16, 0, 51, 0; Benaud 16, 2, 60, 1; Simpson 15, 3, 57, 5. *Second Innings:* Davidson 10·6, 2, 25, 5; McKenzie 14, 3, 26, 3; Guest 2, 0, 8, 0; Benaud 19, 10, 29, 1; Simpson 4, 2, 5, 0; O'Neill 7, 5, 7, 1.
ENGLAND. *First Innings:* Trueman 20, 2, 68, 0; Statham 21·2, 2, 67, 1; Coldwell 15, 1, 41, 1; Titmus 37, 14, 79, 7; Barrington 8, 0, 43, 0. *Second Innings:* Trueman 6, 1, 20, 2; Statham 3, 0, 15, 0; Dexter 3·2, 0, 27, 0.

Umpires: W. Smyth, L. Rowan

1962/3 Fourth Test, Adelaide

January 25, 26, 28, 29, 30   Toss: Australia
Result: MATCH DRAWN

AUSTRALIA

W. M. Lawry, b Illingworth	10	c Graveney b Trueman	16
R. B. Simpson, c Smith b Statham	0	c Smith b Dexter	71
R. N. Harvey, c Statham b Dexter	154	c Barrington b Statham	6
B. C. Booth, c Cowdrey b Titmus	34	c Smith b Dexter	77
N. C. O'Neill, c Cowdrey b Dexter	100	c Cowdrey b Trueman	23
A. K. Davidson, b Statham	46	(10)b Statham	2
B. K. Shepherd, c Trueman b Statham	10	(6)c Titmus b Dexter	13
K. D. Mackay, c Smith b Trueman	1	(7)c Graveney b Trueman	3
*R. Benaud, b Dexter	16	(8)c Barrington b Trueman	48
G. D. McKenzie, c Sheppard b Titmus	15	(9)c Smith b Statham	13
†A. T. W. Grout, not out	1	not out	16
Extras, (lb 5, w 1)	6	(b 1, lb 4)	5
Total	393		293

FALL OF WICKETS. *First Innings:* 1–2, 2–16, 3–101, 4–295, 5–302, 6–331, 7–336, 8–366, 9–383, 10–393. *Second Innings:* 1–27, 2–37, 3–170, 4–175, 5–199, 6–205, 7–228, 8–254, 9–258, 10–293.

ENGLAND

G. Pullar, b McKenzie	9	c Simpson b McKenzie	3
Rev. D. S. Sheppard, st Grout b Benaud	30	c Grout b Mackay	1
K. F. Barrington, b Simpson	63	not out	132
M. C. Cowdrey, c Grout b McKenzie	13	run out	32
*E. R. Dexter, c Grout b McKenzie	61	c Simpson b Benaud	10
T. W. Graveney c Booth b McKenzie	22	not out	36
F. J. Titmus, not out	59		
R. Illingworth, c Grout b McKenzie	12		
†A. C. Smith, c Lawry b Mackay	13		
F. S. Trueman, c Benaud b Mackay	38		
J. B. Statham, b Mackay	1		
Extras, (b 5, lb 5)	10	(b 4, w 5)	9
Total	331	(4 wkts)	223

FALL OF WICKETS. *First Innings:* 1–17, 2–84, 3–117, 4–119, 5–165, 6–226, 7–246, 8–275, 9–327, 10–331. *Second Innings:* 1–2, 2–4, 3–98, 4–122.

BOWLING

ENGLAND. *First Innings:* Trueman 19, 1, 54, 1; Statham 21, 5, 66, 3; Illingworth 20, 3, 85, 1; Dexter 23, 1, 94, 3; Titmus 20·1, 2, 88, 2. *Second Innings:* Trueman 23·3, 3, 60, 4; Statham 21, 2, 71, 3; Illingworth 5, 1, 23, 0; Dexter 17, 0, 65, 3; Titmus 24, 5, 69, 0.
AUSTRALIA. *First Innings:* Davidson 3·4, 0, 30, 0; McKenzie 33, 3, 89, 5; Mackay 27·6, 8, 80, 3; Benaud 18, 3, 82, 1; Simpson 8, 1, 40, 1. *Second Innings:* McKenzie 14, 0, 64, 1; Mackay 8, 2, 13, 1; Benaud 15, 3, 38, 1; Simpson 10, 1, 50, 0; O'Neill 8, 0, 49, 0; Lawry 1, 1, 0, 0; Harvey 1, 1, 0, 0.

Umpires: C. J. Egar, A. Mackley

1962/3 Fifth Test, Sydney

February 15, 16, 18, 19, 20   Toss: England
Result: MATCH DRAWN

ENGLAND

Rev. D. S. Sheppard, c and b Hawke	19	c Harvey b Benaud	68
M. C. Cowdrey, c Harvey b Davidson	2	(5)c Benaud b Davidson	53
K. F. Barrington, c Harvey b Benaud	101	c Grout b McKenzie	94
*E. R. Dexter, c Simpson b O'Neill	47	st Grout b Benaud	6
T. W. Graveney, c Harvey b McKenzie	14	(6)c and b Davidson	3
R. Illingworth, c Grout b Davidson	27	(2)c Hawke b Benaud	18
F. J. Titmus, c Grout b Hawke	34	not out	12
F. S. Trueman, c Harvey b Benaud	30	c Harvey b McKenzie	8
†A. C. Smith, b Simpson	6	c Simpson b Davidson	1
D. A. Allen, c Benaud b Davidson	14		
J. B. Statham, not out	17		
Extras, (b 4, lb 6)	10	(b 1, lb 4)	5
Total	321	(8 wkts dec)	268

FALL OF WICKETS. *First Innings:* 1–5, 2–39, 3–129, 4–177, 5–189, 6–224, 7–276, 8–286, 9–293, 10–321. *Second Innings:* 1–40, 2–137, 3–145, 4–239, 5–247, 6–249, 7–257, 8–268.

AUSTRALIA

W. M. Lawry, c Smith b Trueman	11	not out	45
R. B.Simpson, c Trueman b Titmus	32	b Trueman	0
B. C. Booth, b Titmus	11	(5)b Allen	0
N. C. O'Neill, c Graveney b Allen	73	c Smith b Allen	17
P. J. Burge, lbw b Titmus	103	(6)not out	52
R. N. Harvey, c sub (P. H. Parfitt) b Statham	22	(3)b Allen	28
A. K. Davidson, c Allen b Dexter	15		
*R. Benaud, c Graveney b Allen	57		
G. D. McKenzie, c and b Titmus	0		
N. J. N. Hawke, c Graveney b Titmus	14		
†A. T. W. Grout, not out	0		
Extras, (b 6, lb 5)	11	(b 4, lb 6)	10
Total	349	(4 wkts)	152

FALL OF WICKETS. *First Innings:* 1–28, 2–50, 3–71, 4–180, 5–231, 6–271, 7–299, 8–303, 9–347, 10–349. *Second Innings:* 1–0, 2–39, 3–70, 4–70.

BOWLING
AUSTRALIA. *First Innings:* Davidson 25·6, 4, 43, 3; McKenzie 27, 4, 57, 1; Hawke 20, 1, 51, 2; Benaud 34, 9, 71, 2; Simpson 18, 4, 51, 1; O'Neill 10, 0, 38, 1. *Second Innings:* Davidson 28, 1, 80, 3; McKenzie 8, 0, 39, 2; Hawke 9, 0, 38, 0; Benaud 30, 8, 71, 3; Simpson 4, 0, 22, 0; Harvey 3, 0, 13, 0.
ENGLAND. *First Innings:* Trueman 11, 0, 33, 1; Statham 18, 1, 76, 1; Dexter 7, 1, 24, 1; Titmus 47·2, 9, 103, 5; Allen 43, 15, 87, 2; Illingworth 5, 1, 15, 0. *Second Innings:* Trueman 3, 0, 6, 1; Statham 4, 1, 8, 0; Dexter 4, 1, 11, 0; Titmus 20, 7, 37, 0; Allen 19, 11, 26, 3; Illingworth 10, 5, 8, 0; Barrington 8, 3, 22, 0; Graveney 4, 0, 24, 0.

Umpires: C. J. Egar, L. Rowan

Averages: 1962/3

AUSTRALIA

BATTING	M.	Inns.	N.O.	Runs	H.S.	Av.
P. J Burge	3	6	2	245	103	61·25
B. C. Booth	5	10	2	404	112	50·50
B. K. Shepherd	2	3	1	94	71*	47·00
R. B. Simpson	5	10	1	401	91	44·55
R. N. Harvey	5	10	0	395	154	39·50
K. D. Mackay	3	5	1	148	86*	37·00

BATTING	M.	Inns.	N.O.	Runs	H.S.	Av.
N. C. O'Neill	5	9	0	310	100	34·44
W. M. Lawry	5	10	1	310	98	34·44
R. Benaud	5	7	0	227	57	32·42
A. K. Davidson	5	7	0	158	46	22·57
N. J. N. Hawke	1	1	0	14	14	14·00
B. N. Jarman	3	4	2	23	11*	11·50
C. E. J. Guest	1	1	0	11	11	11·00
G. D. McKenzie	5	7	0	52	16	7·42
A. T. W. Grout	2	3	3	17	16*	—

BOWLING	Overs	Mds.	Runs	Wkts.	Av.
A. K. Davidson	175·6	30	480	24	20·00
G. D. McKenzie	205·3	25	619	20	30·95
R. Benaud	233	58	688	17	40·47
N. J. Hawke	29	1	89	2	44·50
R. B. Simpson	93	18	369	8	46·12
K. D. Mackay	85·6	19	227	4	56·75
N. C. O'Neill	33	8	118	2	59·00

ALSO BOWLED: C. E. J. Guest 18–0–59–0, R. N Harvey 4–1–13–0, W. M. Lawry 1–1–0–0, B. C. Booth 0·2–0–4–0.

ENGLAND

BATTING	M.	Inns.	N.O.	Runs	H.S.	Av.
K. F. Barrington	5	10	2	582	132*	72·75
E. R. Dexter	5	10	0	481	99	48·10
M. C. Cowdrey	5	10	1	394	113	43·77
F. J. Titmus	5	8	3	182	59*	36·40
Rev. D. S. Sheppard	5	10	0	330	113	33·00
T. W. Graveney	3	5	1	116	41	29·00
P. H. Parfitt	2	4	0	112	80	28·00
G. Pullar	4	8	0	170	56	21·25
F. S. Trueman	5	7	0	142	38	20·28
R. Illingworth	2	3	0	57	27	19·00
D. A. Allen	1	1	0	14	14	14·00
A. C. Smith	4	5	1	47	21	11·75
J. B. Statham	5	6	2	29	17*	7·25
B. R. Knight	1	2	1	4	4*	4·00
J. T. Murray	1	2	1	3	3*	3·00
L. J. Coldwell	2	3	1	3	2*	1·50

BOWLING	Overs	Mds.	Runs	Wkts.	Av.
D. A. Allen	62	26	113	5	22·60
F. S. Trueman	158·3	9	521	20	26·05
F. J. Titmus	236·3	54	616	21	29·33
E. R. Dexter	95·2	6	373	11	33·90

BOWLING	Overs	Mds.	Runs	Wkts.	Av.
B. R. Knight	31·5	3	128	3	42·66
J. B. Statham	165·2	16	580	13	44·61
L. J. Coldwell	57	5	159	3	53·00
R. Illingworth	40	9	131	1	131·00
K. F. Barrington	39	6	154	1	154·00

ALSO BOWLED: T. W. Graveney 7–1–34–0.

1965/6 First Test, Brisbane

December 10, 11, 13, 14, 15   Toss: Australia
Result: MATCH DRAWN

AUSTRALIA
W. M. Lawry, c Parks b Higgs   166
I. R. Redpath, b Brown   17
R. M. Cowper, c Barrington
  b Brown   22
P. J. Burge, b Brown   0
*B. C. Booth, c and b Titmus   16
K. D. Walters, c Parks b Higgs   155
T. R. Veivers, not out   56
N. J. N. Hawke, not out   6
†A. T. W. Grout ⎫
P. I. Philpott   ⎬ did not bat
P. J. Allan   ⎭
  Extras, (lb 2, nb 3)   5
  Total (6 wkts dec)   443

FALL OF WICKETS. *First Innings:* 1–51, 2–90, 3–90, 4–125, 5–312, 6–431.

ENGLAND
R. W. Barber, c Walters b Hawke	5	c Veivers b Walters	34
G. Boycott, b Philpott	45	not out	63
J. H. Edrich, c Lawry b Philpott	32	c Veivers b Philpott	37
K. F. Barrington, b Hawke	53	c Booth b Cowper	38
*M. J. K. Smith, b Allan	16	not out	10
†J. M. Parks, c Redpath b Philpott	52		
F. J. Titmus, st Grout b Philpott	60		
D. A. Allen, c Cowper b Walters	3		
D. J. Brown, b Philpott	3		
K. Higgs, lbw b Allan	4		
W. E. Russell, not out	0		
Extras, (b 4, nb 3)	7	(b 2, lb 2)	4
Total	280	(3 wkts)	186

FALL OF WICKETS. *First Innings:* 1–5, 2–75, 3–86, 4–115, 5–191, 6–221, 7–232, 8–253, 9–272, 10–280. *Second Innings:* 1–46, 2–114, 3–168.

BOWLING

ENGLAND. *First Innings:* Brown 21, 4, 71, 3; Higgs 30, 6, 102, 2; Titmus 38, 9, 99, 1; Allen 39, 12, 108, 0; Barber 5, 0, 42, 0; Boycott 4, 0, 16, 0.

AUSTRALIA. *First Innings:* Allan 21, 6, 58, 2; Hawke 16, 7, 44, 2; Walters 10, 1, 25, 1; Philpott 28·1, 3, 90, 5; Cowper 7, 4, 7, 0; Veivers 11, 1, 49, 0. *Second Innings:* Allan 3, 0, 25, 0; Hawke 10, 2, 16, 0; Walters 5, 1, 22, 1; Philpott 14, 1, 62, 1; Cowper 6, 0, 20, 1; Veivers 12, 1, 37, 0.

Umpires: C. J. Egar, L. Rowan

1965/6 Second Test, Melbourne

December 30, 31, January 1, 3, 4   Toss: Australia
Result: MATCH DRAWN

AUSTRALIA

*R. B. Simpson, c Edrich b Allen	59	c Barrington b Knight	67	
W. M. Lawry, c Cowdrey b Allen	88	c Smith b Barber	78	
P. J. Burge, b Jones	5	(4)c Edrich b Boycott	120	
R. M. Cowper, c Titmus b Jones	99	(3)lbw b Jones	5	
B. C. Booth, lbw b Jones	23	b Allen	10	
K. D. Walters, c Parks b Knight	22	c and b Barrington	115	
T. R. Veivers, run out	19	st Parks b Boycott	3	
P. I. Philpott, b Knight	10	b Knight	2	
†A. T. W. Grout, c Barber b Knight	11	c Allen b Barrington	16	
G. D. McKenzie, not out	12	run out	2	
A. N. Connolly, c Parks b Knight	0	not out	0	
Extras, (b 2, lb 7, nb 1)	10	(b 1, lb 3, w 1, nb 3)	8	
Total	358		426	

FALL OF WICKETS. *First Innings:* 1–93, 2–109, 3–203, 4–262, 5–297, 6–318, 7–330, 8–342, 9–352, 10–358. *Second Innings:* 1–120, 2–141, 3–163, 4–176, 5–374, 6–382, 7–385, 8–417, 9–426, 10–426.

ENGLAND

G. Boycott, c McKenzie b Walters	51	not out	5
R. W. Barber, c Grout b McKenzie	48	not out	0
J. H. Edrich, c and b Veivers	109		
K. F. Barrington, c Burge b Veivers	63		
M. C. Cowdrey, c Connolly b Cowper	104		

*M. J. K. Smith, c Grout b McKenzie	41		
†J. M. Parks, c Cowper b McKenzie	71		
B. R. Knight, c Simpson b McKenzie	1		
F. J. Titmus, not out	56		
D. A. Allen, c Grout b Connolly	2		
I. J. Jones, b McKenzie	1		
Extras, (b 4, lb 5, w 2)	11		
Total	558	(0 wkts)	5

FALL OF WICKETS. *First Innings:* 1–98, 2–110, 3–228, 4–333, 5–409, 6–443, 7–447, 8–540, 9–551, 10–558.

BOWLING
ENGLAND. *First Innings:* Jones 24, 4, 92, 3; Knight 26·5, 2, 84, 4; Titmus 31, 7, 93, 0; Allen 20, 4, 55, 2; Barber 6, 1, 24, 0. *Second Innings:* Jones 20, 1, 92, 1; Knight 21, 4, 61, 2; Titmus 22, 6, 43, 0; Allen 18, 3, 48, 1; Barber 17, 0, 87, 1; Barrington 7·4, 0, 47, 2; Boycott 9, 0, 32, 2; Smith 2, 0, 8, 0.
AUSTRALIA. *First Innings:* McKenzie 35·2, 3, 134, 5; Connolly 37, 5, 125, 1; Philpott 30, 2, 133, 0; Walters 10, 2, 32, 1; Simpson 16, 4, 61, 0; Veivers 12, 3, 46, 2; Cowper 3, 0 16, 1. *Second Innings:* McKenzie 1, 0, 2, 0; Connolly 1, 0, 3, 0.

Umpires: C. J. Egar, W. Smyth

1965/6 Third Test, Sydney

January 7, 8, 10, 11   Toss: England
Result: ENGLAND WON BY AN INNINGS AND 93 RUNS

ENGLAND

G. Boycott, c and b Philpott	84
R. W. Barber, b Hawke	185
J. H. Edrich, c and b Philpott	103
K. F. Barrington, c McKenzie b Hawke	1
M. C. Cowdrey, c Grout b Hawke	0
*M. J. K. Smith, c Grout b Hawke	6
D. J. Brown, c Grout b Hawke	1
†J. M. Parks, c Grout b Hawke	13
F. J. Titmus, c Grout b Walters	14
D. A. Allen, not out	50
I. J. Jones, b Hawke	16
Extras, (b 3, lb 8, w 2, nb 2)	15
Total	488

FALL OF WICKETS. *First Innings:* 1–234, 2–303, 3–309, 4–309, 5–317, 6–328, 7–358, 8–395, 9–433, 10–488.

AUSTRALIA

W. M. Lawry, c Parks b Jones	0	c Cowdrey b Brown	33
G. Thomas, c Titmus b Brown	51	c Cowdrey b Titmus	25
R. M. Cowper, st Parks b Allen	60	c Boycott b Titmus	0
P. J. Burge, c Parks b Brown	6	run out	1
*B. C. Booth, c Cowdrey b Jones	8	b Allen	27
D. J. Sincock, c Parks b Brown	29	(7)c Smith b Allen	27
K. D. Walters, st Parks b Allen	23	(6)not out	35
N. J. N. Hawke, c Barber b Brown	0	(9)c Smith b Titmus	2
†A. T. W. Grout, b Brown	0	(10)c Smith b Allen	3
G. D. McKenzie, c Cowdrey b Barber	24	(11)c Barber b Titmus	12
P. I. Philpott, not out	5	(8)lbw b Allen	5
Extras, (b 7, lb 8)	15	(b 3, lb 1)	4
Total	221		174

FALL OF WICKETS. *First Innings:* 1–0, 2–81, 3–91, 4–105, 5–155, 6–174, 7–174, 8–174, 9–203, 10–221. *Second Innings:* 1–46, 2–50, 3–51, 4–86, 5–86, 6–119, 7–131, 8–135, 9–140, 10–174.

BOWLING

AUSTRALIA. *First Innings:* McKenzie 25, 2, 113, 0; Hawke 33·7, 6, 105, 7; Walters 10, 1, 38, 1; Philpott 28, 3, 86, 2; Sincock 20, 1, 98, 0; Cowper 6, 1, 33, 0.
ENGLAND. *First Innings:* Jones 20, 6, 51, 2; Brown 17, 1, 63, 5; Boycott 3, 1, 8, 0; Titmus 23, 8, 40, 0; Barber 2·1, 1, 2, 1; Allen 19; 5, 42, 2. *Second Innings:* Jones 7, 0, 35, 0; Brown 11, 2, 32, 1; Titmus 17·3, 4, 40, 4; Barber 5, 0, 16, 0; Allen 20, 8, 47, 4.

Umpires: C. J. Egar, L. Rowan

1965/6 Fourth Test, Adelaide

January 28, 29, 31, February 1   Toss: England
Result: AUSTRALIA WON BY AN INNINGS AND 9 RUNS

ENGLAND

G. Boycott, c Chappell b Hawke	22	lbw b McKenzie	12
R. W. Barber, b McKenzie	0	c Grout b Hawke	19
J. H. Edrich, c Simpson b McKenzie	5	c Simpson b Hawke	1
K. F. Barrington, lbw b Walters	60	c Chappell b Hawke	102
M. C. Cowdrey, run out	38	c Grout b Stackpole	35

*M. J. K. Smith, b Veivers	29	c McKenzie b Stackpole	5
†J. M. Parks, c Stackpole b McKenzie	49	run out	16
F. J. Titmus, lbw b McKenzie	33	c Grout b Hawke	53
D. A. Allen, c Simpson b McKenzie	2	not out	5
D. J. Brown, c Thomas b McKenzie	1	c and b Hawke	0
I. J. Jones, not out	0	c Lawry b Veivers	8
Extras, (lb 2)	2	(lb 2, nb 8)	10
Total	241		266

FALL OF WICKETS. *First Innings:* 1–7, 2–25, 3–33, 4–105, 5–150, 6–178, 7–210, 8–212, 9–222, 10–241. *Second Innings:* 1–23, 2–31, 3–32, 4–114, 5–123, 6–163, 7–244, 8–253, 9–257, 10–266.

AUSTRALIA

*R. B. Simpson, c Titmus b Jones	225
W. M. Lawry, b Titmus	119
G. Thomas, b Jones	52
T. R. Veivers, c Parks b Jones	1
P. J. Burge, c Parks b Jones	27
K. D. Walters, c Parks b Brown	0
I. M. Chappell, c Edrich b Jones	17
K. R. Stackpole, c Parks b Jones	43
N. J. N. Hawke, not out	20
†A. T. W. Grout, b Titmus	4
G. D. McKenzie, lbw b Titmus	1
Extras, (b 4, lb 3)	7
Total	516

FALL OF WICKETS. *First Innings:* 1–244, 2–331, 3–333, 4–379, 5–383, 6–415, 7–480, 8–501, 9–506, 10–516.

BOWLING

AUSTRALIA. *First Innings:* McKenzie 21·7, 4, 48, 6; Hawke 23, 2, 69, 1; Walters 14, 0, 50, 1; Stackpole 5, 0, 30 0; Chappell 4, 1, 18, 0; Veivers 13, 3, 24, 1. *Second Innings:* McKenzie 18, 4, 53, 1; Hawke 21, 6, 54, 5; Walters 9, 0, 47, 0; Stackpole 14, 3, 33, 2; Chappell 22, 4, 53, 0; Veivers 3·7, 0, 16, 1.

ENGLAND. *First Innings:* Jones 29, 3, 118, 6; Brown 28, 4, 109, 1; Boycott 7, 3, 33, 0; Titmus 37, 6, 116, 3; Allen 21, 1, 103, 0; Barber 4, 0, 30, 0.

Umpires: C. J. Egar, L. Rowan

1965/6 Fifth Test, Melbourne

February 11, 12, 14, 15, 16   Toss: England
Result: MATCH DRAWN

ENGLAND

G. Boycott, c Stackpole b McKenzie	17	lbw b McKenzie	1
R. W. Barber, run out	17	b McKenzie	20
J. H. Edrich, c McKenzie b Walters	85	b McKenzie	3
K. F. Barrington, c Grout b Walters	115	not out	32
M. C. Cowdrey, c Grout b Walters	79	not out	11
*M. J. K. Smith, c Grout b Walters	0		
†J. M. Parks, run out	89		
F. J. Titmus, not out	42		
B. R. Knight, c Grout b Hawke	13		
D. J. Brown, c and b Chappell	12		
I. J. Jones, not out	4		
Extras, (b 9, lb 2, nb 1)	12	(lb 2)	2
Total (9 wkts dec)	485	(3 wkts)	69

FALL OF WICKETS. *First Innings:* 1–36, 2–41, 3–219, 4–254, 5–254, 6–392, 7–419, 8–449, 9–474 *Second Innings:* 1–6, 2–21, 3–34.

AUSTRALIA

W. M. Lawry, c Edrich b Jones	108
*R. B. Simpson, b Brown	4
G. Thomas, c Titmus b Jones	19
R. M. Cowper, b Knight	307
K. D. Walters, c and b Barber	60
I. M. Chappell, c Parks b Jones	19
K. R. Stackpole, b Knight	9
T. R. Veivers, b Titmus	4
N. J. N. Hawke, not out	0
†A. T. W. Grout ⎱ did not bat D. G. McKenzie ⎰	
Extras, (b 6, lb 5, nb 2)	13
Total (8 wkts dec)	543

FALL OF WICKETS. *First Innings:* 1–15, 2–36, 3–248, 4–420, 5–481, 6–532, 7–543, 8–543.

P

BOWLING

AUSTRALIA. *First Innings:* McKenzie 26, 5, 100, 1; Hawke 35, 5, 109, 1; Walters 19, 3, 53, 4; Simpson 5, 1, 20, 0; Stackpole 10, 2, 43, 0; Veivers 15, 3, 78, 0; Chappell 17, 4, 70, 1. *Second Innings:* McKenzie 6, 2, 17, 3; Hawke 4, 1, 22, 0; Walters 2, 0, 16, 0; Stackpole 3, 0, 10, 0; Chappell 2, 0, 2, 0.

ENGLAND. *First Innings:* Brown 31, 3, 134, 1; Jones 29, 1, 145, 3; Knight 36·2, 4, 105, 2; Titmus 42, 12, 86, 1; Barber 16, 0, 60, 1.

Umpires: C. J. Egar, L. Rowan

Averages: 1965/6

AUSTRALIA

BATTING	M.	Inns.	N.O.	Runs	H.S.	Av.
R. B. Simpson	3	4	0	355	225	88·75
W. M. Lawry	5	7	0	592	166	84·57
R. M. Cowper	4	6	0	493	307	82·16
K. D. Walters	5	7	1	410	155	68·33
G. Thomas	3	4	0	147	52	36·75
P. J. Burge	4	6	0	159	120	26·50
K. R. Stackpole	2	2	0	52	43	26·00
T. R. Veivers	4	5	1	83	56*	20·75
I. M. Chappell	2	2	0	36	19	18·00
B. C. Booth	3	5	0	84	27	16·80
N. J. N. Hawke	4	5	3	28	20	14·00
G. D. McKenzie	4	5	1	51	24	12·75
P. I. Philpott	3	4	1	22	10	7·33
A. T. W. Grout	5	5	0	34	16	6·80

PLAYED IN ONE MATCH: A. N. Connolly 0 and 0*, I. R. Redpath 17, D. J. Sincock 29 and 27. P. J. Allan did not bat.

BOWLING	Overs	Mds.	Runs	Wkts.	Av.
N. J. N. Hawke	142·7	29	419	16	26·18
G. D. McKenzie	133·1	20	467	16	29·18
K. D. Walters	79	8	283	9	31·44
R. M. Cowper	22	5	76	2	38·00
P. J. Allan	24	6	83	2	41·50
P. I. Philpott	100·1	9	371	8	46·37
K. R. Stackpole	32	5	116	2	58·00
T. R. Veivers	66·7	11	250	4	62·50
A. N. Connolly	38	5	128	1	128·00
I. M. Chappell	45	9	143	1	143·00

ALSO BOWLED: R. B. Simpson 21–5–81–0, D. J. Sincock 20–1–98–0.

ENGLAND

BATTING	M.	*Inns.*	N.O.	*Runs*	H.S.	*Av.*
K. F. Barrington	5	8	1	464	115	66·28
F. J. Titmus	5	6	2	258	60	64·50
M. C. Cowdrey	4	6	1	267	104	53·40
J. M. Parks	5	6	0	290	89	48·33
J. H. Edrich	5	8	0	375	109	46·87
G. Boycott	5	9	2	300	84	42·85
R. W. Barber	5	9	1	328	185	41·00
D. A. Allen	4	5	2	62	50*	20·66
M. J. K. Smith	5	7	1	107	41	17·83
I. J. Jones	4	5	2	29	16	9·66
B. R. Knight	2	2	0	14	13	7·00
D. J. Brown	4	5	0	17	12	3·40

PLAYED IN ONE MATCH: K. Higgs 4, W. E. Russell 0*.

BOWLING	*Overs*	*Mds.*	*Runs*	*Wkts.*	*Av.*
K. F. Barrington	7·4	0	47	2	23·50
B. R. Knight	83·7	10	250	8	31·25
I. J. Jones	129	15	533	15	35·53
D. J. Brown	108	14	409	11	37·18
G. Boycott	23	4	89	2	44·50
D. A. Allen	137	33	403	9	44·77
K. Higgs	30	6	102	2	51·00
F. J. Titmus	210·3	52	517	9	57·44
R. W. Barber	55·1	2	261	3	87·00

ALSO BOWLED: M. J. K. Smith 2–0–8–0.

1970/1 First Test, Brisbane

November 27, 28, 29, December 1, 2   Toss: Australia
Result: MATCH DRAWN

AUSTRALIA

*W. M. Lawry, c Knott b Snow	4	c Snow b Fletcher	84
K. R. Stackpole, c Knott b Snow	207	c Knott b Shuttleworth	8
I. M. Chappell, run out	59	st Knott b Illingworth	10
K. D. Walters, b Underwood	112	c Luckhurst b Snow	7
I. R. Redpath, c Illingworth b Underwood	22	c and b Underwood	28
A. P. Sheahan, c Knott b Underwood	0	c Shuttleworth b Snow	36
†R. W. Marsh, b Snow	9	b Shuttleworth	14
T. J. Jenner, c Cowdrey b Snow	0	c Boycott b Shuttleworth	2
G. D. McKenzie, not out	3	b Shuttleworth	1

APPENDIX

J. W. Gleeson, c Cowdrey b Snow	0	b Shuttleworth	6
A. L. Thomson, b Snow	0	not out	4
Extras, (b 7, lb 4, nb 6)	17	(b 4, lb 3, nb 7)	14
Total	433		214

FALL OF WICKETS. *First Innings* 1–12, 2–163, 3–372, 4–418, 5–418, 6–421, 7–422, 8–433, 9–433, 10–433. *Second Innings:* 1–30, 2–47, 3–64, 4–137, 5–152, 6–193, 7–199, 8–201, 9–208, 10–214.

ENGLAND

G. Boycott, c Marsh b Gleeson	37	c and b Jenner	16
B. W. Luckhurst, run out	74	not out	20
†A. P. Knott, c Lawry b Walters	73		
J. H. Edrich, c Chappell b Jenner	79		
M. C. Cowdrey, c Chappell b Gleeson	28		
K. W. R. Fletcher, c Marsh b McKenzie	34		
B. L. d'Oliveira, c Sheahan b McKenzie	57		
*R. Illingworth, c Marsh b Thomson	8		
J. A. Snow, c Marsh b Walters	34		
D. L. Underwood, not out	2		
K. Shuttleworth, c Lawry b Walters	7		
Extras, (b 2, lb 7, nb 22)	31	(lb 3)	3
Total	464	(1 wkt)	39

FALL OF WICKETS. *First Innings:* 1–92, 2–136, 3–245, 4–284, 5–336, 6–346, 7–371, 8–449, 9–456, 10–464. *Second Innings:* 1–39.

BOWLING

ENGLAND. *First Innings:* Snow 32·3, 6, 114, 6; Shuttleworth 27, 6, 81, 0; d'Oliveira 16, 2, 63, 0; Illingworth 11, 1, 47, 0; Underwood 28, 6, 101, 3; Cowdrey 1, 0, 10, 0. *Second Innings:* Snow 20, 3, 48, 2; Shuttleworth 17·5, 2, 47, 5; d'Oliveira 7, 5, 7, 0; Illingworth 18, 11, 19, 1; Underwood 20, 10, 23, 1; Cowdrey 2, 0, 8, 0; Fletcher 9, 1, 48, 1.

AUSTRALIA. *First Innings:* McKenzie 28, 5, 90, 2; Thomson 43, 8, 136, 1; Gleeson 42, 15, 97, 2; Jenner 24, 5, 86, 1; Stackpole 4, 0, 12, 0; Walters 5·5, 0, 12, 3. *Second Innings:* McKenzie 3, 0, 6, 0; Thomson 4, 0, 20, 0; Jenner 4·6, 2, 9, 1; Stackpole 4, 3, 1, 0.

Umpires: T. F. Brooks, L. P. Rowan

1970/1 Second Test, Perth

December 11, 12, 13, 15, 16   Toss: Australia
Result: MATCH DRAWN

ENGLAND

G. Boycott, c McKenzie b Gleeson	70	st Marsh b Gleeson	50
B. W. Luckhurst, b McKenzie	131	c Stackpole b Walters	19
J. H. Edrich, run out	47	not out	115
†A. P. E. Knott, c Stackpole b Thomson	24	not out	30
K. W. R. Fletcher, b Walters	22	lbw b Gleeson	0
M. C. Cowdrey, c and b G. Chappell	40	c Marsh b Thomson	1
B. L. d'Oliveira, c Stackpole b Thomson	8	b Gleeson	31
*R. Illingworth, b McKenzie	34	c Marsh b Stackpole	29
J. A. Snow, not out	4		
K. Shuttleworth, b McKenzie	2		
P. Lever, b McKenzie	2		
Extras, (lb 8, w 1, nb 4)	13	(b 2, lb 3, nb 7)	12
Total	397	(6 wkts dec)	287

FALL OF WICKETS. *First Innings:* 1–171, 2–243, 3–281, 4–291, 5–310, 6–327, 7–389, 8–389, 9–393, 10–397. *Second Innings:* 1–60, 2–98, 3–98, 4–101, 5–152, 6–209.

AUSTRALIA

*W. M. Lawry, c Illingworth b Snow	0	(2)not out	38
K. R. Stackpole, c Lever b Snow	5	(1)c sub (J. H. Hampshire) b Snow	0
I. M. Chappell, c Knott b Snow	50	c sub (J. H. Hampshire) b Snow	17
K. D. Walters, c Knott b Lever	7	b Lever	8
I. R. Redpath, c and b Illingworth	171	not out	26
A. P. Sheahan, run out	2		
G. S. Chappell, c Luckhurst b Shuttleworth	108		
†R. W. Marsh, c d'Oliviera b Shuttleworth	44		
G. D. McKenzie, c Lever b d'Oliveira	7		
J. W. Gleeson, c Knott b Snow	15		

A. L. Thomson, not out	12		
Extras, (b 5, lb 4, nb 10)	19	(b 4, lb 4, nb 3)	11
Total	440	(3 wkts)	100

FALL OF WICKETS *First Innings:* 1–5, 2–8, 3–17, 4–105, 5–107, 6–326, 7–393, 8–408, 9–426, 10–440 *Second Innings:* 1–0, 2–20, 3–40.

BOWLING
AUSTRALIA. *First Innings:* McKenzie 31·4, 4, 66, 4; Thomson 24, 4, 118, 2; G. Chappell 24, 4, 54, 1; Gleeson 32, 10, 78, 1; Walters 11, 1, 35, 1; Stackpole 11, 2, 33, 0. *Second Innings:* McKenzie 18, 2, 50, 0; Thomson 25, 3, 71, 1; G. Chappell 4, 1, 17, 0; Gleeson 32, 11, 68, 3; Walters 7, 1, 26, 1; Stackpole 15, 3, 43, 1.
ENGLAND. *First Innings:* Snow 33·5, 3, 143, 4; Shuttleworth 28, 4, 105, 2; Lever 21, 3, 78, 1; d'Oliveira 17, 1, 41, 1; Illingworth 13, 2, 43, 1; Boycott 1, 0, 7, 0; Fletcher 1, 0, 4, 0. *Second Innings:* Snow 9, 4, 17, 2; Shuttleworth 3, 1, 9, 0; Lever 5, 2, 10, 1; d'Oliveira 4, 2, 5, 0; Illingworth 4, 2, 12, 0; Fletcher 4, 0, 18, 0; Cowdrey 3, 0, 18, 0.

Umpires: T. F. Brooks, L. P. Rowan

The Third Test at Melbourne was abandoned without a ball being bowled.

1970/1 Fourth Test, Sydney

January 9, 10, 12, 13, 14   Toss: England
Result: ENGLAND WON BY 299 RUNS

ENGLAND

G. Boycott, c Gleeson b Connolly	77	not out	142
B. W. Luckhurst, lbw b Gleeson	38	c I. Chappell b McKenzie	5
J. H. Edrich, c Gleeson b G. Chappell	55	run out	12
K. W. R. Fletcher, c Walters b Mallett	23	c Stackpole b Mallett	8
B. L. d'Oliveira, c Connolly b Mallett	0	c I. Chappell b G. Chappell	56
*R. Illingworth, b Gleeson	25	st Marsh b Mallett	53
†A. P. E. Knott, st Marsh b Mallett	6	not out	21
J. A. Snow, c Lawry b Gleeson	37		
P. Lever, c Connolly b Mallett	36		
D. L. Underwood, c G. Chappell b Gleeson	0		

R. G. D. Willis, not out	15		
Extras, (b 5, lb 2, w 1, nb 12)	20	(b 9, lb 4, nb 9)	22
Total	332	(5 wkts dec)	319

FALL OF WICKETS. *First Innings:* 1–116, 2–130, 3–201, 4–205, 5–208, 6–219, 7–262, 8–291, 9–291, 10–332. *Second Innings:* 1–7, 2–35, 3–48, 4–181, 5–276.

AUSTRALIA

*W. M. Lawry, c Edrich b Lever	9	not out	60
I. M. Chappell, c Underwood b Snow	12	c d'Oliveira b Snow	0
I. R. Redpath, c Fletcher b d'Oliveira	64	c Edrich b Snow	6
K. D. Walters, c Luckhurst b Illingworth	55	c Knott b Lever	3
G. S. Chappell, c and b Underwood	15	b Snow	2
K. R. Stackpole, c Boycott b Underwood	33	c Lever b Snow	30
†R. W. Marsh, c d'Oliveira b Underwood	8	c Willis b Snow	0
A. A. Mallett, b Underwood	4	c Knott b Willis	6
G. D. McKenzie, not out	11	retired hurt	6
J. W. Gleeson, c Fletcher b d'Oliveira	0	b Snow	0
A. N. Connolly, b Lever	14	c Knott b Snow	0
Extras (nb 11)	11	(b 2, nb 1)	3
Total	236		116

FALL OF WICKETS. *First Innings:* 1–14, 2–38, 3–137, 4–160, 5–189, 6–199, 7–208, 8–208, 9–219, 10–236. *Second Innings:* 1–1, 2–11, 3–14, 4–21, 5–66, 6–66, 7–86, 8–116, 9–116.

BOWLING

AUSTRALIA. *First Innings:* McKenzie 15, 3, 74, 0; Connolly 13, 2, 43, 1; Gleeson 29, 7, 83, 4; G. Chappell 11, 4, 30, 1; Mallett 16·7, 5, 40, 4; Walters 3, 1, 11, 0; Stackpole 7, 2, 31, 0. *Second Innings:* McKenzie 15, 0, 65, 1; Connolly 14, 1, 38, 0; Gleeson 23, 4, 54, 0; G. Chappell 15, 5, 24, 1; Mallett 19, 1, 85, 2; Walters 2, 0, 14, 0; Stackpole 6, 1, 17 0.
ENGLAND. *First Innings:* Snow 14, 6, 23, 1; Willis 9, 2, 26, 0; Lever 8·6, 1, 31, 2; Underwood 22, 7, 66, 4; Illingworth 14, 3, 59, 1; d'Oliveira 9, 2, 20, 2. *Second Innings:* Snow 17·5, 5, 40, 7; Willis 3, 2, 1, 1; Lever 11, 1, 24, 1; Underwood 8, 2, 17, 0; Illingworth 9, 5, 9, 0; d'Oliveira 7, 3, 16, 0; Fletcher 1, 0, 6, 0.

Umpires: T. F. Brooks, L. P. Rowan

1970/1 Fifth Test, Melbourne

January 21, 22, 23, 25, 26   Toss: Australia
Result: MATCH DRAWN

AUSTRALIA

*W. M. Lawry, c Snow b Willis	56	c sub (K. Shuttleworth) b Snow	42
K. R. Stackpole, c Lever b d'Oliveira	30	c Knott b Willis	18
I. M. Chappell, c Luckhurst b Snow	111	b Underwood	30
I. R. Redpath, b Snow	72	c Knott b Snow	5
K. D. Walters, b Underwood	55	not out	39
G. S. Chappell, c Edrich b Willis	3	not out	20
†R. W. Marsh, not out	92		
K. J. O'Keeffe, c Luckhurst b Illingworth	27		
J. W. Gleeson, c Cowdrey b Willis	5		
J. R. F. Duncan, c Edrich b Illingworth	3		
A. L. Thomson, not out	0		
Extras, (b 10, lb 17, nb 12)	39	(b 8, lb 3, nb 4)	15
Total (9 wkts dec)	493	(4 wkts dec)	169

FALL OF WICKETS. *First Innings:* 1–64, 2–266, 3–269, 4–310, 5–314, 6–374, 7–471, 8–477, 9–480. *Second Innings:* 1–51, 2–84, 3–91, 4–132.

ENGLAND

G. Boycott, c Redpath b Thomson	12	not out	76
B. W. Luckhurst, b Walters	109		
J. H. Edrich, c Marsh b Thomson	9	not out	74
M. C. Cowdrey, c and b Gleeson	13		
B. L. d'Oliveira, c Marsh b Thomson	117		
*R. Illingworth, c Redpath b Gleeson	41		
†A. P. E. Knott, lbw b Stackpole	19		
J. A. Snow, b I. Chappell	1		
P. Lever, run out	19		
D. L. Underwood, c and b Gleeson	5		
R. G. D. Willis, not out	5		
Extras, (b 17, lb 14, nb 11)	42	(b 1, lb 8, nb 2)	11
Total	392	(0 wkt)	161

FALL OF WICKETS. *First Innings:* 1–40, 2–64, 3–88, 4–228, 5–306, 6–340, 7–354, 8–362, 9–379, 10–392.

BOWLING

ENGLAND. *First Innings:* Snow 29, 6, 94, 2; Lever 25, 6, 79, 0; d'Oliveira 22, 6, 71, 1; Willis 20, 5, 73, 3; Underwood 19, 4, 78, 1; Illingworth 13, 0, 59, 2. *Second Innings:* Snow 12, 4, 21, 2; Lever 12, 1, 53, 0; Willis 10, 1, 42, 1; Underwood 12, 0, 38, 1.

AUSTRALIA. *First Innings:* Thomson 34, 5, 110, 3; Duncan 14, 4, 30, 0; G. Chappell 8, 0, 21, 0; O'Keeffe 31, 11, 71, 0; Gleeson 25, 7, 60, 3; Stackpole 17·5, 4, 41, 1; Walters 5, 2, 7, 1; I. Chappell 3, 0, 10, 1. *Second Innings:* Thomson 11, 5, 26, 0; G. Chappell 5, 0, 19, 0; O'Keeffe 19, 3, 45, 0; Gleeson 3, 1, 18, 0; Stackpole 13, 2, 28, 0; Walters 7, 1, 14, 0.

Umpires: L. P. Rowan, M. G. O'Connell

1970/1 Sixth Test, Adelaide

January 29, 30, February 1, 2, 3   Toss: England
Result: MATCH DRAWN

ENGLAND

G. Boycott, run out	58	not out	119
J. H. Edrich, c Stackpole b Lillee	130	b Thomson	40
K. W. R. Fletcher, b Thomson	80	b Gleeson	5
†A. P. E. Knott, c Redpath b Lillee	7		
B. L. d'Oliveira, c Marsh b G. Chappell	47	c Walters b Thomson	5
J. H. Hampshire, c Lillee b G. Chappell	55	lbw b Thomson	3
*R. Illingworth, b Lillee	24	not out	48
J. A. Snow, b Lillee	38		
P. Lever, b Thomson	5		
D. L. Underwood, not out	1		
R. G. D. Willis, c Walters b Lillee	4		
Extras, (b 1, lb 5, w 4, nb 11)	21	(lb 4, w 1, nb 8)	13
Total	470	(4 wkts dec)	233

FALL OF WICKETS. *First Innings:* 1–107, 2–276, 3–289, 4–289, 5–385, 6–402, 7–458, 8–465, 9–465, 10–470. *Second Innings:* 1–103, 2–128, 3–143, 4–151.

AUSTRALIA

K. R. Stackpole, b Underwood	87	b Snow	136
*W. M. Lawry, c Knott b Snow	10	c Knott b Willis	21
I. M. Chappell, c Knott b Lever	28	c Willis b Underwood	104
I. R. Redpath, c Lever b Illingworth	9	not out	21
K. D. Walters, c Knott b Lever	8	not out	36
G. S. Chappell, c Edrich b Lever	0		
†R. W. Marsh, c Knott b Willis	28		
A. A. Mallett, c Illingworth b Snow	28		
J. H. Gleeson, c Boycott b Willis	16		
D. K. Lillee, c Boycott b Lever	10		
A. L. Thomson, not out	6		
Extras, (lb 2, nb 3)	5	(b 2, lb 3, nb 5)	10
Total	235	(3 wkts)	328

FALL OF WICKETS. *First Innings:* 1–61, 2–117, 3–131, 4–141, 5–145, 6–163, 7–180, 8–219, 9–221, 10–235. *Second Innings:* 1–65, 2–267, 3–271.

BOWLING

AUSTRALIA. *First Innings:* Thomson 29·7, 6, 94, 2; Lillee 28·3, 0, 84, 5; Walters 9, 2, 29, 0; G. Chappell 18, 1, 54, 2; Gleeson 19, 1, 78, 0; Mallett 20, 1, 63, 0; Stackpole 12, 2, 47, 0. *Second Innings:* Thomson 19, 2, 79, 3; Lillee 7, 0, 40, 0; Walters 3, 0, 5, 0; G. Chappell 5, 0, 27, 0; Gleeson 16, 1, 69, 1; Mallett 1, 1, 0, 0.

ENGLAND. *First Innings:* Snow 21, 4, 73, 2; Lever 17·1, 2, 49, 4; Underwood 21, 6, 45, 1; Willis 12, 3, 49, 2; Illingworth 5, 2, 14, 1. *Second Innings:* Snow 17, 3, 60, 1; Lever 17, 4, 49, 0; Underwood 35, 7, 85, 1; Willis 13, 1, 48, 1; Illingworth 14, 7, 32, 0; d'Oliveira 15, 4, 28, 0; Fletcher 4, 0, 16, 0.

Umpires: T. F. Brooks, M. G. O'Connell

1970/1 Seventh Test, Sydney

February 12, 13, 14, 16, 17   Toss: Australia
Result: ENGLAND WON BY 62 RUNS

ENGLAND

J. H. Edrich, c G. Chappell b Dell	30	c I. Chappell b O'Keeffe	57
B. W. Luckhurst, c Redpath b Walters	0	c Lillee b O'Keeffe	59
K. W. R. Fletcher, c Stackpole b O'Keeffe	33	c Stackpole b Eastwood	20
J. H. Hampshire, c Marsh b Lillee	10	c I. Chappell b O'Keeffe	24
B. L. d'Oliveira, b Dell	1	c I. Chappell b Lillee	47

*R. Illingworth, b Jenner	42	lbw b Lillee	29
†A. P. E. Knott, c Stackpole b O'Keeffe	27	b Dell	15
J. A. Snow, b Jenner	7	c Stackpole b Dell	20
P. Lever, c Jenner b O'Keeffe	4	c Redpath b Jenner	17
D. L. Underwood, not out	8	c Marsh b Dell	0
R. G. D. Willis, b Jenner	11	not out	2
Extras, (b 4, lb 4, w 1, nb 2)	11	(b 3, lb 3, nb 6)	12
Total	184		302

FALL OF WICKETS. *First Innings:* 1–5, 2–60, 3–68, 4–69, 5–98, 6–145, 7–156, 8–165, 9–165, 10–184. *Second Innings:* 1–94, 2–130, 3–158, 4–165, 5–234, 6–251, 7–276, 8–298, 9–299, 10–302.

AUSTRALIA

K. H. Eastwood, c Knott b Lever	5	b Snow	0
K. R. Stackpole, b Snow	6	b Illingworth	67
†R. W. Marsh, c Willis b Lever	4	c Underwood	16
*I. M. Chappell, b Willis	25	c Knott b Lever	6
I. R. Redpath, c and b Underwood	59	c Hampshire b Illingworth	14
K. D. Walters, st Knott b Underwood	42	c d'Oliveira b Willis	1
G. S. Chappell, b Willis	65	st Knott b Illingworth	30
K. J. O'Keeffe, c Knott b Illingworth	3	b d'Oliveira	12
T. J. Jenner, b Lever	30	c Fletcher b Underwood	4
D. K. Lillee, c Knott b Willis	6	c Hampshire b d'Oliveira	0
A. R. Dell, not out	3	not out	3
Extras, (lb 5, w 1, nb 10)	16	(b 2, nb 5)	7
Total	264		160

FALL OF WICKETS. *First Innings:* 1–11, 2–13, 3–32, 4–66, 5–147, 6–162, 7–178, 8–235, 9–239, 10–264. *Second Innings:* 1–0, 2–22, 3–71, 4–82, 5–96, 6–131, 7–142, 8–154, 9–154, 10–160.

BOWLING
AUSTRALIA. *First Innings:* Lillee 13, 5, 32, 1; Dell 16, 8, 32, 2; Walters 4, 0, 10, 1; G. Chappell 3, 0, 9, 0; Jenner 16, 3, 42, 3; O'Keeffe 24, 8, 48, 3. *Second Innings:* Lillee 14, 0, 43, 2; Dell 26·7, 3, 65, 3; Walters 5, 0, 18, 0; Jenner 21, 5, 39, 1; O'Keeffe 26, 8, 96, 3; Eastwood 5, 0, 21, 1; Stackpole 3, 1, 8, 0.
ENGLAND. *First Innings:* Snow 18, 2, 68, 1; Lever 14·6, 3, 43, 3; d'Oliveira 12, 2, 24, 0; Willis 12, 1, 58, 3; Underwood 16, 3, 39, 2;

Illingworth 11, 3, 16, 1. *Second Innings:* Snow 2, 1, 7, 1; Lever 12, 2, 23, 1; d'Oliveira 5, 1, 15, 2; Willis 9, 1, 32, 1; Underwood 13·6, 5, 28, 2; Illingworth 20, 7, 39, 3; Fletcher 1, 0, 9, 0.

Umpires: T. F. Brooks, L. P. Rowan

Averages: 1970/1

AUSTRALIA

BATTING	M.	Inns.	N.O.	Runs	H.S.	Av.
K. R. Stackpole	6	12	0	627	207	52·25
I. R. Redpath	6	12	2	497	171	49·70
W. M. Lawry	5	10	2	324	84	40·50
I. M. Chappell	6	12	0	452	111	37·66
K. D. Walters	6	12	2	373	112	37·30
G. S. Chappell	5	8	1	243	108	34·71
R. W. Marsh	6	9	1	215	92*	26·87
A. L. Thomson	4	5	4	22	12*	22·00
G. D. McKenzie	3	5	3	28	11*	14·00
K. J. O'Keeffe	2	3	0	42	27	14·00
A. A. Mallett	2	3	0	38	28	12·66
A. P. Sheahan	2	3	0	38	36	12·66
T. J. Jenner	2	4	0	36	30	9·00
J. W. Gleeson	5	7	0	42	16	6·00
D. K. Lillee	2	3	0	16	10	5·33

PLAYED IN ONE MATCH: A. N. Connolly 14 and 0, A. R. Dell 3* and 3*, J. R. F. Duncan, 3, K. H. Eastwood 5 and 0.

BOWLING	Overs	Mds.	Runs	Wkts.	Av.
A. R. Dell	42·7	11	97	5	19·40
D. K. Lillee	62·3	5	199	8	24·87
K. D. Walters	61·5	8	181	7	25·85
T. J. Jenner	65·6	15	176	6	29·33
A. A. Mallett	56·7	8	188	6	31·33
J. W. Gleeson	221	57	605	14	43·21
K. J. O'Keeffe	100	30	260	6	43·33
G. D. McKenzie	110·4	14	351	7	50·14
G. S. Chappell	93	15	255	5	51·00
A. L. Thomson	189·7	33	654	12	54·50

ALSO BOWLED: I. M. Chappell 3–0–10–1, A. N. Connolly 27–3–81–1, J. R. F. Duncan 14–4–30–0, K. H. Eastwood 5–0–21–1, K. R. Stackpole 92·5–20–261–2.

ENGLAND

BATTING	M.	Inns.	N.O.	Runs	H.S.	Av.
G. Boycott	5	10	3	657	142*	93·85
J. H. Edrich	6	11	2	648	130	72·00
B. W. Luckhurst	5	9	1	455	131	56·87
R. Illingworth	6	10	1	333	53	37·00
B. L. d'Oliveira	6	10	0	369	117	36·90
A. P. E. Knott	6	9	2	222	73	31·71
K. W. R. Fletcher	5	9	0	225	80	25·00
J. A. Snow	6	7	1	141	38	23·50
J. H. Hampshire	2	4	0	92	55	23·00
M. C. Cowdrey	3	4	0	82	40	20·50
R. G. D. Willis	4	5	3	37	15*	18·50
P. Lever	5	6	0	83	36	13·83
D. L. Underwood	5	6	3	16	8*	5·33
K. Shuttleworth	2	2	0	9	7	4·50

BOWLING	Overs	Mds.	Runs	Wkts.	Av.
J. A. Snow	225·5	47	708	31	22·83
R. G. D. Willis	88	16	329	12	27·41
D. L. Underwood	194·6	50	520	16	32·50
P. Lever	143·5	25	439	13	33·76
K. Shuttleworth	75·5	13	242	7	34·57
R. Illingworth	132	43	349	10	34·90
B. L. d'Oliveira	114	29	290	6	48·33

ALSO BOWLED: G. Boycott 1–0–7–0, M. C. Cowdrey 6–0–36–0, K. W. R. Fletcher 20–1–101–1.

1974/5 First Test, Brisbane

November 29, 30, December 1, 3, 4   Toss: Australia
Result: AUSTRALIA WON BY 166 RUNS

AUSTRALIA

I. R. Redpath, b Willis	5	b Willis	25
W. J. Edwards, c Amiss b Hendrick	4	c Knott b Willis	5
*I. M. Chappell, c Greig b Willis	90	c Fletcher b Underwood	11
G. S. Chappell, c Fletcher b Underwood	58	b Underwood	71
R. Edwards, c Knott b Underwood	32	c Knott b Willis	53
K. D. Walters, c Lever b Willis	3	not out	62
†R. W. Marsh, c Denness b Hendrick	14	not out	46
T. J. Jenner, c Lever b Willis	12		
D. K. Lillee, c Knott b Greig	15		

217

M. H. N. Walker, not out	41		
J. R. Thomson, run out	23		
Extras, (lb 4, nb 8)	12	(b 1, lb 7, w 1, nb 6)	15
Total	309	(5 wkts dec)	288

FALL OF WICKETS. *First Innings:* 1–7, 2–10, 3–110, 4–197, 5–202, 6–205, 7–228, 8–229, 9–257, 10–309. *Second Innings:* 1–15, 2–39, 3–59, 4–173, 5–190.

ENGLAND

D. L. Amiss, c Jenner b Thomson	7	c Walters b Thomson	25
B. W. Luckhurst, c Marsh b Thomson	1	c I. Chappell b Lillee	3
J. H. Edrich, c I. Chappell b Thomson	48	b Thomson	6
*M. H. Denness, lbw b Walker	6	c Walters b Thomson	27
K. W. R. Fletcher, b Lillee	17	c G. Chappell b Jenner	19
A. W. Greig, c Marsh b Lillee	110	b Thomson	2
†A. P. E. Knott, c Jenner b Walker	12	b Thomson	19
P. Lever, c I. Chappell b Walker	4	c Redpath b Lillee	14
D. L. Underwood, c Redpath b Walters	25	c Walker b Jenner	30
R. G. D. Willis, not out	13	not out	3
M. Hendrick, c Redpath b Walker	4	b Thomson	0
Extras, (b 5, lb 2, w 3, nb 8)	18	(b 8, lb 3, w 2, nb 5)	18
Total	265		166

FALL OF WICKETS. *First Innings:* 1–9, 2–10, 3–33, 4–57, 5–130, 6–162, 7–168, 8–226, 9–248, 10–265. *Second Innings:* 1–18, 2–40, 3–44, 4–92, 5–94, 6–94, 7–115, 8–162, 9–163, 10–166.

BOWLING

ENGLAND. *First Innings:* Willis 21·5, 3, 56, 4; Lever 16, 1, 53, 0; Hendrick 19, 3, 64, 2; Greig 16, 2, 70, 1; Underwood 20, 6, 54, 2. *Second Innings:* Willis 15, 3, 45, 3; Lever 18, 4, 58, 0; Hendrick 13, 2, 47, 0; Greig 13, 2, 60 0; Underwood 26, 6, 63, 2.
AUSTRALIA. *First Innings:* Lillee 23, 6, 73, 2; Thomson 21, 5, 59, 3; Walker 24·5, 2, 73, 4; Walters 6, 1, 18, 1; Jenner 6, 1, 24, 0. *Second Innings:* Lillee 12, 2, 25, 2; Thomson 17·5, 3, 46, 6; Walker 9, 4, 32, 0; Walters 2, 2, 0, 0; Jenner 16, 5, 45, 2.

Umpires: R. C. Bailhache, T. F. Brooks

1974/5 Second Test, Perth

December 13, 14, 15, 17   Toss: Australia
Result: AUSTRALIA WON BY NINE WICKETS

ENGLAND

D. Lloyd, c G. Chappell b Thomson	49	c G. Chappell b Walker	35
B. W. Luckhurst, c Mallett b Walker	27	(7)c Mallett b Lillee	23
M. C. Cowdrey, b Thomson	22	(2)lbw b Thomson	41
A. W. Greig, c Mallett b Walker	23	c G. Chappell b Thomson	32
K. W. R. Fletcher, c Redpath b Lillee	4	c Marsh b Thomson	0
*M. H. Denness, c G. Chappell b Lillee	2	(3)c Redpath b Thomson	20
†A. P. E. Knott, c Redpath b Walters	51	(6)c G. Chappell b Lillee	18
F. J. Titmus, c Redpath b Walters	10	c G. Chappell b Mallett	61
C. M. Old, c G. Chappell b I. Chappell	7	c Thomson b Mallett	43
G. G. Arnold, run out	1	c Mallett b Thomson	4
R. G. D. Willis, not out	4	not out	0
Extras, (w 3, nb 5)	8	(lb 4, w 1, nb 11)	16
Total	208		293

FALL OF WICKETS. *First Innings:* 1–44, 2–99, 3–119, 4–128, 5–132, 6–132, 7–194, 8–201, 9–202, 10–208. *Second Innings:* 1–62, 2–106, 3–124, 4–124, 5–154, 6–156, 7–219, 8–285, 9–293, 10–293.

AUSTRALIA

I. R. Redpath, st Knott b Titmus	41	not out	12
W. J. Edwards, c Lloyd b Greig	30	lbw b Arnold	0
*I. M. Chappell, c Knott b Arnold	25	not out	11
G. S. Chappell, c Greig b Willis	62		
R. Edwards, b Arnold	115		
K. D. Walters, c Fletcher b Willis	103		
†R. W. Marsh, c Lloyd b Titmus	41		
M. H. N. Walker, c Knott b Old	19		
D. K. Lillee, b Old	11		
A. A. Mallett, c Knott b Old	0		
J. R. Thomson, not out	11		
Extras, (b 7, lb 14, nb 2)	23		
Total	481	(1 wkt)	23

FALL OF WICKETS. *First Innings:* 1–64, 2–101, 3–113, 4–192, 5–36 2
6–416, 7–449, 8–462, 9–462, 10–481. *Second Innings:* 1–4.

BOWLING
AUSTRALIA. *First Innings:* Lillee 16, 4, 48, 2; Thomson 15, 6, 45, 2;
Walker 20, 5, 49, 2; Mallett 10, 3, 35, 0; Walters 2·3, 0, 13, 2; I. M.
Chappell 2, 0, 10, 1. *Second Innings:* Lillee 22, 5, 59, 2; Thomson 25, 4,
93, 5; Walker 24, 7, 76, 1; Mallett 11·1, 4, 32, 2; Walters 9, 4, 17, 0.
ENGLAND. *First Innings:* Willis 22, 0, 91, 2; Arnold 27, 1, 129, 2;
Old 22·6, 3, 85, 3; Greig 9, 0, 69, 1; Titmus 28, 3, 84, 2. *Second Innings:*
Willis 2, 0, 8, 0; Arnold 1·7, 0, 15, 1.

Umpires: R. C. Bailhache, T. F. Brooks

1974/5 Third Test, Melbourne

December 26, 27, 28, 30, 31   Toss: Australia
Result: MATCH DRAWN

ENGLAND

D. L. Amiss, c Walters b Lillee	4	c I. Chappell b Mallett	90
D. Lloyd, c Mallett b Thomson	14	c and b Mallett	44
M. C. Cowdrey, lbw b Thomson	35	c G. Chappell b Lillee	8
J. H. Edrich, c Marsh b Mallett	49	c Marsh b Thomson	4
*M. H. Denness, c Marsh b Mallett	8	c I. Chappell b Thomson	2
A. W. Greig, run out	28	c G. Chappell b Lillee	60
†A. P. E. Knott, b Thomson	52	c Marsh b Thomson	4
F. J. Titmus, c Mallett b Lillee	10	b Mallett	0
D. L. Underwood, c Marsh b Walker	9	c I. Chappell b Mallett	4
R. G. D. Willis, c Walters b Thomson	13	b Thomson	15
M. Hendrick, not out	8	not out	0
Extras, (lb 2, w 1, nb 9)	12	(b 2, lb 9, w 2)	13
Total	242		244

FALL OF WICKETS. *First Innings:* 1–4, 2–34, 3–110, 4–110, 5–141,
6–157, 7–176, 8–213, 9–232, 10–242. *Second Innings:* 1–115, 2–134,
3–152, 4–156, 5–158, 6–165, 7–178, 8–182, 9–238, 10–244.

AUSTRALIA

I. R. Redpath, c Knott b Greig	55	run out	39
W. J. Edwards, c Denness b Willis	29	lbw b Greig	0
G. S. Chappell, c Greig b Willis	2	(4)lbw b Titmus	61
R. Edwards, c Cowdrey b Titmus	1	(5)c Lloyd b Titmus	10

K. D. Walters, c Lloyd b Greig	36	(6)c Denness b Greig	32
*I. M. Chappell, lbw b Willis	36	(3)lbw b Willis	0
†R. W. Marsh, c Knott b Titmus	44	c Knott b Greig	40
M. H. N. Walker, c Knott b Willis	30	not out	23
D. K. Lillee, not out	2	c Denness b Greig	14
A. A. Mallett, run out	0	not out	0
J. R. Thomson, b Willis	2		
Extras, (b 2, lb 2)	4	(b 6, lb 9, nb 4)	19
Total	241	(8 wkts)	238

FALL OF WICKETS. *First Innings:* 1–65, 2–67, 3–68, 4–121, 5–126, 6–173, 7–237, 8–237, 9–238, 10–241. *Second Innings:* 1–4, 2–5, 3–106, 4–120, 5–121, 6–171, 7–208, 8–235.

BOWLING
AUSTRALIA. *First Innings:* Lillee 20, 2, 70, 2; Thomson 22·4, 4, 72, 4; Walker 24, 10, 36, 1; Walters 7, 2, 15, 0; Mallett 15, 3, 37, 2. *Second Innings:* Lillee 17, 3, 55, 2; Thomson 17, 1, 71, 4; Walker 11, 0, 45, 0; Mallett 24, 6, 60, 4.
ENGLAND. *First Innings:* Willis 21·7, 4, 61, 5; Hendrick 2·6, 1, 8, 0; Underwood 22, 6, 62, 0; Greig 24, 2, 63, 2; Titmus 22, 11, 43, 2. *Second Innings:* Willis 14, 2, 56, 1; Underwood 19, 7, 43, 0; Greig 18, 2, 56, 4; Titmus 29, 10, 64, 2.

Umpires: R. C. Bailhache, T. F. Brooks

1974/5 Fourth Test, Sydney

January 4, 5, 6, 8, 9   Toss: Australia
Result: AUSTRALIA WON BY 171 RUNS

AUSTRALIA

I. R. Redpath, hit wkt b Titmus	33	c sub (C. M. Old) b Underwood	105
R. B. McCosker, c Knott b Greig	80		
*I. M. Chappell, c Knott b Arnold	53	(2)c Lloyd b Willis	5
G. S. Chappell, c Greig b Arnold	84	(3)c Lloyd b Arnold	144
R. Edwards, b Greig	15	not out	17
K. D. Walters, lbw b Arnold	1	(4)b Underwood	5
†R. W. Marsh, b Greig	30	(6)not out	7
M. H. N. Walker, c Greig b Arnold	30		
D. K. Lillee, b Arnold	8		
A. A. Mallett, lbw b Greig	31		
J. R. Thomson, not out	24		
Extras, (lb 4, w 1, nb 11)	16	(lb 2, w 1, nb 3)	6
Total	405	(4 wkts dec)	289

FALL OF WICKETS. *First Innings:* 1–96, 2–142, 3–199, 4–251, 5–255, 6–305, 7–310, 8–332, 9–368, 10–405. *Second Innings:* 1–15, 2–235, 3–242, 4–280.

ENGLAND

D. L. Amiss, c Mallett b Walker	12	c Marsh b Lillee	37
D. Lloyd, c Thomson b Lillee	19	c G. Chappell b Thomson	26
M. C. Cowdrey, c McCosker b Thomson	22	c I. Chappell b Walker	1
*J. H. Edrich, c Marsh b Walters	50	not out	33
K. W. R. Fletcher, c Redpath b Walker	24	c Redpath b Thomson	11
A. W. Greig, c G. Chappell b Thomson	9	st Marsh b Mallett	54
†A. P. E. Knott, b Thomson	82	c Redpath b Mallett	10
F. J. Titmus, c Marsh b Walters	22	c Thomson b Mallett	4
D. L. Underwood, c Walker b Lillee	27	c and b Walker	5
R. G. D. Willis, b Thomson	2	b Lillee	12
G. G. Arnold, not out	3	c G. Chappell b Mallett	14
Extras, (b 15, lb 7, w 1)	23	(b 13, lb 3, nb 5)	21
Total	295		228

FALL OF WICKETS. *First Innings:* 1–36, 2–46, 3–69, 4–108, 5–123, 6–180, 7–240, 8–273, 9–285, 10–295. *Second Innings:* 1–68, 2–70, 3–74, 4–103, 5–136, 6–156, 7–158, 8–175, 9–201, 10–228.

BOWLING

ENGLAND. *First Innings:* Willis 18, 2, 80, 0; Arnold 29, 7, 86, 5; Greig 22·7, 2, 104, 4; Underwood 13, 3, 54, 0; Titmus 16, 2, 65, 1. *Second Innings:* Willis 11, 1, 52, 1; Arnold 22, 3, 78, 1; Greig 12, 1, 64, 0; Underwood 12, 1, 65, 2; Titmus 7·3, 2, 24, 0.

AUSTRALIA. *First Innings:* Lillee 19·1, 2, 66, 2; Thomson 19, 3, 74, 4; Walker 23, 2, 77, 2; Mallett 1, 0, 8, 0; Walters 7, 2, 26, 2; I. M. Chappell 4, 0, 21, 0. *Second Innings:* Lillee 21, 5, 65, 2; Thomson 23, 7, 74, 2; Walker 16, 5, 46, 2; Mallett 16·5, 9, 21, 4; I. M. Chappell 3, 2, 1, 0.

Umpires: R. C. Bailhache, T. F. Brooks

1974/5 Fifth Test, Adelaide

January 25, 26, 27, 29, 30   Toss: England
Result: AUSTRALIA WON BY 163 RUNS

AUSTRALIA

I. R. Redpath, c Greig b Underwood	21	b Underwood	52
R. B. McCosker, c Cowdrey b Underwood	35	c Knott b Arnold	11
*I. M. Chappell, c Knott b Underwood	0	c Knott b Underwood	41
G. S. Chappell, lbw b Underwood	5	c Greig b Underwood	18
K. D. Walters, c Willis b Underwood	55	not out	71
†R. W. Marsh, c Greig b Underwood	6	c Greig b Underwood	55
T. J. Jenner, b Underwood	74	not out	14
M. H. N. Walker, run out	41		
D. K. Lillee, b Willis	26		
A. A. Mallett, not out	23		
J. R. Thomson, b Arnold	5		
Extras, (b 4, lb 4, nb 5)	13	(lb 4, nb 6)	10
Total	304	(5 wkts dec)	272

FALL OF WICKETS. *First Innings:* 1–52, 2–52, 3–58, 4–77, 5–84, 6–164, 7–241, 8–259, 9–295, 10–304. *Second Innings:* 1–16, 2–92, 3–128, 4–133, 5–245.

ENGLAND

D. L. Amiss, c I. Chappell b Lillee	0	c Marsh b Lillee	0
D. Lloyd, c Marsh b Lillee	4	c Walters b Walker	5
M. C. Cowdrey, c Walker b Thomson	26	c Mallett b Lillee	3
*M. H. Denness, c Marsh b Thomson	51	c Jenner b Lillee	14
K. W. R. Fletcher, c I. Chappell b Thomson	40	lbw b Lillee	63
A. W. Greig, c Marsh b Lillee	19	lbw b Walker	20
†A. P. E. Knott, c Lillee b Mallett	5	not out	106
F. J. Titmus, c G. Chappell b Mallett	11	lbw b Jenner	20
D. L. Underwood, c Lillee b Mallett	0	c I. Chappell b Mallett	0
G. G. Arnold, b Lillee	0	b Mallett	0

R G D Willis, not out	11	b Walker	3
Extras, (lb 2, nb 3)	5	(b 3, lb 3, nb 1)	7
Total	172		241

FALL OF WICKETS. *First Innings:* 1–2, 2–19, 3–66, 4–90, 5–130, 6–147, 7–155, 8–156, 9–161, 10–172. *Second Innings:* 1–0, 2–8, 3–10, 4–33, 5–76, 6–144, 7–212, 8–213, 9–217, 10–241.

BOWLING
ENGLAND. *First Innings:* Willis 10, 0, 46, 1; Arnold 12·2, 3, 42, 1; Underwood 29, 3, 113, 7; Greig 10, 0, 63, 0; Titmus 7, 1, 27, 0. *Second Innings:* Willis 5, 0, 27, 0; Arnold 20, 1, 71 1; Underwood 26 5, 102, 4; Greig 2, 0, 9, 0; Titmus 13, 1, 53, 0.
AUSTRALIA. *First Innings:* Lillee 12·5, 2, 49, 4; Thomson 15, 1, 58, 3; Walker 5, 1, 18, 0; Jenner 5, 0, 28, 0; Mallett 9, 4, 14, 3. *Second Innings:* Lillee 14, 3, 69, 4; Walker 20, 3, 89, 3; Jenner 15, 4, 39, 1; Mallett 25, 10, 36, 2; I. M. Chappell 1, 0, 1, 0.

Umpires: R. C. Bailhache, T. F. Brooks

1974/5 Sixth Test, Melbourne

February 8, 9, 10, 12, 13   Toss: Australia
Result: ENGLAND WON BY AN INNINGS AND 4 RUNS

AUSTRALIA

I. R. Redpath, c Greig b Lever	1	c Amiss b Greig	83
R. B. McCosker, c Greig b Lever	0	c Cowdrey b Arnold	76
*I. M. Chappell, c Knott b Old	65	c Knott b Greig	50
G. S. Chappell, c Denness b Lever	1	b Lever	102
R. Edwards, c Amiss b Lever	0	c Knott b Arnold	18
K. D. Walters, c Edrich b Old	12	b Arnold	3
†R. W. Marsh, b Old	29	c Denness b Lever	1
M. H. N. Walker, not out	20	c and b Greig	17
D. K. Lillee, c Knott b Lever	12	(11)not out	0
A. A. Mallett, b Lever	7	(9)c Edrich b Greig	0
G. Dymock, c Knott b Greig	0	(10)c Knott b Lever	0
Extras, (b 2, lb 1 nb 2)	5	(b 9, lb 5, w 4, nb 5)	23
Total	152		373

FALL OF WICKETS. *First Innings:* 1–0, 2–5, 3–19, 4–23, 5–50, 6–104, 7–115, 8–141, 9–149, 10–152. *Second Innings:* 1–111, 2–215, 3–248, 4–289, 5–297, 6–306, 7–367, 8–373, 9–373, 10–373.

ENGLAND

D. L. Amiss, lbw b Lillee	0
M. C. Cowdrey, c Marsh b Walker	7
J. H. Edrich, c I. Chappell b Walker	70
*M. H. Denness, c and b Walker	188
K. W. R. Fletcher, c Redpath b Walker	146
A. W. Greig, c sub (T. J. Jenner) b Walker	89
†A. P. E. Knott, c Marsh b Walker	5
C. M. Old, b Dymock	0
D. L. Underwood, b Walker	11
G. G. Arnold, c Marsh b Walker	0
P. Lever, not out	6
Extras, (b 4, lb 2, nb 1)	7
Total	529

FALL OF WICKETS. *First Innings:* 1–4, 2–18, 3–167, 4–359, 5–507, 6–507, 7–508, 8–514, 9–514, 10–529.

BOWLING

ENGLAND. *First Innings:* Arnold 6, 2, 24, 0; Lever 11, 2, 38, 6; Old 11, 0, 50, 3; Greig 9·7, 1, 35, 1. *Second Innings:* Arnold 23, 6, 83, 3; Lever 16, 1, 65, 3; Old 18, 1, 75, 0; Greig 31·7, 7, 88, 4; Underwood 18, 5, 39, 0.

AUSTRALIA. *First Innings:* Lillee 6, 2, 17, 1; Walker 42·2, 7, 143, 8; Dymock 39, 6, 130, 1; Walters 23, 3, 86, 0; Mallett 29, 8, 96, 0; I. M. Chappell 12, 1, 50, 0.

Umpires: R. C. Bailhache, T. F. Brooks

Averages: 1974/5

AUSTRALIA

BATTING	M.	Inns.	N.O.	Runs	H.S.	Av.
G. S. Chappell	6	11	0	608	144	55·27
T. J. Jenner	2	3	1	100	74	50·00
M. H. N. Walker	6	8	3	221	41*	44·20
I. R. Redpath	6	12	1	472	105	42·90
K. D. Walters	6	11	2	383	103	42·55
R. B. McCosker	3	5	0	202	80	40·40
I. M. Chappell	6	12	1	387	90	35·18
R. W. Marsh	6	11	2	313	55	34·77
R. Edwards	5	9	1	261	115	32·62
J. R. Thomson	5	5	2	65	24*	21·66
D. K. Lillee	6	8	2	88	26	14·66

BATTING	M	*Inns.*	N.O.	*Runs*	H.S.	*Av.*
A. A. Mallett	5	7	2	61	31	12·20
W. J. Edwards	3	6	0	68	30	11·33

PLAYED IN ONE TEST: G. Dymock 0, 0.

BOWLING	*Overs*	*Mds.*	*Runs*	*Wkts.*	*Av.*
J. R. Thomson	175·1	34	592	33	17·93
A. A. Mallett	140·6	47	339	17	19·94
D. K. Lillee	182·6	36	596	25	23·84
M. H. N. Walker	218·7	46	684	23	29·73
K. D. Walters	56·3	14	175	5	35·00

ALSO BOWLED: I. M. Chappell 22–3–83–1, G. Dymock 39–6–130–1, T. J. Jenner 42–10–136–3.

ENGLAND

BATTING	M.	*Inns.*	N.O.	*Runs*	H.S.	*Av.*
J. H. Edrich	4	7	1	260	70	43·33
A. W. Greig	6	11	0	446	110	40·54
A. P. E. Knott	6	11	1	364	106*	36·40
K. W. R. Fletcher	5	9	0	324	146	36·00
M. H. Denness	5	9	0	318	188	35·33
D. Lloyd	4	8	0	196	49	24·50
D. L. Amiss	5	9	0	175	90	19·44
M. C. Cowdrey	5	9	0	165	41	18·33
F. J. Titmus	4	8	0	138	61	17·25
C. M. Old	2	3	0	50	43	16·66
R. G. D. Willis	5	10	5	76	15	15·20
B. W. Luckhurst	2	4	0	54	27	13·50
D. L. Underwood	5	9	0	111	30	12·33
P. Lever	2	3	1	24	14	12·00
M. Hendrick	2	4	2	12	8*	6.00
G. G. Arnold	4	7	1	22	14	3·66

BOWLING	*Overs*	*Mds.*	*Runs*	*Wkts.*	*Av.*
P. Lever	61	8	214	9	23·77
R. G. D. Willis	140·4	15	522	17	30·70
D. L. Underwood	185	42	595	17	35·00
C. M. Old	51·6	4	210	6	35·00
G. G. Arnold	141·1	23	528	14	37·71
A. W. Greig	168·6	20	681	17	40·05
F. J. Titmus	122·3	30	360	7	51·42

ALSO BOWLED: M. Hendrick 34·6–6–119–2.

Test appearances in Australia 1946-75

ENGLAND

D. A. Allen	5	62 (1); 65 (4)
D. L. Amiss	5	74 (5)
K. V. Andrew	1	54 (1)
R. Appleyard	4	54 (4)
G. G. Arnold	4	74 (4)
T. E. Bailey	14	50 (4); 54 (5); 58 (5)
R. W. Barber	5	65 (5)
K. F. Barrington	10	62 (5); 65 (5)
A. V. Bedser	11	46 (5); 50 (5); 54 (1)
G. Boycott	10	65 (5); 70 (5)
D. J. Brown	4	65 (4)
F. R. Brown	5	50 (5)
D. B. Close	1	50 (1)
L. J. Coldwell	2	62 (2)
D. C. S. Compton	13	46 (5); 50 (4); 54 (4)
M. C. Cowdrey	27	54 (5); 58 (5); 62 (5); 65 (4); 70 (3); 74 (5)
M. H. Denness	5	74 (5)
J. G. Dewes	2	50 (2)
E. R. Dexter	7	58 (2); 62 (5)
B. L. d'Oliveira	6	70 (6)
J. H. Edrich	15	65 (5); 70 (6); 74 (4)
W. J. Edrich	9	46 (5); 54 (4)
T. G. Evans	16	46 (4); 50 (5); 54 (4); 58 (3)
L. B. Fishlock	1	46 (1)
K. W. R. Fletcher	10	70 (5); 74 (5)
P. A. Gibb	1	46 (1)
T. W. Graveney	10	54 (2); 58 (5); 62 (3)
A. W. Greig	6	74 (6)
W. R. Hammond	4	46 (4)
J. H. Hampshire	2	70 (2)
J. Hardstaff	1	46 (1)
M. Hendrick	2	74 (2)
K. Higgs	1	65 (1)
L. Hutton	15	46 (5); 50 (5); 54 (5)
J. T. Ikin	5	46 (5)
R. Illingworth	10	62 (2); 70 (6)
I. J. Jones	4	65 (4)
B. R. Knight	3	62 (1); 65 (2)
A. P. E. Knott	12	70 (6); 74 (6)
J. C. Laker	4	58 (4)

P. Lever	7	70 (5); 74 (2)
D. Lloyd	4	74 (4)
P. J. Loader	2	58 (2)
G. A. R. Lock	4	58 (4)
B. W. Luckhurst	7	70 (5); 74 (2)
A. J. W. McIntyre	1	50 (1)
P. B. H. May	10	54 (5); 58 (5)
C. A. Milton	2	58 (2)
J. B. Mortimore	1	58 (1)
J. T. Murray	1	62 (1)
C. M. Old	2	74 (2)
P. H. Parfitt	2	62 (2)
W. G. A. Parkhouse	2	50 (2)
J. M. Parks	5	65 (5)
G. Pullar	4	62 (4)
P. E. Richardson	4	58 (4)
W. E. Russell	1	65 (1)
D. S. Sheppard	7	50 (2); 62 (5)
K. Shuttleworth	2	70 (2)
R. T. Simpson	6	50 (5); 54 (1)
A. C. Smith	4	62 (4)
M. J. K. Smith	5	65 (5)
T. P. B. Smith	2	46 (2)
J. A. Snow	6	70 (6)
J. B. Statham	14	54 (5); 58 (4); 62 (5)
R. Swetman	2	58 (2)
R. Tattersall	2	50 (2)
F. J. Titmus	14	62 (5); 65 (5); 74 (4)
F. S. Trueman	8	58 (3); 62 (5)
F. H. Tyson	7	54 (5); 58 (2)
D. L. Underwood	10	70 (5); 74 (5)
W. Voce	2	46 (2)
J. H. Wardle	4	54 (4)
J. J. Warr	2	50 (2)
C. Washbrook	10	46 (5); 50 (5)
W. Watson	2	58 (2)
R. G. D. Willis	9	70 (4); 74 (5)
D. V. P. Wright	10	46 (5); 50 (5)
N. W. D. Yardley	5	46 (5)

AUSTRALIA

P. J. Allan	1	65 (1)
K. A. Archer	3	50 (3)
R. G. Archer	4	54 (4)
S. G. Barnes	4	46 (4)

R. Benaud	15	54 (5); 58 (5); 62 (5)
B. C. Booth	8	62 (5); 65 (3)
D. G. Bradman	5	46 (5)
P. J. P. Burge	9	54 (1); 58 (1); 62 (3); 65 (4)
J. W. Burke	9	50 (2); 54 (2); 58 (5)
G. S. Chappell	11	70 (5); 74 (6)
I. M. Chappell	14	65 (2); 70 (6); 74 (6)
A. N. Connolly	2	65 (1); 70 (1)
R. M. Cowper	4	65 (4)
A. K. Davidson	13	54 (3); 58 (5); 62 (5)
A. R. Dell	1	70 (1)
B. Dooland	2	46 (2)
J. R. F. Duncan	1	70 (1)
G. Dymock	1	74 (1)
K. H. Eastwood	1	70 (1)
R. Edwards	5	74 (5)
W. J. Edwards	3	74 (3)
L. E. Favell	6	54 (4); 58 (2)
F. W. Freer	1	46 (1)
J. W. Gleeson	5	70 (5)
A. T. W. Grout	12	58 (5); 62 (2); 65 (5)
C. E. J. Guest	1	62 (1)
R. A. Hamence	1	46 (1)
M. R. Harvey	1	46 (1)
R. N. Harvey	20	50 (5); 54 (5); 58 (5); 62 (5)
A. L. Hassett	10	46 (5); 50 (5)
N. J. N. Hawke	5	62 (1); 65 (4)
G. B. Hole	4	50 (1); 54 (3)
J. B. Iverson	5	50 (5)
B. N. Harman	3	62 (3)
T. J. Jenner	4	70 (2); 74 (2)
I. W. Johnson	13	46 (4); 50 (5); 54 (4)
W. A. Johnston	9	50 (5); 54 (4)
L. F. Kline	2	58 (2)
G. R. A. Langley	2	54 (2)
W. M. Lawry	15	62 (5); 65 (5); 70 (5)
D. K. Lillee	8	70 (2); 74 (6)
R. R. Lindwall	15	46 (4); 50 (5); 54 (4); 58 (2)
S. J. E. Loxton	3	50 (3)
C. L. McCool	5	46 (5)
R. B. McCosker	3	74 (3)
C. C. McDonald	7	54 (2); 58 (5)
G. D. McKenzie	12	62 (5); 65 (4); 70 (3)
K. D. Mackay	8	58 (5); 62 (3)
L. V. Maddocks	3	54 (3)
A. A. Mallett	7	70 (2); 74 (5)

R. W. Marsh	12	70 (6); 74 (6)
I. Meckiff	4	58 (4)
K. R. Miller	14	46 (5); 50 (5); 54 (4)
J. A. R. Moroney	1	50 (1)
A. R. Morris	14	46 (5); 50 (5); 54 (4)
K. J. O'Keeffe	2	70 (2)
N. C. O'Neill	10	58 (5); 62 (5)
P. I. Philpott	3	65 (3)
I. R. Redpath	13	65 (1); 70 (6); 74 (6)
G. F. Rorke	2	58 (2)
A. P. Sheahan	2	70 (2)
B. K. Shepherd	2	62 (2)
R. B. Simpson	9	58 (1); 62 (5); 65 (3)
D. J. Sincock	1	65 (1)
K. N. Slater	1	58 (1)
K. R. Stackpole	8	65 (2); 70 (6)
D. Tallon	10	46 (5); 50 (5)
G. Thomas	3	65 (3)
A. L. Thomson	4	70 (4)
J. R. Thomson	5	74 (5)
E. R. H. Toshack	5	46 (5)
G. E. Tribe	3	46 (3)
T. R. Veivers	4	65 (4)
M. H. N. Walker	6	74 (6)
K. D. Walters	17	65 (5); 70 (6); 74 (6)
W. Watson	1	54 (1)

Test batting averages in Australia 1946-75

ENGLAND

	M.	Inns.	N.O.	Runs	H.S.	Av.	100	50	Ct/St
K. F. Barrington	10	18	3	1046	132*	69·73	4	6	9
G. Boycott	10	19	5	957	142*	68·35	2	8	5
J. H. Edrich	15	26	3	1283	130	55·78	4	7	11
J. B. Mortimore	1	2	1	55	44*	55·00	—	—	—
L. Hutton	15	28	5	1170	156*	50·86	2	7	13
J. M. Parks	5	6	0	290	89	48·33	—	3	12/3
B. W. Luckhurst	7	13	1	509	131	42·41	2	2	5
R. W. Barber	5	9	1	328	185	41·00	1	—	4
A. W. Greig	6	11	0	446	110	40·54	1	3	12
P. B. H. May	10	19	0	756	113	39·78	2	4	7
J. Hardstaff	1	2	0	76	67	38·00	—	1	—
B. L. d'Oliveira	6	10	0	369	117	36·90	1	2	4
M. C. Cowdrey	27	48	3	1618	113	35·95	4	6	28
W. J. Edrich	9	18	0	642	119	35·66	1	4	3
E. R. Dexter	7	14	0	499	99	35·64	—	5	2
M. H. Denness	5	9	0	318	188	35·33	1	1	6
A. P. E. Knott	12	20	3	586	106*	34·47	1	4	43/4
F. J. Titmus	14	22	5	578	61	34·00	—	1	8
D. C. S. Compton	13	25	4	703	147	33·47	2	3	6
T. W. Graveney	10	18	2	528	111	33·00	1	2	15
R. T. Simpson	6	12	1	360	156*	32·72	1	1	4
R. Illingworth	8	13	1	390	53	32·50	—	1	4
N. W. D. Yardley	5	10	2	252	61	31·50	—	2	3
K. W. R. Fletcher	10	18	0	549	146	30·50	1	2	6
D. S. Sheppard	7	13	0	381	113	29·30	1	2	2
P. H. Parfitt	2	4	0	112	80	28·00	—	1	—
C. Washbrook	10	20	0	536	112	26·80	1	2	3
F. R. Brown	5	8	0	210	79	26·25	—	2	4
D. Lloyd	4	8	0	196	49	24·50	—	—	6
J. A. Snow	6	7	1	141	38	23·50	—	—	2
T. E. Bailey	14	26	3	536	88	23·30	—	3	7
J. H. Hampshire	2	4	0	92	55	23·00	—	1	3
R. Appleyard	4	5	3	44	19*	22·00	—	—	4
J. H. Wardle	4	6	1	109	38	21·80	—	—	1
G. Pullar	4	8	0	170	56	21·25	—	2	—
W. R. Hammond	4	8	0	168	37	21·00	—	—	6
P. E. Richardson	4	8	0	162	68	20·25	—	1	—
D. L. Amiss	5	9	0	175	90	19·44	—	1	3
W. G. A. Parkhouse	2	4	0	77	28	19·25	—	—	1

APPENDIX

	M.	Inns.	N.O.	Runs	H.S.	Av.	100	50	Ct/St
D. A. Allen	5	6	2	76	50*	19·00	—	1	2
J. T. Ikin	5	10	0	184	60	18·40	—	1	3
W. Watson	2	4	0	72	40	18·00	—	—	—
M. J. K. Smith	5	7	1	107	41	17·83	—	—	4
F. S. Trueman	8	13	0	217	38	16·69	—	—	10
C. M. Old	2	3	0	50	43	16·66	—	—	—
R. G. D. Willis	9	15	8	113	15*	16·14	—	—	4
R. Swetman	2	4	0	56	41	14·00	—	—	3/0
T. G. Evans	16	30	4	363	49	13·96	—	—	38/0
P. Lever	7	9	1	107	36	13·37	—	—	7
J. C. Laker	4	7	2	62	22*	12·40	—	—	—
P. A. Gibb	1	2	0	24	13	12·00	—	—	1/0
A. C. Smith	4	5	1	47	21	11·75	—	—	13/0
J. B. Statham	14	20	6	160	36*	11·42	—	—	6
F. H. Tyson	7	11	1	114	37*	11·40	—	—	2
A. V. Bedser	11	20	5	159	27*	10·60	—	—	7
D. L. Underwood	10	15	3	127	30	10·58	—	—	4
I. J. Jones	4	5	2	29	16	9·66	—	—	—
C. A. Milton	2	4	0	38	17	9·50	—	—	1
W. Voce	2	3	1	19	18	9·50	—	—	1
G. A. R. Lock	4	8	1	60	21	8·57	—	—	1
T. P. B. Smith	2	4	0	32	24	8·00	—	—	1
L. B. Fishlock	1	2	0	14	14	7·00	—	—	1
D. V. P. Wright	10	15	4	70	15*	6·36	—	—	2
B. R. Knight	3	4	1	18	13	6·00	—	—	1
M. Hendrick	2	4	2	12	8*	6·00	—	—	—
J. G. Dewes	2	4	0	23	9	5·75	—	—	—
K. V. Andrew	1	2	0	11	6	5·50	—	—	0/0
R. Tattersall	2	3	0	16	10	5·33	—	—	1
K. Shuttleworth	2	2	0	9	7	4·50	—	—	1
A. J. W. McIntyre	1	2	0	8	7	4·00	—	—	1
K. Higgs	1	1	0	4	4	4·00	—	—	—
G. G. Arnold	4	7	1	22	14	3·66	—	—	—
P. J. Loader	2	4	2	7	6*	3·50	—	—	—
D. J. Brown	4	5	0	17	12	3·40	—	—	—
J. T. Murray	1	2	1	3	3*	3·00	—	—	1/0
L. J. Coldwell	2	3	1	3	2*	1·50	—	—	—
J. J. Warr	2	4	0	4	4	1·00	—	—	—
D. B. Close	1	2	0	1	1	0·50	—	—	1

PLAYED IN ONE TEST: W. E. Russell 0*.

AUSTRALIA

	M.	Inns.	N.O.	Runs	H.S.	Av.	100	50	Ct/St
D. M. Bradman	5	8	1	680	234	97·14	2	3	3
R. G. Cowper	4	6	0	493	307	82·16	1	2	2
S. G. Barnes	4	6	0	443	234	73·83	1	1	4
C. C. McDonald	7	13	1	705	170	58·75	2	2	3
C. L. McCool	5	7	2	272	104*	54·40	1	1	3
R. B. Simpson	9	15	1	756	225	54·00	1	6	13
W. M. Lawry	15	27	3	1226	166	51·08	3	8	9
K. R. Stackpole	8	14	0	679	207	48·50	2	2	11
G. S. Chappell	11	19	1	851	144	47·27	4	6	17
B. K. Shepherd	2	3	1	94	71*	47·00	—	1	1
K. D. Walters	17	30	5	1166	155	46·64	3	6	9
A. R. Morris	14	24	1	1047	206	45·52	5	2	3
K. R. Miller	14	23	3	901	145*	45·05	2	2	7
I. R. Redpath	13	25	3	986	171	44·81	2	6	17
M. H. N. Walker	6	8	3	221	41*	44·20	—	—	5
A. L. Hassett	10	16	0	698	128	43·62	1	4	7
R. N. Harvey	20	37	4	1402	167	42·48	3	6	20
N. C. O'Neill	10	16	2	592	100	42·28	1	5	3
R. B. McCosker	3	5	0	202	80	40·40	—	2	1
B. C. Booth	8	15	2	488	112	37·53	2	1	3
P. J. P. Burge	9	15	3	441	120	36·75	2	1	5
G. Thomas	3	4	0	147	52	36·75	—	2	1
I. M. Chappell	14	26	1	875	111	35·00	2	6	21
R. Edwards	5	9	1	261	115	32·62	1	1	—
R. W. Marsh	12	20	3	528	92*	31·05	—	2	29/4
R. A. Hamence	1	2	1	31	30*	31·00	—	—	—
K. A. Archer	3	5	0	152	48	30·40	—	—	—
L. V. Maddocks	3	5	0	150	69	30·00	—	1	7/0
K. D. Mackay	8	10	1	266	86*	29·55	—	2	3
J. W. Burke	9	18	4	405	101*	28·92	1	1	8
D. J. Sincock	1	2	0	56	29	28·00	—	—	—
R. Benaud	15	21	0	507	64	24·14	—	3	20
A. K. Davidson	13	17	0	409	71	24·05	—	1	16
G. B. Hole	4	7	0	166	63	23·71	—	2	3
I. W. Johnson	13	20	4	373	77	23·31	—	2	9
T. J. Jenner	4	7	1	136	74	22·66	—	1	5
L. E. Favell	6	10	1	203	54	22·55	—	1	3
A. L. Thomson	4	5	4	22	12*	22·00	—	—	—
J. R. Thomson	5	5	2	65	24*	21·66	—	—	3
R. R. Lindwall	15	22	3	409	100	21·52	1	1	10
M. R. Harvey	1	2	0	43	31	21·50	—	—	—
T. R. Veivers	4	5	1	83	56*	20·75	—	1	3
D. Tallon	10	14	2	213	92	17·75	—	1	24/4
G. E. Tribe	3	3	1	35	25*	17·50	—	—	—

	M.	Inns.	N.O.	Runs	H.S.	Av.	100	50	Ct/St
R. G. Archer	4	7	0	117	49	16·71	—	—	4
B. Dooland	2	3	0	49	29	16·33	—	—	2
A. T. W. Grout	12	14	3	170	74	15·45	—	1	39/6
S. J. E. Loxton	3	5	0	75	32	15·00	—	—	7
N. J. N. Hawke	5	6	3	42	20	14·00	—	—	3
K. J. O'Keeffe	2	3	0	42	27	14·00	—	—	—
A. P. Sheahan	2	3	0	38	36	12·66	—	—	1
A. A. Mallett	7	10	2	99	31	12·37	—	—	9
D. K. Lillee	8	11	2	104	26	11·55	—	—	4
B. N. Jarman	3	4	2	23	11*	11·50	—	—	7/0
W. J. Edwards	3	6	0	68	30	11·33	—	—	—
C. E. J. Guest	1	1	0	11	11	11·00	—	—	—
W. Watson	1	2	0	21	18	10·50	—	—	—
G. D. McKenzie	12	17	4	131	24	10·07	—	—	8
P. I. Philpott	3	4	1	22	10	7·33	—	—	2
G. R. A. Langley	2	3	0	21	16	7·00	—	—	9/0
J. W. Gleeson	5	7	0	42	16	6·00	—	—	4
W. A. Johnston	9	14	4	54	12*	5·40	—	—	2
E. R. H. Toshack	5	5	2	14	6	4·66	—	—	3
A. N. Connolly	2	4	1	14	14	4·66	—	—	2
J. R. F. Duncan	1	1	0	3	3	3·00	—	—	—
K. H. Eastwood	1	2	0	5	5	2·50	—	—	—
I. Meckiff	4	4	0	9	5	2·25	—	—	1
J. B. Iverson	5	7	3	3	1*	0·75	—	—	2
G. Dymock	1	2	0	0	0	0·00	—	—	—
J. A. R. Moroney	1	2	0	0	0	0·00	—	—	—

PLAYED IN TWO TESTS: L. F. Kline §4* and 1*, G. F. Rorke 2* and 0*.
PLAYED IN ONE TEST: A. R. Dell 3* and 3*, F. W. Freer 28*, K. N. Slater 1*.
PLAYED IN ONE TEST BUT DID NOT BAT: P. J. Allan.
§Held two catches.

Test bowling averages in Australia 1946-75

ENGLAND

	Overs	Mds.	Runs	Wkts.	Av.	5wI	10wM	runs per 100 balls/balls	wicket
R. Appleyard	79	22	224	11	20·36	—	—	35	57
J. C. Laker	127·6	24	318	15	21·20	1	—	31	68
F. R. Brown	109	12	389	18	21·61	1	—	45	48
J. A. Snow	225·5	47	708	31	22·83	2	—	39	58
J. H. Wardle	70·6	15	229	10	22·90	1	—	40	57
F. H. Tyson	205	18	776	31	25·03	2	1	47	53
T. E. Bailey	223·5	33	763	28	27·25	—	—	43	64
F. S. Trueman	245·3	20	797	29	27·48	1	—	41	68
P. J. Loader	60·2	10	193	7	27·57	—	—	40	69
D. B. Close	7	1	28	1	28·00	—	—	50	56
R. G. D. Willis	218·4	31	851	29	29·34	1	—	49	29
L. Hutton	3·6	—	30	1	30·00	—	—	100	30
A. V. Bedser	478·3	76	1489	47	31·68	2	1	39	81
J. B. Statham	412·5	44	1365	43	31·74	2	—	41	77
D. L. Underwood	379·6	92	1115	33	33·78	1	1	37	34
E. R. Dexter	95·2	6	373	11	33·90	—	—	49	69
B. R. Knight	115·4	13	378	11	34·36	—	—	41	84
K. Shuttleworth	75·5	13	242	7	34·57	1	—	40	86
C. M. Old	51·6	4	210	6	35·00	—	—	51	35
I. J. Jones	129	15	533	15	35·53	1	—	52	69
D. A. Allen	199	59	516	14	36·85	—	—	32	114
D. J. Brown	108	14	409	11	37·18	—	—	47	79
N. W. D. Yardley	114	15	372	10	37·20	—	—	41	91
G. G. Arnold	141·1	23	528	14	37·71	1	—	47	38
A. W. Greig	168·6	20	681	17	40·05	—	—	51	40
F. J. Titmus	569·1	136	1493	37	40·35	2	—	33	123
J. B. Mortimore	11	1	41	1	41·00	—	—	47	88
R. Illingworth	172	53	480	11	43·63	—	—	35	125
D. V. P. Wright	343·2	29	1490	34	43·82	2	—	54	81
G. Boycott	24	4	96	2	48·00	—	—	50	96
B. L. d'Oliveira	114	28	290	6	48·33	—	—	32	152
K. Higgs	30	6	102	2	51·00	—	—	43	120
L. J. Coldwell	57	5	159	3	53·00	—	—	35	152
W. J. Edrich	118·3	13	511	9	56·77	—	—	54	105
M. Hendrick	34·6	6	119	2	59·50	—	—	43	139
P. Lever	204·5	33	653	10	65·30	1	—	40	164
R. Tattersall	68·5	12	257	4	64·25	—	—	47	137
K. F. Barrington	46·4	6	201	3	67·00	—	—	54	124
T. W. Graveney	13	1	68	1	68·00	—	—	65	104
G. A. R. Lock	126·2	25	376	5	75·20	—	—	37	202
R. W. Barber	55·1	2	261	3	87·00	—	—	59	147
T. P. B. Smith	47	1	218	2	109·00	—	—	58	188
D. C. S. Compton	28	2	121	1	121·00	—	—	54	224
J. J. Warr	73	6	281	1	281·00	—	—	48	584

ALSO BOWLED: M. C. Cowdrey 7·3–0–45–0, J. T. Ikin 7–0–48–0, M. J. K. Smith 2–0–8–0, W. Voce 44–1–161–0.

AUSTRALIA

	Overs	Mds.	Runs	Wkts.	Av.	5wI	10wM	runs per 100 balls/ balls	balls/ wicket
G. B. Hole	6	0	13	1	13·00	—	—	27	48
J. B. Iverson	138·4	29	320	21	15·23	1	—	29	53
R. G. Archer	97·6	32	215	13	16·53	—	—	27	60
I. Meckiff	112·2	24	292	17	17·17	1	—	33	53
J. R. Thomson	175·1	34	592	33	17·93	2	—	42	42
A. E. Dell	42·7	11	97	5	19·40	—	—	28	69
K. R. Miller	317·5	65	878	43	20·41	1	—	35	59
W. A. Johnston	295·3	66	845	41	20·60	2	—	36	58
G. F. Rorke	70·5	17	165	8	20·62	—	—	29	71
K. H. Eastwood	5	0	21	1	21·00	—	—	53	40
A. K. Davidson	430·3	91	1156	51	22·66	3	—	34	68
A. A. Mallett	197·5	55	527	23	22·91	—	—	33	69
R. R. Lindwall	419·2	68	1301	54	24·09	1	—	39	62
D. K. Lillee	245·1	41	795	33	24·09	1	—	41	59
F. W. Freer	20	3	74	3	24·66	—	—	46	53
E. R. H. Toshack	178·4	50	437	17	25·70	1	—	31	84
C. L. McCool	182	27	491	18	27·27	1	—	34	81
N. J. N. Hawke	171·7	30	508	18	28·22	2	—	37	76
R. Benaud	583·1	146	1649	58	28·43	3	—	35	80
I. W. Johnson	347·4	95	860	29	29·65	1	—	31	96
M. H. N. Walker	218·7	46	684	23	29·73	1	—	39	76
K. D. Walters	197	30	639	21	30·42	—	—	41	75
J. W. Burke	30	11	63	2	31·50	—	—	26	120
G. D. McKenzie	449	59	1437	43	33·41	—	—	40	84
T. J. Jenner	107·6	25	312	9	34·66	—	—	36	96
R. M. Cowper	22	5	76	2	38·00	—	—	43	88
P. J. Allan	24	6	83	2	41·50	—	—	43	96
J. W. Gleeson	221	57	605	14	43·21	—	—	34	126
K. J. O'Keeffe	100	30	260	6	43·33	—	—	33	133
K. D. Mackay	130·6	33	306	7	43·71	—	—	29	149
B. Dooland	98	9	351	8	43·87	—	—	45	98
P. I. Philpott	100·1	9	371	8	46·37	1	—	46	100
K. N. Slater	32	9	101	2	50·50	—	—	39	128
G. S. Chappell	93	15	255	5	51·00	—	—	34	149
A. L. Thomson	189·7	33	654	12	54·50	—	—	43	127
R. B. Simpson	114	23	450	8	56·25	1	—	49	114
T. R. Veivers	66·7	11	250	4	62·50	—	—	47	134
N. C. O'Neill	35	9	126	2	63·00	—	—	45	140
I. M. Chappell	70	12	236	3	78·66	—	—	42	187
K. R. Stackpole	124·5	25	377	4	94·25	—	—	38	249
A. N. Connolly	65	8	209	2	104·50	—	—	40	260
G. Dymock	39	6	130	1	130·00	—	—	42	312
G. E. Tribe	95	9	330	2	165·00	—	—	43	380

ALSO BOWLED: S. G. Barnes 7–0–23–0, B. C. Booth 0·2–0–4–0, J. R. F. Duncan 14–4–30–0, C. E. J. Guest 18–0–59–0, R. N. Harvey 4–1–13–0, A. L. Hassett 0·6–0–4–0, L. F. Kline 25–6–77–0, W. M. Lawry 1–1–0–0, S. J. E. Loxton 9–1–26–0, D. J. Sincock 20–1–98–0.

Hundreds series by series

A=Adelaide   B=Brisbane   M=Melbourne   P=Perth   S=Sydney
a=1st innings   b=2nd innings
(Thus 2b=second innings of second Test Match of that tour)

ENGLAND				AUSTRALIA			
			1946/7				
W. J. Edrich	119	2b	S	D. G. Bradman	187	1a	B
C. Washbrook	112	3b	M	A. L. Hassett	128	1a	B
D. C. S. Compton	147	4a	A	S. G. Barnes	234	2a	S
D. C. S. Compton	103	4b	A	D. G. Bradman	234	2a	S
L. Hutton	122*	5a	S	C. L. McCool	104*	3a	M
				A. R. Morris	155	3b	M
				R. R. Lindwall	100	3b	M
				A. R. Morris	122	4a	A
				K. R. Miller	141*	4a	A
				A. R. Morris	124*	4b	A
			1950/1				
L. Hutton	156*	4a	A	K. R. Miller	145*	3a	S
R. T. Simpson	156*	5a	M	A. R. Morris	206	4a	A
				J. W. Burke	101*	4b	A
			1954/5				
P. B. H. May	104	2b	S	A. R. Morris	153	1a	B
M. C. Cowdrey	102	3a	M	R. N. Harvey	162	1a	B
T. W. Graveney	111	5a	S				
			1958/9				
P. B. H. May	113	2a	M	R. N. Harvey	167	2a	M
M. C. Cowdrey	100*	3b	S	C. C. McDonald	170	4a	A
				C. C. McDonald	133	5a	M
			1962/3				
M. C. Cowdrey	113	2a	M	B. C. Booth	112	1a	B
D. S. Sheppard	113	2b	M	B. C. Booth	103	2b	M
K. F. Barrington	132*	4b	A	R. N. Harvey	154	4a	A
K. F. Barrington	101	5a	S	N. C. O'Neill	100	4a	A
				P. J. P. Burge	103	5a	S

237   R

ENGLAND   AUSTRALIA

1965/6

ENGLAND				AUSTRALIA			
J. H. Edrich	109	2a	M	W. M. Lawry	166	1a	B
M. C. Cowdrey	104	2a	M	K. D. Walters	155	1a	B
R. W. Barber	185	3a	S	P. J. Burge	120	2b	M
H. Edrich	103	3a	S	K. D. Walters	115	2b	M
K. F. Barrington	102	4b	A	R. B. Simpson	225	4a	A
K. F. Barrington	115	5a	M	W. M. Lawry	119	4a	A
				W. M. Lawry	108	5a	M
				R. M. Cowper	307	5a	M

1970/1

ENGLAND				AUSTRALIA			
B. W. Luckhurst	131	2a	P	K. R. Stackpole	207	1a	B
J. H. Edrich	115*	2b	P	K. D. Walters	112	1a	B
G. Boycott	142*	4b	S	I. R. Redpath	171	2a	P
B. W. Luckhurst	109	5a	M	G. S. Chappell	108	2a	P
B. L. d'Oliveira	117	5a	M	I. M. Chappell	111	5a	M
J. H. Edrich	130	6a	A	K. R. Stackpole	136	6b	A
B. Boycott	119*	6b	A	I. M. Chappell	104	6b	A

1974/5

ENGLAND				AUSTRALIA			
A. W. Greig	110	1a	B	R. Edwards	115	2a	P
A. P. E. Knott	106*	5b	A	K. D. Walters	103	2a	P
M. H. Denness	188	6a	M	I. R. Redpath	105	4b	S
K. W. R. Fletcher	146	6a	M	G. S. Chappell	144	4b	S
				G. S. Chappell	102	6b	M

Total 1946–75: 33   Total 1946–75: 43

Five wickets in an innings series by series

ENGLAND				AUSTRALIA			

1946/7

ENGLAND				AUSTRALIA			
D. V. P. Wright	5–167	1a	B	K. R. Miller	7–60	1a	B
D. V. P. Wright	7–105	5a	S	E. R. H. Toshack	6–82	1b	B
				I. W. Johnson	6–42	2a	S
				C. L. McCool	5–109	2b	S
				R. R. Lindwall	7–63	5a	S
				C. L. McCool	5–44	5b	S

1950/1

ENGLAND				AUSTRALIA			
F. R. Brown	5–49	5a	M	W. A. Johnston	5–35	1a	B
A. V. Bedser	5–46	5a	M	J. B. Iverson	6–27	3b	S
A. V. Bedser	5–59	5b	M				

1954/5

ENGLAND				AUSTRALIA			
F. H. Tyson	6–85	2b	S	W. A. Johnston	5–25	3b	M
J. B. Statham	5–60	3a	M				
F. H. Tyson	7–27	3b	M				
J. H. Wardle	5–79	5a	S				

1958/9

ENGLAND				AUSTRALIA			
J. B. Statham	7–57	2a	M	A. K. Davidson	6–64	2a	M
J. C. Laker	5–107	3a	S	I. Meckiff	6–38	2b	M
				R. Benaud	5–83	3a	S
				R. Benaud	5–91	4a	A

1962/3

ENGLAND				AUSTRALIA			
F. S. Trueman	5–62	2b	M	R. Benaud	6–115	1a	B
F. J. Titmus	7–79	3a	S	A. K. Davidson	6–75	2a	M
F. J. Titmus	5–103	5a	S	R. B. Simpson	5–57	3a	S
				A. K. Davidson	5–25	3b	S
				G. D. McKenzie	5–89	4a	A

1965/6

ENGLAND				AUSTRALIA			
D. J. Brown	5–62	3a	S	P. I. Philpott	5–90	1a	B
I. J. Jones	6–118	4a	A	G. D. McKenzie	5–134	2a	M
				N. J. N. Hawke	7–105	3a	S
				G. D. McKenzie	6–48	4a	A
				N. J. N. Hawke	5–54	4b	A

ENGLAND				AUSTRALIA			
			1970/1				
J. A. Snow	6–114	1a	B	D. K. Lillee	5–84	6a	A
K. Shuttleworth	5–47	1b	B				
J. A. Snow	7–40	4b	S				
			1974/5				
R. G. D. Willis	5–61	3a	M	J. R. Thomson	6–46	1b	B
G. G. Arnold	5–86	4a	S	J. R. Thomson	5–93	2b	P
D. L. Underwood	7–113	5a	A	M. H. N. Walker	8–143	6a	M
P. Lever	6–38	6a	M				
Total 1946–75: 23				Total 1946–75: 27			

Comparative striking rates series by series

RUNS PER 100 BALLS

SERIES		1st Test	2nd Test	3rd Test	4th Test	5th Test	6th Test	7th Test	Eng	Aus
1946/7	E	37	39	40	36	36	—	—	38	—
	A	51	48	53	54	46	—	—	—	51
1950/1	E	40	34	34	37	43	—	—	37	—
	A	47	42	41	49	39	—	—	—	44
1954/5	E	34	35	35	32	49	—	—	36	—
	A	58	47	45	38	47	—	—	—	47
1958/9	E	23	33	33	36	44	—	—	33	—
	A	34	37	33	46	46	—	—	—	39
1962/3	E	38	47	33	47	34	—	—	39	—
	A	49	38	43	44	31	—	—	—	41
1965/6	E	41	48	50	38	48	—	—	45	—
	A	40	44	34	51	44	—	—	—	43
1970/1	E	39	36	—	43	35	47	34	39	—
	A	39	46	—	33	48	37	34	—	40
1974/5	E	39	40	39	43	42	44	—	41	—
	A	42	56	35	53	54	46	—	—	47

BALLS PER WICKET

SERIES		1st Test	2nd Test	3rd Test	4th Test	5th Test	6th Test	7th Test	Eng	Aus
1946/7	E	127	173	89	130	79	—	—	111	—
	A	42	81	104	124	69	—	—	—	83
1950/1	E	33	47	129	99	53	—	—	64	—
	A	30	50	71	72	88	—	—	—	61
1954/5	E	147	44	38	60	51	—	—	56	—
	A	70	64	67	91	108	—	—	—	75
1958/9	E	83	78	102	123	83	—	—	92	—
	A	75	55	90	70	50	—	—	—	68
1962/3	E	111	79	83	77	116	—	—	91	—
	A	109	122	57	91	96	—	—	—	91
1965/6	E	183	100	61	101	154	—	—	103	—
	A	88	116	98	75	115	—	—	—	95
1970/1	E	110	165	—	56	107	118	59	83	—
	A	130	125	—	108	174	115	71	—	113
1974/5	E	88	98	86	93	77	58	—	83	—
	A	55	66	66	61	49	121	—	—	65

Results of all first-class matches tour by tour

1946/7 and 1950/1

		1946/7				1950/1			
Western Australia		WA	366	48-1		MCC	434-9d	121-3d	
		MCC	477	—	D	WA	236	207-4	D
Combined XI		C.XI	462	—		No match			
		MCC	302	—	D				
South Australia	(1)	MCC	506-5d	—		SA	350	185-3d	
		SA	266	276-8	D	MCC	351-9d	186-3	W
	(2)	MCC	577	152-2		MCC	211	220	
		SA	443	—	D	SA	126	153	W
Victoria	(1)	MCC	358	279-7d		MCC	306-9d	79-4	
		V	189	204	W	V	331	—	D
	(2)	MCC	355	118		V	441	234	
		V	327	—	D	MCC	414	36-1	D
Australian XI		MCC	314	—		A.XI	526-9d	—	
		A.XI	327-5	—	D	MCC	321	173-3	D
New South Wales	(1)	NSW	156-2	—		NSW	509-3d	140-2d	
		MCC	165-4d	—	D	MCC	339	143-2	D
	(2)	NSW	342	262-6d		NSW	333	130-6	
		MCC	266	205-3	D	MCC	553-8d	—	D
Queensland		Q	400	230-6d		Q	305	5-1	
		MCC	310	238-6	D	MCC	291	—	D
Combined XI in Tasmania		MCC	278	353-9d		C.XI	289	103	
Tasmania		C.XI	374	145-2	D	MCC	382-7d	13-0	W
Tasmania		MCC	467-5d	—		T	192	229	
		T	103	129-6	D	MCC	234	188-1	W

P	W	L	D		P	W	L	D
12	1	—	11		11	4	—	7

1954/5 and 1958/9

		1954/5				1958/9			
Western Australia		WA	103	255		MCC	351	146-4d	
		MCC	321	40-3	W	WA	221	124-3	D
Combined XI		C.XI	86	163		MCC	349	257-4	
		MCC	311	—	W	C.XI	260	—	D
South Australia	(1)	MCC	246	181		SA	165	194	
		SA	254	152	W	MCC	245	115-1	W
	(2)	SA	185	123		MCC	276	195-9d	
		MCC	451	—	W	SA	223	138-9	D
Victoria	(1)	MCC	312	236-5d		MCC	396	149-3d	
		V	277	88-3	D	V	252	206	W
	(2)	V	113	—		V	286	180	
		MCC	90-1	—	D	MCC	313	156-1	W
Australian XI		MCC	205	—		MCC	319	257-3d	
		A.XI	167-7	—	D	A.XI	128	103	W

1954/5

New South Wales (1)	MCC	252	327	
	NSW	382	78–2	D
(2)	NSW	172	314–8d	
	MCC	172	269	L
Queensland	MCC	304	288	
	Q	288	25–2	D
Combined XI in	C.XI	221	184–6d	
Tasmania	MCC	242	99–2	D
Tasmania	MCC	427–7d	133–6d	
	T	117	200	W

P	W	L	D
12	5	1	6

1958/9

NSW	391–7d	—	
MCC	177	356–6	D
NSW	215	44–0	
MCC	303	—	D
MCC	151	71–4	
Q	210	—	D
MCC	384–9d	162–4	
C.XI	241	—	D
MCC	229–7d	—	
T	94–4	—	D

P	W	L	D
12	4	—	8

1962/3

Western Australia	MCC	303	49–0	
	WA	77	274	W
Combined XI	MCC	157	270	
	C.XI	317	115–0	L
South Australia (1)	SA	335	283–7d	
	MCC	508–9d	95–1	D
(2)	MCC	586–5d	167–6d	
	SA	450	113–4	D
Victoria (1)	V	340	175	
	MCC	336	180–5	W
(2)	MCC	375	218–5d	
	V	307	188–9	D
Australian XI	MCC	633–7d	68–5d	
	A.XI	451	201–4	D
New South Wales (1)	MCC	348	104	
	NSW	532–6d	—	L
(2)	No match			
Queensland	Q	433–7d	94–7	
	MCC	581–6d	—	D
Combined XI in	MCC	331–7d	116–1d	
Tasmania	C.XI	77	57	W
Tasmania	Not first-class			

P	W	L	D
10	3	2	5

1965/6

MCC	447–5d	156–5d	
WA	303–9d	291	W
MCC	379–7d	205–4d	
C.XI	231–5d	322–6	D
SA	103	364	
MCC	310	158–4	W
SA	459–7d	253–4d	
MCC	444	270–4	W
V	384–7d	165	
MCC	211	306	L
No match			
No match			
MCC	527–6d	2–1	
NSW	288	240	W
NSW	488	—	
MCC	329	472–6	D
MCC	452–5d	123–2d	
Q	222	325–8	D
C.XI	199	273–1	
MCC	471–9d	—	D
MCC	371–9d	289–7	
T	322	—	D

P	W	L	D
10	4	1	5

1970/1

Western Australia	WA	257–5d	285	
	MCC	258–3	256–6	D
Combined	No match			
South Australia (1)	MCC	451–9d	235–4	
	SA	649–9d	—	D
(2)	SA	297–2d	338–7d	
	MCC	238	336–8	D

1974/5

WA	265–8d	346–5d	
MCC	314–5d	177	L
No match			
SA	247	320	
MCC	349–9d	82–3	D
SA	270–6d	222–6d	
MCC	277–2d	210–6	D

		1970/1				1974/5			
Victoria	(1)	MCC	142	341		v	293–8d	174–8	
		v	304–8d	180–4	L	MCC	392–9d	—	D
	(2)	No match				No match			
Australian XI		No match				No match			
New South Wales	(1)	NSW	410–5d	—		NSW	338	174	
		MCC	204	325–1	D	MCC	332–7d	181–4	W
	(2)	No match				MCC	315–5d	266–7d	
						NSW	157	237	W
Queensland		Q	360	—		MCC	258	175	
		MCC	418–4	—	D	Q	226	161	W
Combined XI in		MCC	184–4	—		MCC	204–4d	—	
Tasmania		C.XI	—	—	D	C.XI	189–5	—	D
Tasmania		MCC	316–4d	72–1		T	164	105	
		T	164	223	W	MCC	341–4d	—	W

P	W	L	D		P	W	L	D
8	1	1	6		9	4	1	4

SUMMARY

		P	W	L	D
Western Australia		8	3	1	4
Combined XI		5	1	1	3
South Australia	(1)	8	4	—	4
	(2)	8	3	—	5
Victoria	(1)	8	3	2	3
	(2)	5	1	—	4
Australian XI		5	1	—	4
New South Wales	(1)	8	2	1	5
	(2)	6	1	1	4
Queensland		8	1	—	7
Combined XI in Tasmania		8	2	—	6
Tasmania		7	4	—	3
		84	26	6	52

Index

245